GOD OR NOTHING

Robert Cardinal Sarah
with Nicholas Diat

God or Nothing

A Conversation on Faith

Translated by Michael J. Miller

IGNATIUS PRESS   SAN FRANCISCO

Original French edition:
Dieu ou rien: Entretien sur la foi
© 2015 by Librairie Arthème Fayard, Paris

Cover photo of Robert Cardinal Sarah by Stefano Spaziani

Cover design by Roxanne Mei Lum

To Monsignor Louis Barry,
whose courage made him so great.

To Brother Vincent,
and to all those who take turns without a break at his bedside.

For nothing is impossible with God.

—Luke 1:37

Let all of you then live together, one in mind and heart, mutually giving honor to God in yourselves, whose temples you have become.

—Saint Augustine, *Rule*

Because the man of the world wants to change his place, his destiny, his idols, and to change them perpetually, the friend of God must remain and stay in the place where God has put him. Indeed, between the friends of God and the world there is an antithesis and a rupture. What the one chooses, the other rejects. Otherwise there would no longer be two camps, but only one: the world.

—Father Jérôme, *Écrits monastiques*

CONTENTS

INTRODUCTION

God is found by the low paths.

—Father Jérôme, *Car toujours dure longtemps ...*

There are radical encounters that change some aspect of our way of looking at things. My encounter with Robert Cardinal Sarah was definitely of this sort. There was no before and after, but the obvious fact of being with a man of God.

Father Jérôme, a monk at the Abbey of Notre-Dame de Sept-Fons of the Order of Cistercians of the Strict Observance, wrote in *L'art d'être disciple* (The art of being a disciple), "Do not ask your master to talk just for the sake of talking. Ask him about the problems of human destiny and other related problems, problems that are still relevant today. How does he himself experience them? How does he manage to accept them with courage and peace of mind? Ask him what he knows with certainty, what he no longer questions, what he considers indisputable and unchanging. Have him talk about the drama of his true self, not about the artificial role that may be imposed on him by circumstances. Have him talk about his disappointments and his hopes, about his religious faith, his trust in God, his prayer. Ask him how and to what extent he has been freed of himself by giving himself. Find out the source of his clear-sighted self-denial. Let him confide in you what he learns in his silence. Let him tell you where his tears come from and what makes him smile. Get to the heart of this man. And if he agrees to take up his schoolbooks or his apprenticeship tools again in order to help you, thank him by your docility."

Over these months of interviews with Robert Cardinal Sarah, I tried to put into practice the simple yet demanding instructions of Father Jérôme. This saintly Trappist monk was writing to a novice to encourage him to try to understand his master's counsel and requests better.

Robert Cardinal Sarah is an extraordinary spiritual master. A man great in his humility, a gentle and firm guide, a priest who never tires of speaking about the God he loves.

Robert Cardinal Sarah has had an exceptional life, even though he sincerely thinks that it is, on the whole, rather commonplace.

Robert Cardinal Sarah is a friend of God, a merciful and forgiving man, a man of silence, a good man.

When I think back to the long hours that we spent together working on this book, I always come back to those first moments, when he spoke to me about his childhood in the most remote parts of Guinea, deep in the bush, at the ends of the world, about the little village of Ourous, about the half-light of the church, about the missionaries, about his parents and his people, the Coniaguis.

I am certain God had his eye on the cardinal in a special way; I also think that his expectations are immense. But God can rest assured, because the cardinal loves him in the most beautiful way a man can love his Father.

In this book, the new prefect of the Congregation for Divine Worship and the Discipline of the Sacraments talks a lot about Benedict XVI. With admiration, gratitude, and joy.

But the pontiff to whom Robert Cardinal Sarah feels closest is Paul VI. There is, so to speak, a mysterious parallel between Giovanni Battista Montini and this son of Africa. Their spiritualities, their theologies converge on the same simple and ascetic road to God.

Certainly, in the final hours of his reign, Paul VI chose a priest with little experience to make him the youngest bishop in the world. The name of this man was Father Sarah. But the relation between them was more extensive, more secret, more profound. The link between Paul VI and Cardinal Sarah is found in their spirit of childhood, docility, and radicalism in following the demands of truth, whatever the cost.

During his general audience on September 1, 1976, Paul VI was able to say, "To build the Church, we must labor, we must suffer. The Church must be a strong people, a people of courageous witnesses, a people that knows how to suffer for its faith and for spreading it throughout the world, in silence, gratuitously, and always through love." Two years later, Paul VI left this world. Yet these few words could be spoken once again by Cardinal Sarah, who has never forgotten that "the Church must be a strong people", for nothing in his life was ever easy or free. A man who lived through one of the bloodiest dictatorial regimes in Africa appreciates better than anyone the value of this meditation of Paul VI from the year 1963, when the successor of Peter was just starting on his path: "Does God speak to the troubled soul or to the peaceful soul? We know perfectly well that in order to listen to his voice, a bit of calm and tranquility must reign. We must keep ourselves far from all intimidating excitement or nervousness and be ourselves. That is the essential thing: within ourselves! Consequently, the encounter is not outside but within ourselves."

If the reader should take away one thing from this book, it is no doubt what the cardinal confided regarding the moment when it seemed impossible for him to accept his episcopate, given all of Guinea's political, economic, and social difficulties. Robert Sarah then left for a hermitage, far from the commotion and troubles, to be alone with God, fasting from all food and water for several days, the Eucharist and the Bible his sole companions. The whole personality of the child from Ourous, guided by Spiritan missionaries, is found here. And nowhere else. His message really is that of Paul VI, who was not afraid to declare in 1970, "It is necessary that everyone learn to pray both in himself and by himself. A Christian must know how to have a personal prayer life. Every soul is a temple. And when do we enter into this temple of our consciousness to worship God who is present there? Would we be empty souls, even though Christian, souls that are not present to themselves, forgetting the mysterious and ineffable encounter, the filial and inebriating dialogue that God, the one God in three Persons, deigns to offer to us within ourselves?"

Many extraordinary things happened in the life of Cardinal Sarah, in particular the origins of his priestly vocation. Nothing in the animistic surroundings in which he grew up predisposed him to leave his village to enter a minor seminary at age eleven. The day when he left his parents, taking with him only a small bag, marked the beginning of a long and tumultuous crossing, as if obscure forces were trying in every possible way to prevent this young adolescent from becoming a priest: poverty, separation from his family, a Marxist dictatorship, military persecution, the storm that raged in the Church, the ill winds of ideology.... Yet this man stood firm because he thought that God would always be near him.

Like the monks, he knows that the monotony and repetition of the passing days is also the hidden mainspring of the authentic encounter with God. How often the course of his life demonstrated to him that God was waiting for him still farther ahead. . . .

Starting from a primitive religion, Robert Sarah has reached the heights of Christianity. These days, he is still absolutely the same: humble, attentive, and determined. John Paul II often said that we must not conserve strength on this earth, because we will have eternity in which to rest. Robert Sarah, too, thinks that his work will not be finished until the moment of his death. He is on earth to serve God and to help men.

In 2010, Benedict XVI entrusted to him the Pontifical Council *Cor unum*, which is in charge of the pope's charitable efforts. He made this decision confident that this man from a small, fragile nation would be able to understand better than anyone the life of the poor. The former pope was quite right! For Robert Sarah did not learn about poverty in books, in the living rooms of middle-class people seeking to assuage their consciences, or in lecture halls full of puffed-up egos, feverishly trying to change the world by their undisciplined wills. . . . He was born into a poor family who had nothing, and he was able to pursue his studies thanks to the help of French missionaries who gave him everything.

Sometimes, the cardinal's thinking seems tough and too demanding. It is certainly a great mystery how someone can be so radical only to arrive at last at a happy medium. Robert Sarah displays a gentle and angelic stubbornness in all things.

"Be of good cheer—you would not seek Me if you had not found Me", wrote Pascal in his *Pensées*.

The cardinal's will is always turned toward God alone. For Robert Sarah's constant desire is to be with him in prayer. He believes in the value of prayer. That is easy to say, but for this man, it has been his heartbeat for his entire life. Even more, the spiritual son of intrepid missionaries thinks that prayer is simply a marvelous transposition of acts of friendship. He too can say, as Paul VI did on a pastoral journey to the Philippines, "Jesus Christ teaches us that the love of God is inseparable from love of neighbor. The apostle must thirst for a love that is ever more real, more universal. His love for his brothers, and especially for the weakest and poorest, will be rooted in the love that God has for us, and especially for 'the least of these his brethren'. Loving God is not personal insurance; it is an imperative to share."

Far from his native land, in Rome, Robert Sarah's heart has always remained close to his African brothers and to all who suffer from war, sickness, and hunger. In the fall of 2014, when Pope Francis appointed him to his new position, the cardinal was saddened. Others would have been overjoyed by such a brilliant promotion; they would have paraded like a peacock on display.... Robert Sarah sought nothing. He did not ask for anything. He simply wanted to continue to serve the poor.

By his personal simplicity, Robert Sarah gives evidence of an unspectacular but fundamental success. This man's subtle and self-effacing piety has an ageless simplicity. His relationship with God is obvious, for it has been sustained by a whole lifetime of fidelity, constancy, love, and trust. He is a resistance fighter, a past master in the art of not calling attention to himself, and yet he possesses indescribable strength.

The son of Claire and Alexandre Sarah sometimes resembles a monk about to set out on a great journey to meet his God, his love. He is peaceful and confident, in spite of the little concerns and sufferings that are quickly dispatched by the fiery blade of his faith.

Surely the friends of God are always hidden in his shadow. Robert Sarah is a regular visitor of God's house, and he knows many ways in.

Nicolas Diat
Rome, January 25, 2015

I

SIGNS FROM GOD
IN THE LIFE OF AN AFRICAN CHILD

"What surprises me", God says, "is hope.
And I cannot get over it.
This little hope that seems like nothing at all.
This little girl hope,
Who is immortal."

—Charles Péguy, *La Porche du mystère*
de la deuxième vertu

NICOLAS DIAT: This first question in our interview concerns your birth in Ourous, in the heart of the highlands of Guinea. It is not easy to understand how a child from the African countryside was able to become a cardinal....

ROBERT CARDINAL SARAH: You are quite right! It is difficult to grasp what I have become today, considering my modest beginnings.

When I think about the animistic milieu, so deeply attached to its customs, from which the Lord took me in order to make me into a Christian, a priest, a bishop, a cardinal, and one of the close collaborators of the pope, I am overcome with emotion.

I was born on June 15, 1945, in Ourous, one of the smallest villages in Guinea, in the north of the country, near the border of Senegal. It is a mountainous region that is far from the capital of Conakry and often regarded as unimportant by the administrative and political authorities.

In fact, my home is about 310 miles distant from Conakry. The trip to the capital takes an entire day along especially difficult roads. During the rainy season, sometimes the cars get stuck. The journey may be interrupted for long hours, the time it takes to get the vehicle out of the mud, only for it to get bogged down again a little farther on. At the time when I was born, most of the roads were no more than simple dirt paths.

My years in Ourous were the most precious time of my life in Guinea. I grew up in that isolated place, where I went to school to earn a primary school diploma. We followed the same curriculum as little French children, and so I learned that my ancestors were Gauls. . . .

At the time, the Holy Ghost Fathers, members of the Congregation of the Holy Spirit—founded in the eighteenth century by Claude Poullart des Places and reformed in the nineteenth century by Father François Libermann—had already converted many animists to the Christian faith. These missionaries had come to our region because Islam was not widespread there; they saw it as a possible field for evangelization. In Conakry, for example, efforts to convert people were almost fruitless because the Muslims had long been the dominant group there.

Today, my village is almost entirely Christian and has close to 1,000 inhabitants.

At the beginning of the twentieth century—the mission was founded in 1912—the chief of Ourous welcomed the Holy Ghost Fathers with true generosity. He gave them more than 100 acres of land to promote the establishment of Catholic worship. By farming this land, the missionaries obtained the resources necessary to cover the costs of running the mission and providing for the boarding-school students. Six months after the arrival of the Holy Ghost Fathers, one of them was brutally carried off by an untimely death. Remember that hygiene at the time was very basic. Cases of malaria, in particular, were still common.

In such a setting, these men of God made great sacrifices and suffered many deprivations, without ever complaining and with unending generosity. The villagers helped them to build their huts. Then, little by little, they built a church together. This place of worship was decorated by Father Fautrard, who had just been appointed to Ourous by Bishop Raymond Lerouge, the first vicar apostolic of Conakry.

My father watched the construction of the mission and the church. He told me the story of how he had been chosen along with seven other young boys, animists like himself, to carry to the village the bell that had arrived by boat at Conakry. By working in shifts for a week, they completed the arduous journey.

Later, my father, Alexandre, was baptized and married on the same day, April 13, 1947, that is, two years after my birth.

What was life like for your people, the Coniaguis, that small ethnic group from the north of Guinea?

The Coniaguis are a people made up almost exclusively of farmers and livestock breeders, who have managed to preserve their traditions. Where do they come from? According to some researchers, the Coniaguis are related to the Yolas of Casamance, whose language is said to be almost identical to theirs. Now the Yolas, according to oral tradition, are the descendants of Guélowar Bamana. In fact, the Yolas or Biagares, whose territory extends to Koli and borders on the land of the Bassaris, live on the bank of the Geba River, opposite Bissau. According to storytellers' oral tradition, a young Coniagui girl, Guélowar Bamana, was at the origin of the Gabu or Kaabu dynasties, said to go back to the thirteenth century, and also of all the populations of the Sine region, that is, Senegal, Guinea-Bissau, the Gambia, and the northwest of Guinea-Conakry. "In those days, the king's son married a young woman who appeared mysteriously in the bush: she was descended from the spirits and did not speak Mandingue. They taught her to speak and eat in the manner of the Mandingues, that is, the Malinkés. Out of their union four girls were born, who married the kings of Djimana, Pinda, Sama, and Sine, respectively. Only male descendants can be emperors of Gabu, but through the matrilineal line."

My ancestors were basically animists, faithful to the rituals and secular festivals that still set the tempo of their existence.

During my childhood, we lived in round, one-room brick huts covered by wattle and daub, surrounded by a "veranda" where we usually ate our meals. We owned one or two other small huts nearby where we stored rice, fonio, peanuts, millet, and other crops. We had fields and rice paddies; the earth's yield served to feed the village families, and the surplus was sold at the market. It was a simple, humble, secure life without conflicts. Community living and caring for the needs of others were of the utmost importance.

Villagers organized themselves into groups of fifteen to twenty people to help each other with their work in the fields. During the growing and harvest seasons, each group set aside certain days to work the fields of each of its members in turn, according to a mutually agreed-on calendar. When a work cycle was complete, each having welcomed the group in his field, we started over again, until the end of the growing season.

This solidarity allowed each member to receive effective aid from his group when it was his turn. Occasionally a family would invite a few extra villagers to help them work in the fields. The family would then offer some millet beer or mead and a midday meal to the friends who had joined them.

Could you describe the ancient religious rituals of your ancestors, in particular the important rite of passage into adult life?

The Coniagui people are very religious and devoted to God, who is called *Ounou*. However, they can come into contact with him only through their ancestors.

The God of my ancestors is the Creator of the universe and of all that exists. He is the Supreme Being, ineffable, incomprehensible, invisible, and intangible. Yet he is at the center of our lives and permeates our entire existence. It is common in Coniagui culture to encounter theophoric names such as *Mpooun* ("God's second"), *Taoun* ("God's third"), *Ounouted* ("God is the one who knows"), and *Ounoubayerou* ("are you God?").

Religious and ritual life is essentially divided into two spheres: funeral rites, on the one hand, and initiation rites, on the other.

The funeral rites consist of sacrificial offerings, consisting of libations of animal blood or of millet beer. These offerings are poured out on the ground or at the foot of a sacred tree, on an altar or on a wooden stele representing the village ancestors. The objective is to appease the spirits, to give thanks to God, and to ask supernatural forces for blessings. In fact, there are three rites or types of offerings. The *rhavanhë* performed at funerals is an indispensable moment, for it opens the door of the village of ancestors to those who passed away at a certain age; they do not celebrate the *rhavanhë* for those who have died at a very young age or as adolescents, probably because of their innocence, that is, their inability to do serious and deliberate evil—after their death, they are readmitted to the ancestors' village without there being need for a sacrifice. Then there is the *sadhëkha*, celebrated as a thank offering for blessings received, for example, on the occasion of a birth, or to ask for a blessing on important actions. Finally, the purpose of the *tchëva* is to obtain the end of natural disasters such as drought and invading clouds of devastating crickets that devour the crops and the leaves and fruits of trees. It consists of a nocturnal procession through the fields and the village to ask for God's protection over the farms and the work done there. This ritual resembles the rogation processions that were held in the Catholic Church until the Vatican II Council and that still exist in other countries, such as Mexico. It is celebrated by women and presided over by the *loukoutha*, repre - sented by a special ceremonial mask; the *loukoutha* is a spirit in human form, dressed in natural fibers or leaves so as not to be seen or recognized by the women and non-initiated children.

Additionally, a young man's initiation ceremony is a critical moment in the life of the Coniagui people. It is preceded by the circumcision ritual, designed as a test of physical endurance. Even though circumcision is performed around the age of twelve without anesthetics, the boy must not cry, no matter how much pain he experiences. This operation begins a two- to three-year transition period to prepare the boy for his initiation; the goal is to bring about a radical transformation of the boy from childhood to adulthood. The adolescent then becomes a man who is fully responsible for himself and for his community.

Folk dances start Saturday afternoon and last all night. Then the adolescents are led into the forest, where they stay for a week to be trained in suffering and to learn endurance, self-denial for the sake of the common good, and scrupulous respect for the elderly, older men and women. Initiation is an apprenticeship in the customs, traditions, and manners of the community. The adolescents also learn how to treat certain diseases with medicinal plants.

Initiation might appear to be a good thing; in reality, however, this ritual is a ruse, a hoax that uses lies, violence, and fear. The physical trials and humiliations are such that they do not lead to a real transformation or a free assimilation of the teachings, which ought to involve the intellect, the conscience, and the heart. The process instills servile submission to traditions, for fear of being cast out for not conforming to the rules. During the initiation rite, the keepers of the traditions lead the women to believe that the young adolescent dies and is reborn to a new life. According to animist beliefs, the initiate is eaten by a spirit, the *nh'ëmba*, and then restored to the community with a new spirit. The ceremony for the return to the village is especially solemn, because the young man appears for the first time before the community, physically pretending to be a different man endowed with new powers.

The initiation rite is an obsolete practice that is incapable of answering life's most important questions or of showing a Guinean man how to be integrated properly into a world full of challenges.

Indeed, a culture that does not promote the ability to make progress and to be open to other social realities, so as to welcome its own transformation serenely, becomes closed in on itself. Yet an initiation rite makes us slaves to our milieu, walled up in fear and in the past.

The Spiritan missionaries enabled my people to understand that Jesus alone truly gives us the gift of being born again, born "of water and the Spirit", as Christ says to Nicodemus (Jn 3:5).

Initiation has always been a secret rite that entails knowledge and customs reserved exclusively for the initiated. An esoteric education in a secret circle of initiates cannot help but give rise to doubts about its value, its substance, and its real ability to transform a man. The Church has always opposed this kind of gnosis. What is worse, with regard to the initiation of girls, some practices must be prohibited. Indeed, the ritual seriously violates the dignity of a woman: in a perverse way, the initiation rite ruins the most intimate aspect of her physical integrity.

For my part, I was brought into the forest by my uncle, Samuel MPouna Coline, who is still alive.

In fact, Father had agreed to let me be initiated, provided that the ceremony be brief. As a seminarian, it was unthinkable that I should miss Mass for a whole week. Father and I were already convinced that the Mass was the only moment that transforms man on this earth. My own initiation therefore lasted merely three days....

How do you view your childhood in Ourous when you look back on it today? What was your daily routine like at the time?

My childhood was very happy, without a doubt. I grew up in an atmosphere of peace and innocent naïveté in a small village with the mission of the Holy Ghost Fathers at its center.

I lived in a pious, serene, and peaceful family in which God was present and the Virgin Mary was venerated with devotion.

Like many villagers, my parents were farmers. To this day I greatly respect a job well done, after seeing them work so hard and joyfully. They rose early in the morning to go into the fields, and I left with them by six o'clock. When I was around seven years old, I could no longer accompany them because after Mass I had to go to school. I must say that we were not rich; the fruit of our labor allowed us to be fed and clothed and guaranteed us a subsistence wage. My parents' unselfishness, their honesty, humility, generosity, and the nobility of their feelings, their faith, the intensity of their prayer life, and most of all their trust in God made a deep impression on me. I never saw them come into conflict with anyone.

I also remember playing soccer, hide-and-seek, hoop, and, most of all, endless dances by the light of the moon. How can I forget the hours my friends and I spent at our elders' sides, listening to the tales and legends of the Coniagui culture? It was like a school for us children; these wonderful moments were a gift that helped us to assimilate our values and traditions. Festive ceremonies full of bright colors occurred regularly. I remember very clearly the big harvest festivals. We would empty our storehouses without any worries about running out....

Anyone could come into our hut, at any time of day or night. Everyone was welcome to share a meal at our table. Father's and Mother's greatest happiness, their greatest joy, was to see our guests happy, welcomed royally in our little home. For them, there was a divine blessing and an immense joy in the simple act of welcoming others; our little three-person family would thus become for a few days "as many as the stars of heaven" (Heb 11:12).

Love, generosity, and the joy of opening the doors of one's home to neighbors or to strangers always tend to enlarge our hearts; "our heart is wide", Saint Paul said to the Corinthians (2 Cor 6:11). Selflessness was at the center of everything. For example, I still remember that Father had a friend who came from afar each year to spend the Christmas and Easter holidays at our house. He and his family stayed as long as they wished; Mother was always available, with a ready smile and a lot of tact.

Please describe the years you spent at the French school in your village.

Starting at age seven, I went to primary school after morning Mass. At the time, we could speak our native language at home and French in the classroom or on the playground. If we broke this rule, we were punished with "the mark", a sort of small necklace made of unfinished wood that symbolized our mistake.... But in fact, children were proud to go to school, to learn the French language and culture. Our ambition was actually to be open to everything that leads to knowledge and to the world of science.

Friendships between schoolmates were strong; you could even say that there was great unity among the youth. We fought sometimes, but it was never serious. Today I have lost many of those friends, who died rather young; others still live in the village or in various regions of Guinea. I have many fond memories of this simple time, marked by the heroism of the missionaries, whose lives were totally imbued with God.

I was an only child, surrounded by affection without being overprotected. My parents never punished me; I felt an inexhaustible tenderness and affectionate veneration for them. Despite their return to the Father's house, I still feel the love that keeps us profoundly united.

I also remember my maternal grandmother, who was baptized at the end of her life, at the very moment of her death. She was baptized with the name Rose, the patron saint of her parish. My grandmother agreed to be baptized when the priest explained to her that she would thus be able to see us again in heaven. At first, she did not understand the meaning of baptism; it was a great joy for me when she became a child of God, for I was sure that we would one day go to live together in heaven, side by side.

In Ourous, the Holy Ghost Fathers seem ultimately to be at the center of your life. . . .

Indeed, as I told you, I was born on June 15, 1945, and I received the Sacrament of Confirmation on June 15, 1958, in Bingerville, at the hands of Archbishop Boivin of Abidjan. I was baptized at the age of two, on July 20, 1947, by a Holy Ghost Father, and I was ordained a priest on July 20, 1969, by another Spiritan, Bishop Raymond-Marie Tchidimbo.

I owe my entrance into Christ's family entirely to the exceptional dedication of the Holy Ghost Fathers. I will always admire these men, who had left France, their families, and their ties to bring the love of God to the ends of the earth.

The first three missionaries who founded Saint Rose mission in Ourous were Fathers Joseph Orcel, Antoine Reeb, and Firmin Montels. They arrived around the time of the Easter celebrations in 1912 and presented themselves to the commander of the French Circle of Youkounkoun, who refused to receive them. They continued their travels and arrived in Ithiou. From there, they crossed the river and reached Ourous, where they were welcomed with open arms.

For three months, they camped in the forest. They lacked everything, suffering from hunger and the hostility of the commander of the Circle located about a mile from Ourous. Every morning after Mass, Father Orcel, with trowel and hammer in hand, built the temporary hut that would house them. Six months later, Father Montels became seriously ill from physical exhaustion; he was called back to God on September 2, 1912, thus becoming the "foundation stone" of the mission.

Every evening, the Fathers of Ourous gathered the children near a large cross set up in the mission courtyard, as if to symbolize the heart and center of the village. We could see it from far away: we oriented our entire lives by it! It was around this cross that we received our cultural and spiritual education. There, as the sun slowly set, the missionaries introduced us to the Christian mysteries.

Under the protection by the great cross of Ourous, we were being prepared by God for the painful incidents of revolutionary persecution that the Church in my country would face throughout the rule of Sékou Touré. His dictatorship drove the populace to exhaustion, lies, brutality, mediocrity, and spiritual poverty.

The Church in Guinea experienced a terrible Way of the Cross. The entire young nation was transformed into a valley of tears. Although we owe some thanks to Sékou Touré for his role in winning our independence, how can we forget his atrocious crimes, like the Boiro camp, where many prisoners died after being brutally tortured, humiliated, and eliminated in the name of a revolution orchestrated by a bloodthirsty ruler who was obsessed by the specter of conspiracy?

The physical experience of the cross is a grace that is absolutely necessary for our growth in the Christian faith and a providential opportunity to conform ourselves to Christ so as to enter into the depths of the ineffable. We understand, therefore, that in piercing the Heart of Jesus, the soldier's spear revealed a great mystery, for it went farther than the Heart of Christ. It revealed God; it passed, so to speak, through the very center of the Trinity.

I thank the missionaries who made me understand that the Cross is the center of the world, the heart of mankind, and the place where our stability is anchored. In fact, there is only one steadfast point in this world to guarantee man's balance and steadiness. Everything else is moving, changing, ephemeral, and uncertain: "Stat Crux, dum volvitur orbis" (Only the Cross stands, and the world revolves around it). Calvary is the highest point in the world, from which we can see everything with new eyes, the eyes of faith, love, and martyrdom: the eyes of Christ.

In Ourous, we had been impressed by this presence of the cross, which was taken down at the time of Séjou Touré's revolution and replaced with the national flag. It was finally restored to its place after the dictator's death.

When the cross was toppled, it caused indescribable suffering for the faithful Christians. By that time, the clinic, the priests' house, and that of the Sisters of the Sacred Heart of Versailles, the schools, and the cemetery had already been confiscated and nationalized.

During my childhood, the Fathers taught us the catechism of Pius X, first in our own language, then in French during the last two years of preparation for the diploma. They told us about the Bible and Church history. We children asked a lot of questions, and the Holy Ghost Fathers talked about their assignments in other countries. As night fell, we would sing evening prayer; then they blessed us, and we returned to our huts. You might think I am describing an idyllic world, but this is what it was really like.

My parents never missed a Sunday service. I was an altar boy, first only on Sundays, then Father Marcel Bracquemond asked me to come every day to serve the Mass at six o'clock. He had noticed that I liked the Divine Office. In order to help us perform our duties as altar servers, the Father Superior, Martin Martinière, had assigned one of the older boys, Barnabé Martin Tany, to teach us the initial prayers at the foot of the altar. Then, after Mass, I would return home for breakfast, and then I went to school.

What led to your priestly vocation and your decision to enter the seminary?

If I look for the source of my priestly vocation, how can I help but see, like Saint John Paul II, that "it throbs in the Cenacle in Jerusalem"? From the Upper Room, during Jesus' last supper with his disciples, "on the night when he was betrayed" (1 Cor 11:23), "the immense night of origins" and the night of this first celebration of the Eucharist, flows the lifeblood that feeds every vocation: the vocation of the apostles and their successors as well as that of every man. My priestly vocation is found in the first Eucharist, as is every priest's. So I was set apart, called to serve God and the Church, from my mother's womb. In each of my daily celebrations of the Eucharist, I hear resounding in my heart the words that Jesus spoke to the apostles, on the memorable day of the washing of their feet, the institution of the priesthood and of the Eucharist, as if those words had been spoken to me also: "Do you know what I have done to you? You call me Teacher and Lord; and you are right, for so I am. If I then, your Lord and Teacher, have washed your feet, you also ought to wash one another's feet. For I have given you an example, that you also should do as I have done to you" (Jn 13:12–15). I am certain that on that night Jesus was thinking of me, too, and had already placed his hand on my head.

It was in the context of the daily Eucharist that Father Bracquemond, no doubt seeing my ardent desire to know God and probably impressed by my love of prayer and my faithful attendance at daily Mass, asked me if I wanted to enter the seminary. With the astonishment and spontaneity characteristic of children, I replied that I would very much like to, without the slightest idea of what I was committing myself to, for I had never left my little village and did not know anything about life in a seminary.

He explained to me that it was a house upheld by the prayers and affection of the entire Church. This place, he told me, would prepare me and other youths to become a priest like him. With this simple explanation, my joy at the thought of becoming a priest someday swelled my heart with both wonder and "madness"!

The priest asked me to talk about it with my parents, Alexandre and Claire, whom he knew very well.

I went to see Mother first, to tell her that I might perhaps be able to enter the seminary. She had no idea what the seminary was but was curious as to why I wanted to go there. I explained to her that it was about entering a special school that would prepare me to become a priest so as to be consecrated to God, like the Holy Ghost Fathers.... With her eyes wide open, she then told me that I must have lost my mind to say such a thing, or else I must not have understood the priest's words. To my mother and the inhabitants of the village, all priests were necessarily white.... In fact, it seemed impossible to her that a black man could become a priest! Hence it was clear that I had misunderstood Father Marcel Bracquemond's words. So she advised me to talk to my father about it, convinced that I had just said something extremely foolish and unrealistic.

That same day, I went out to find Father in the field, and he had the same reaction.... I tried to tell him that it was indeed Father Bracquemond who had persuaded me that, yes, I could become a priest like him. With a smile that was both tender and mocking, Father held me close to his heart, as if to console me for his skepticism. He was certain that I was telling him about a dream I had had the previous night! My request seemed impossible to him, too: a black man cannot become a priest of the Catholic Church. This nonsensical idea, he thought, could only be the product of my childish naïveté. But I insisted that these were Father Bracquemond's very own words.... So they decided to go and ask him to verify the authenticity of this story. He assured them that I had not lied and that he had in fact suggested to me the idea of becoming a priest and, first of all, entering the minor seminary to be trained! My parents were absolutely dumbfounded. That evening, by the light of the moon, they suggested that I leave for a year, showing that they had no idea how many years of study might be required at a seminary.

I was eleven and had just earned my certificate of primary studies. At the time, young seminarians from Guinea had to go to Ivory Coast for their formation. I was enthusiastic, proud, and happy, without knowing anything about the life awaiting me at the Saint Augustine Seminary in Bingerville.

As I left my parents, I could sense that the flow of time was changing. I noticed that my ties with Ourous were gradually breaking, while others would develop between the Lord and me, who possessed nothing but a young heart already enamored of him. I was my parents' only child, and I understood that they were making a very difficult sacrifice. With their own hands, they made a small suitcase for me, holding some underwear and a few shirts, nothing more. The priests helped me to plan the trip, and one of them accompanied me to Labé, a small town 150 miles from Ourous, to take a truck that would bring me to Conakry. I had the opportunity to travel with another seminarian, Alphonse Sara Tylé, who had enrolled at Bingerville a short time before. He was for me a valuable and reassuring companion at the start of this extraordinary adventure.

I had never left my village; I knew nobody at all besides the inhabitants of Ourous. I felt lost in Conakry. Yet along this path that was leading us to God, I was always supported by the joy of entering the seminary and by the encouragement of Alphonse, who was older. I told myself that if he had left and then come back, it must be a rich experience. We took a large boat, the *Foucault*, on a four-day journey that brought us to Abidjan after sailing past the Loos Islands and along the coasts of Sierra Leone and Liberia. Obviously, I did not know how to swim. I was therefore very surprised to see such a vehicle, heavily loaded with merchandise and passengers, "driving" on the water. What a discovery! There were many travelers and a lot of luggage, and an exuberant mood prevailed. I embarked with a dozen Guinean seminarians whose names I will never forget: Adrien Tambassa, Pascal Lys, Maximin Bangoura, Richard Bangoura, Camille Camara, Alphonse Sara Tylé, Joseph Mamidou, Yves Da Costa, and Jean-Marie Touré. I was the youngest....

We traveled in the hold, where the heat was suffocating. It was impossible to eat. The smell from the engines and the kitchens made us nauseated; the little greasy food that we were able to eat soon became food for the fish! Nothing would stay down. The only pleasant, special moments over the course of the four-day journey were during the hour of Holy Mass, celebrated by the ship's chaplain in a chapel in the first-class section. In that atmosphere of luxury and well-being, free from the ship's pitching and tossing, we wished that Mass would last for hours and hours. Unfortunately, once Mass was over, we went for a walk along the bridge for a few minutes, then returned to the hold, which had become a veritable inferno.

We arrived in the port of Abidjan feeling very tired. A car immediately brought us to the Saint Augustine Minor Seminary. After that difficult journey, the real adventure was beginning.

Wasn't your departure for the minor seminary somewhat abrupt, separating you from the world of your family?

Due to an unfortunate set of circumstances, my first year went very badly. Until Christmas, my studies went well. Then I became ill. Anemic and weak, I was treated without anyone really knowing what I was suffering from. The superiors threatened to send me back to my family because I did not have a strong enough constitution. At the time, seminarians were required to have the "3 H's": holiness, head knowledge, and health, in order to continue formation for the priesthood. I must admit that I possessed not one of these 3 H's!

Fearing dismissal from the seminary because of my shortcomings, I asked the nun who was my nurse to tell the Father Superior that I was doing better, but that was only a pious, well-meaning lie. I did not want to go back home and leave on a bad note. In fact, the doctors were treating me blindly. The Father Superior ended up asking specialists to perform several further tests. It was then discovered that I was infested with hookworms that were eating away at me little by little. The correct treatment freed me from those parasites, and I began to regain my strength. In June, the Father Superior, after consulting with my professors, authorized me to return for a second academic year after the holidays, on the express condition that I catch up on my first year and do well in my second year.

Soon it was time for summer vacation, and we took the boat back to Guinea. I was wary about admitting to my parents that I had been so ill because I was afraid they would tell me sternly, "Robert, it is out of the question that you return to Bingerville!" I dreaded hearing those terrible words. Now back home, my mother saw that I was weak and had lost weight. But I found a way to explain my physical state. "The demands of sports and daily physical labor and the rigors of seminary life have made me so thin," I dared to say, and I went on brazenly, "but I am very happy there, and I have some very good friends among my classmates. And then, Mother, I must get used to this beautiful new life little by little, even if it takes enormous effort!"

I was very lucky, because my parents never opposed my vocation. However, some of their friends, worried about their old age, sought to persuade them that it was imprudent for them to let their only child become a priest. They even went so far as to provoke them to anxiety with troubling questions: Have you thought about your old age? Who then will take care of you when you are no longer able to work to meet your needs? Furthermore, you will never have grandchildren.... Have you thought about this?

With God's help, sustained by daily prayer, Mother and Father never showed me their misgivings because they did not want to oppose my heart's desire. My parents understood the depth of my joy and did nothing to frustrate God's plan for me. As Christians, they reflected that if my path were really leading me to the seminary, the Lord would guide me to the end.

After summer vacation, I once again happily embarked for Bingerville for my second year of seminary. It was September 27, 1958, on board the *Mermoz*.

At that time, Guinea was agitating to gain its independence. Everywhere in the country people were shouting, "We prefer freedom in poverty to opulence in slavery." My homeland, having chosen immediate independence, cut off all ties with France. Many of my fellow countrymen thought that the first glimmers of the dawn of liberty were now on the horizon. France, under General de Gaulle's leadership, nervous and unhappy about this decision by the Guinean government, was, therefore, preparing to leave with its weapons and baggage. There was an atmosphere of joy and happiness, euphoria and troubling realism, all at once.

In the midst of this uncertainty, we once again took the boat for Abidjan and Bingerville. The 1958–1959 school year went as usual; my grades were very good, though not excellent. I had managed for the most part to fill in the gaps in my learning, and I was admitted to the third year to continue my formation as a future priest.

Then, once again, summer vacation in Guinea loomed on the horizon, as always preceded by four days of fasting and penance, because for most of us the journey by boat was a real ordeal. Seasickness was our loyal traveling companion. We hated it, but it was fond of us and would not let us go!

The 1959–1960 school year was the last year at Saint Augustine's in Bingerville for the Guinean seminarians. Father Thépaut had been replaced by Father Messner as rector of the seminary. Three African priests, Jacques Nomel, Louis Grandouillet, and Pierre-Marie Coty, were then appointed professors at the seminary. We were happy and proud to see these African models among our instructors! These young priests were the pride and consolation of the white missionaries, who thus tasted the fruits of their sacrifices. The men whom they had educated were now participating in the formation of the African clergy. I remember that in Bingerville there was an excellent atmosphere of work and ecclesial communion. But we Guineans had to cut our school year short. Boats departed for Conakry less frequently due to the revolutionary policies of Sékou Touré, who was becoming more radical and closing Guinea off from the world. We had to leave Ivory Coast in early June aboard the *Général Mangin* from Libreville.

What memories do you still have of these years in Ivory Coast?

I only spent three years at Saint Augustine Minor Seminary, 1957 to 1960. The academic program was rigorous and identical to the one in

French middle and high schools, since the seminarians had to pass the same official exams as their student colleagues. Our professors gave equal attention to our intellectual, cultural, and spiritual education. Sports and daily manual labor were also an important part of the program.

However, daily Mass was the focus of our day. It was carefully prepared for and celebrated with fervor and solemnity, especially on Sundays. Special attention was paid to our liturgical education, so that we might understand the mysteries we were celebrating. Training in silence, discipline, and communal life helped to mold the seminarians, preparing them to develop their own interior life and to become true stewards of the mysteries of God. We learned to live together as a family, avoiding regionalism or tribalism. We constantly had to change our companion during our daily walks or recreation, so as to get used to living in brotherly communion with everybody, without privileging or preferring anyone. We thus were able to train to become the future priests of multicultural, multiethnic, and multiracial Christian communities. The priests wanted the Eucharist to make us blood brothers, one family, one people, one race, that of the children of God. The present archbishop of Abidjan, Jean-Pierre Cardinal Kutwa, was my classmate.

Guinea gained its independence in October 1958, and because of strained relations and the lack of cooperation between Sékou Touré and Félix Houphouët-Boigny, we had to return to Guinea to a combined seminary and middle school run by the Holy Ghost Fathers.

From that moment on, was your seminary formation affected by the troubles in Guinean politics?

Yes indeed, we are all affected by the sociopolitical and historical context in which we live. God shapes us in a given environment, through happy or unhappy events and through his chosen intermediaries. He knows how to lead us through the trials and tribulations of history.

Given the political troubles, Archbishop Gérard de Milleville of Conakry decided to repatriate us from the seminary in Bingerville to the Saint Mary of Dixinn seminary and middle school. The latter is located in a district in Conakry by the same name. In order to facilitate our life as future priests and the discernment of our vocation, he housed us in the novitiate of the Sisters of Saint Joseph of Cluny, near the middle school in Dixinn, so that we might receive our intellectual, emotional, and spiritual formation in a setting of partial solitude. The Sisters of Cluny no longer had any novices; the building was therefore vacant, ready to welcome a little group of seminarians. Since they were attending a school where young Christians, Muslims, and Africans who practiced traditional religions were present, it was important to teach the young seminarians the habit of frequent "encounters" with Jesus. Thus, the Sisters' novitiate was transformed into a seminary, and Father Louis Barry was placed in charge as the rector.

As the one primarily responsible for the seminary, he was concerned about setting an example, so that our discipline, piety, and desire to become better acquainted with God would grow a little more each day. He wanted to instill in us a love of righteousness and humility. Like Saint Paul, he tacitly exhorted us through his example to devote ourselves to "whatever is true, whatever is honorable, whatever is just, whatever is pure, whatever is lovely, whatever is gracious, if there is any excellence, if there is anything worthy of praise", as it says in the Letter to the Philippians; for the Apostle of the Gentiles also said, "What you have learned and received and heard and seen in me, do" (Phil 4:8–9).

As I would later discover in my own experience as a priest, he wanted to make each of us, even at our young age, despite our frailties, not only an *alter Christus*, but, much more, *ipse Christus*, Christ himself.

We took courses with the other students, as the Guinean government required. Unfortunately, after a year, the middle school was confiscated and nationalized by the State, as were all Church-owned schools, charitable works, and property. This measure by the revolutionary Guinean government immediately provoked energetic protests from Archbishop Gérard de Milleville. He was therefore promptly expelled from the country for having defended the rights of the Church. Subsequently, for several months, the seminarians were compelled to stay in their respective parishes, where the Fathers tried to give them a few courses. Under pressure from the regime and given all sorts of difficulties connected with the persecutions, many seminarians abandoned their vocation in order to attend State schools.

Along with several other fellow students who wanted to consecrate their lives to the Lord, I persevered, for I really believed that my path was the priesthood. After repeated negotiations, our new bishop, Archbishop Tchidimbo, managed to enroll us in the State school in Kindia so that we might return to a regular academic life.

The year was already well under way, and we had to pass our *brevet* (middle school examination). How could we pass the exam after missing more than six months of classes? For it was only in March 1962 that a dozen seminarians, the meager remnant of the group from Dixinn, were able to reach Kindia, ninety miles from Conakry. We went to work converting the premises of a dilapidated former youth center into a livable home with study rooms, a game room, and refectory. The Fathers' dedication allowed us rapidly to convert the two largest rooms into dormitories. The seminary came back to life under the patronage of Saint Joseph and the leadership of Father Alphonse Gilbert.

His heart overflowing with affection for each of us, he succeeded in restoring guidance to our life as future priests. His gentleness and his homilies drew us to Jesus and urged us to have a real, increasingly intimate relationship with God. I was personally struck by the example, human qualities, and intense interior life of this missionary. Whenever one of us had a fit of anger or bitterness or behaved in a manner unbefitting a Christian, Father Gilbert asked him to go pray before the Blessed Sacrament, so that he could examine his conscience face to face with Jesus and allow himself to be calmed by the Lord's gentle presence.

After waiting patiently for many months, Archbishop Tchidimbo also succeeded in obtaining authorization to reopen the seminary and to provide courses for seminarians in grades ten and eleven, that is, the year leading up to the baccalaureate. Also, Father Gérard Vieira, who was firmly committed to the training of the future African clergy, came from Conakry every week to teach mathematics, as did Father Maurice de Chalendar to give courses in Latin and Greek. Both of them stayed with us a full day. They were also great models of priestly life and intellectual integrity. At the archbishop's request, Father Lein, the pastor in Mamou, made himself available to teach philosophy to the oldest students and Latin to the youngest. In 1963, reinforcements came from the Diocese of Luçon in France, in the form of Fathers Joseph Bregeon and Emmanuel Rabaud. Thus we benefited from a great team of qualified and devoted priests, who assisted us not only in our academic work but especially in the task of discerning God's will.

Once again we can see the importance of the Holy Ghost Fathers in your life. How would you describe the spirituality that they passed on to you?

I believe that what impressed me most profoundly, since I was very young, even before my years of catechism classes, was the regularity of their prayer life. I will never forget the spiritual rigor of their daily routine.

The days of the Spiritans were ordered like those of monks. Very early in the morning, they were in church to pray together and individually. Then each one celebrated Mass at his altar, assisted by a server. After breakfast, they saw to their work. At noon, they met again in the church for midday prayer and the Angelus. As soon as they finished their meal, they returned once again to the church for thanksgiving and a visit to the Blessed Sacrament. After a rest period, I used to watch with curiosity as they prayed individually, at around four in the afternoon, while reading from a little book. As you may guess, it was the recitation of the breviary.... At the end of the day, around 7 P.M., came evening prayer with everyone, and then dinner. At 9 P.M., around the great cross, one of the Fathers would gladly come spend time with us, answering our questions and trying to introduce us to the Christian life, spiritual values, and sacred history. We always finished our vigil with a song. I still remember the one that usually ended our days, entitled "Before Going to Sleep beneath the Stars". This song prepared us to get down on our knees humbly before God to receive his forgiveness and protection during the night. The melody is still alive today in my heart.

Ourous was home to great and holy missionaries; they were completely consumed by the fire of God's love. They had exceptional human, intellectual, and spiritual qualities, but all died very young.

As I already told you, Father Firmin Montels, the founder, breathed his last on September 2, 1912, only six months after founding the parish. At the moment when he died, he was singing "O Salutaris Hostia, quae caeli pandis ostium. Bella praemunt hostilia, da robur, fer auxilium" (O Saving Victim, opening wide the gate of heav'n to us below! Our foes press on from every side; Your aid supply, Your strength bestow). This priest was a great artist and, according to many accounts, a saint. His days were quite full, with four hours dedicated to teaching catechism each day. He compelled himself to make the Way of the Cross every day and to spend several hours in adoration of the Blessed Sacrament each week. Not to mention the daily work of learning the local language.

When I look back at the past and the early days of the mission, or at Guinea in general, when I consider one by one the exceptional gifts from Providence, I know that God truly guided and adopted us. I remember how enthralled I was when I saw the Holy Ghost Fathers walking every afternoon while reading their breviaries.... I never tired of watching them, with a sense of awe. This may seem naïve fifty years later, but I do not deny what God made known to me.

Every day, the Holy Ghost Fathers lived by the rhythm of the Divine Office, Mass, work, and the rosary, and they never shirked their duties as men of God. As a small child, I told myself that if the Fathers went to church so regularly, it must be because they were certain to encounter someone there and to speak to him with complete confidence. Obviously, my ambition was to be able to encounter Christ, too. When I entered the seminary, I was able to accept the difficulties because of my certainty that one day I would encounter Jesus in prayer, just like the missionaries.

How many times I was profoundly gripped by the silence that reigned in the church during the Fathers' prayers! At first, settled in the back of the building, I watched these men and wondered what they were doing, kneeling or sitting in the half-light, not saying anything.... But they seemed to be listening and conversing with someone in the semi-darkness of the church, lit by candles. I was truly fascinated by their practice of prayer and the peaceful atmosphere it engendered. I think that it is fair to say that there is a true heroism, greatness, and nobility in this life of regular prayer. Man is great only when he is on his knees before God.

Of course they were not perfect. These men had their moods, their human limitations, but I want to pay tribute to these religious men for their generous gift of their lives, their asceticism, and their humility. In all the seminaries run by the missionaries, like the one in Sebikhotane for example, I found this desire to seek Christ deeply in this daily intimate conversation. The way they established contact with the local people was a model of tact and practical thinking. Without this intimacy with heaven, their missionary work could not have been fruitful.

The sufferings they endured were not in vain. My parish, the most remote in the country, was the one that produced the greatest number of vocations in Guinea! This confirms the prophetic words that Father Orcel wrote to his bishop on August 15, 1925, thirteen years after the founding of Saint Rose mission: "I would not be at all surprised to see vocations take shape among our children. As for me, I think that vocations are the reward for serious training in the family and in the mission."

The Holy Ghost Fathers had a profound impact on Guinean Catholicism. How could we forget the way these priests took care of everyone, even the most wretched lepers? They touched them and treated them, even though the patients gave off an unbearable smell. They taught them the catechism, considering that the sick, too, had the right to be instructed in the mysteries of the faith and to receive Christ's sacraments.

Despite the political sufferings that accompanied Sékou Touré's Marxist dictatorship, the Church in Guinea stood fast, for she was founded on the rock, on the sacrifices of missionaries, and on the joy of the Gospel. Communist doctrine never got the better of the priests who traveled on foot to the smallest villages, accompanied by a few catechists, carrying their suitcase-chapel on their heads! The humility of the Spiritans' faith was the strongest defense against the egalitarian aberrations of the revolutionary Marxist ideology of the State Party in Guinea. A handful of zealous and courageous Guinean priests kept the flame of the Gospel burning.

Have you stayed in touch with the Holy Ghost Fathers from this period?

Certainly, the most influential priest used by God to reveal to me my vocation was Father Marcel Bracquemond. He still lives in France. In 2012, I invited him to join us for the centennial celebrations of the parish in Ourous, and, in August 2014, I visited him in his retirement home in Brittany.

He was unable to accept my invitation to attend the centennial in Ourous because of his age and the long roads, which are still very difficult to travel. But I did receive the following letter from him: "I received, via my religious superiors, your charming invitation to the celebration of the centennial of Saint Rose parish in Ouros, of which I have fond memories of having seen your courage as a server fetching the cruets, while menaced by a snake on top of the credence table. This courage is perhaps what brought you to the attention of the Holy Father Benedict XVI. The expulsion in May 1967 separated us.... I had other assignments. Now, at the age of eighty-six, still blessed with enough good health to help in the parish ministry in Brittany, a thoroughly delightful region, I apologize for turning down your invitation, because of the hundreds of miles of roads separating Ourous from Conakry and on account of the attitude of some now-influential Christians during the unhappy circumstances that preceded the expulsion.... Nonetheless, I wish to tell your uncle Samuel Coline, whose marriage to Marie Panaré I blessed, that I remember her often in my prayers, and I ask that a dwelling place may be granted to her in Christ's kingdom. Cardinal

Sarah, I assure you of my prayers: may you continue for a long time to
be as courageous as when I knew you, and may God's will be done
to the extent of the authority that the Church bestows on you."

How could I forget this young priest who was the first to speak to me
about the seminary and my vocation? How could I forget that he helped
my parents plan the long journey toward my new life, a journey that has
never stopped since then....

All these years, your parents seem to have assisted you fervently....

Yes, my parents always supported my vocation and then my priestly
ministry with their humble, powerful prayers. Even though they are now
deceased, Father and Mother continue to watch over me from heaven.
They are truly the most profound sign of God's presence in my life.

To demonstrate his kindness and unfailing support, God willed that
their deaths should fall on a day before or after an anniversary relating to
my priesthood. This providential coincidence convinced me that they
would constantly be at my side, from heaven, still surrounding me with
their prayers as they had done on earth. I was consecrated bishop of
Conakry on December 8, 1979, and Father died on December 7, 1991,
at the very moment when I was celebrating the Eucharist for the twelfth
anniversary of my episcopate. I was ordained to the priesthood on
July 20, 1969, and Mother died on July 21, 2007, the day after my thirty-
eighth anniversary of priestly ordination.

Yes, I was quite shaken by her death. I have never been in so much
pain in all my life. I suddenly felt totally alone. I was in Abruzzo for a
spiritual retreat when Mother passed away in Conakry. The morning
of her death, she had tried to reach me by phone, but I was outside of
Rome. Late that afternoon, in the arms of a nun, Sister Marie-Renée,
she went peacefully to the Father's house.

A few hours after her death, Archbishop Vincent Coulibaly of Conakry told me the news. That evening, on July 21, 2007, I felt as though
I had been cut off from the roots of my whole life. My sadness seemed
unbearable. Once I returned to Rome, I was able to leave for Conakry soon after, on Monday, July 23. The whole populace, both Christians and Muslims, welcomed me with such brotherly compassion that
I had the impression that God was flooding me with consolation. I will
never forget the friendly support offered by the entire population of my

country. Their affection and expressions of sympathy were profoundly fraternal, as if my people were replacing the brothers and sisters I never had. The kindness shown by all of Guinea touched me to the very core.

I returned to Rome at peace, for I felt that my parents would continue to be at the center of my life. They had always lived as faithful Christians, docile to the will of God.

At the time of my departure for Rome in 2001, Mother had behaved quite admirably. I was very afraid to leave her alone, as she was beginning to grow old. Therefore, I entrusted to a nun and friend the painful task of telling her about my new appointment in Rome, as secretary of the Congregation for the Evangelization of Peoples. I was so sad that I did not have the strength necessary to tell her myself. Upon hearing the news of my future position in the service of the universal Church, Mother responded with lucid faith: "I thank God who gave me one child, and the Lord always takes him far from me to do his work. I thank the pope, for there are many bishops in the world, and he thought of my son to be beside him. But will Robert be up to the task that the Supreme Pontiff will assign to him? Will he be able to perform correctly the duties that the pope wishes to entrust to him? And who will succeed him as archbishop of Conakry? I pray that God will find a good successor for him." Mother's act of faith overwhelmed me, giving me wings at the moment when I was about to fly far away from her for God's glory. While I was resisting so as to stay in Guinea, Mother was encouraging me to obey.

One week after I left Conakry, she had a fall and broke her hip.... She had to go to the emergency room. When I learned the news by telephone, I was distraught; despite the painful fracture, she still tried to reassure me. In fact, my parents created an atmosphere of peace, serene tranquility, and religious respect around my vocation, so as to allow me to walk with God, listening only to his voice whispering to me at every moment, as it did to Abraham, "Walk before me, and be blameless" (Gen 17:1).

Father and Mother were a great blessing and a precious treasure to me; God blessed them abundantly, granting them the immense joy of participating in the ceremonies of my priestly ordination and then my episcopal consecration. My only disappointment was that Father did not live to see with us the extraordinary pastoral visit of John Paul II to Guinea. He died two months before the pope's arrival in February 1992. On the other hand, Mother had the honor of seeing him and greeting him.

For all these divine gifts I give thanks to God. I deserved nothing, but God often chooses the lowly. He deigned to look upon a little boy from a poor village. I never would have imagined that God could accomplish all that he has done for me. But who could ever know where God is leading us? Look at Saint Paul: in his rage against the Christians, did he know where he was going while on the road to Damascus? And Saint Augustine, a fiercely ambitious young man eager for honors and pleasures, who was torn between his desires and his aspirations, between his flesh and his spirit, did he understand what he was seeking when he left Africa for Milan? We are all the objects of this extraordinary manifestation of God's mercy. His goodwill toward us is boundless!

Baccalaureate in hand, did you leave very quickly for France?

Indeed, Archbishop Tchidimbo had decided that I must continue discerning my vocation in France. In September 1964, I left Conakry after earning my baccalaureate to begin my studies in philosophy and theology at the seminary in Nancy. Bishop Pirolet of Lorraine agreed to accept seminarians from other countries: there were three of us Guineans, but there was also a boy from Laos, Antoine Biengta, and another from Korea, Joseph Ho.

There were around one hundred of us seminarians, and there was a very friendly atmosphere. Even though I had been introduced to French culture to a great extent, I still had to make another physical and cultural adjustment.... There was a big difference between France and Africa. It was very cold, and for the first time, wide-eyed with amazement, I saw snow fall.

I noticed that relationships were different, lacking the warmth of my country. Yet those years of studying Scholastic philosophy were a wonderful experience, in an enriching intercultural atmosphere. The professors worked diligently for our formation.

When I arrived in Nancy, the first signs of the May 1968 protests were looming on the horizon.... The Constitution on the Sacred Liturgy, *Sacrosanctum concilium*, had been published the previous year, on December 4, 1963. This document was already thought to hold the keys to a modern adaptation of the liturgy. The tradition of wearing clerical garb was no longer necessarily observed—the Roman collar was replaced by a turtleneck sweater—and eventually priestly identity itself began to lose its visibility and disappear into anonymity; the cassock was slowly transformed into a liturgical vestment that was taken off as soon as ceremonies were over. Yet I did not always realize the seriousness of these first signs of upheaval, because there was a fine generosity in our relations, a deep desire to pray. For us foreigners, the welcome was truly touching. We felt completely integrated into God's family.

During the holidays we stayed as guests on farms or at the homes of our classmates' families—to work there, to earn a bit of money, and to cover our personal expenses for the school year, as Archbishop Tchidimbo wished.

During all those years, I never encountered any racism. Once, in Compiègne, where I was staying with the parents of a classmate, Gilles Silvy-Leligois, someone in the street called me a dirty Negro. My friend was furious and wanted his father to intervene. I had to calm his anger, pleading with him to ignore this irrational, unjust act of aggression. And to set him at ease, I added, "I am unquestionably a Negro; however, I am not dirty!" I realized that it must have been a Frenchman who had had to leave Africa with a lot of bitterness and some personal injuries. To tell the truth, it was my one and only personal experience of a racist attack in France.

During those years in France, were there events that had a particular impact on you?

I will never forget my spiritual director, Father Louis Denis, a holy priest and a very gentle man. His heart and mind overflowed with wisdom! He was an invaluable help to me on my path to the priesthood, while I was separated from my parents, without any news. I remember, too, that in Nancy I saw a cardinal for the first time in my life.... It was a great servant of the Holy See, Eugène Cardinal Tisserant, who maintained strong ties with his roots in Lorraine. He always stayed at our seminary when he was passing through Nancy. The cardinal greatly impressed me with the breadth of his knowledge; and yet he was not aloof. On the contrary, his homilies were exemplary. We were neither frightened nor overwhelmed by his stature, because he knew how to remain simple and accessible.

My greatest joy during that period was meeting the family of André and Françoise Mallard, with their three girls, Claire, Agnès, and Béatrice, who considered me their older brother. Their kindness to me was such that, wherever my studies led me—from Nancy to Jerusalem, via Sébik-hotane in Senegal and Rome—my adoptive parents came to visit me to demonstrate their closeness and affection. They were of course present in Conakry for my episcopal consecration.

I was in effect adopted by them and spoiled like one of their own. The void caused by the separation from my parents was filled by their tact, their support, and the warmth of their love. They were truly a second family to me; the bond remains to this day and grows stronger year by year.

How did you stay in touch with your parents, who were still living in Ourous?

You have to understand that I did not go back home for the holidays, including the summer vacations. Guinea was in the midst of a revolution, and the trip was very expensive. After our country declared its independence, the Holy Ghost Fathers were practically forbidden to conduct social, educational, medical, or any other activities. They were all expelled from Guinea in May 1967.

The separation from my family became even more unfortunate. I could not write to them, for fear of jeopardizing my parents, who would have been suspected of having foreign ties. They could have been accused, then arrested, and perhaps put into prison for collaborating with foreign enemies, who, according to the government, were regularly plotting to overthrow the revolutionary government in Guinea....

The only opportunities to hear news were Archbishop Tchidimbo's visits to Nancy. He passed on information about the development of the situation in Guinea. Our bishop brought us letters from our loved ones; we could also give him private messages. But during those three years of seminary in Nancy, he could never give me a single letter from my parents, since they lived over three hundred miles away from the capital of Guinea! The time went by slowly without any communication with my family.

During the vacations, we worked on farms or in workshops to earn a bit of money, which allowed us to cover our personal costs. So it was that I worked on a farm not far from Nancy but also in Longwy. Archbishop Tchidimbo was uncompromising in his management of the money that we earned; he did not want us to keep even one cent of our wages.

One day, the eldest of us three Guineans failed to obey the bishop's instructions and kept his money to buy a motorcycle! When Archbishop Tchidimbo learned that our classmate had used his summer savings for that purchase, he flew into a rage that was difficult to calm. What was worse, the bishop became angry with the whole group, including those who had followed his instructions, like myself.... Today I laugh about it, but at the time, I was completely depressed. We had no news from our parents, and, instead of encouraging us, our pastor had just stridently lectured us, without distinguishing the guilty from the innocent.

I then went through a period of doubts. In my profound confusion, I vaguely considered the possibility of leaving the seminary. I went to see my spiritual director, Father Denis, to tell him about my disappointment. He declared to me, "Listen, Robert. I have known four bishops in Nancy, and each had his faults, which can be difficult, and his virtues, which are very edifying. You will not be a priest for the bishop's sake but for Christ and for the Church. You must continue serenely, with complete confidence, with and for Christ, with your bishop or in spite of him. Certainly, he is the one who will call you to the priesthood, but you will be a priest for the Church. Today, you must get along with Archbishop Tchidimbo, and in the future you will have to learn to cope with his successor's personality." The only surprise was that Archbishop Tchidimbo's successor, by a mysterious decree of God, turned out to be me....

In any case, I stayed on at the seminary with joy and enthusiasm. It is true, Archbishop Tchidimbo was very strict, intensely upright, and endlessly demanding. He used to come visit us at the minor seminary in Kindia. I remember that he insisted on the importance of spiritual qualities, and especially good character, moral integrity, and honesty. I can still hear him thunder to the class: "The first reason to expel a seminarian is for duplicity, the second, for duplicity, and the third, for duplicity." His stern language was somewhat frightening, but he wanted any man called to the priesthood to be upright and to have integrity. Saint Gregory the Great wrote in a homily, "Woe to the sinner who walks the earth by a double path." The sinner walks along two paths when his conduct contradicts his words, for then, inevitably, what he is looking for belongs to the world and to its vices.

Archbishop Tchidimbo believed that honesty was an indispensable trait that a bishop could never compromise. He had been formed in

Chevilly-Larue by the Holy Ghost Fathers, and he belonged to Father Libermann's "valiant society". Despite his severity, he meant a lot to me; he had a generous heart and was capable of being kind and very thoughtful.

Why did you leave Nancy before the end of your theology studies?

Indeed, I ought to have finished my theology studies in Nancy. Moreover, I remember that at the end of my studies in philosophy, I seriously considered earning a bachelor's degree in that subject, which I liked very much. However, Archbishop Tchidimbo asked me not to pursue that plan.

Obedience helped me to mature. It redirected my attention and my heart's desire toward the Sacred Scriptures. Furthermore, my desire to be a priest became more attuned with my new aspiration to study the Word of God. Thanks to a Protestant German friend, Horst Bültzingslöwen, I gradually discovered the study of the Bible. At the time, Horst was studying biblical exegesis at the University of Tübingen, and we often spent our vacation together with the Mallards, who owned a second home on the coast, near Arromanches-les-Bains. Little by little, I was inoculated with the virus of biblical studies, which grew increasingly contagious until the end of my theological studies!

However, relations between Guinea and France, especially the relationship between Sékou Touré and General de Gaulle, were becoming so complicated that I had to leave Nancy. Once again, my country's political troubles obliged me to change my place of study abruptly; so I left for Senegal and went to the seminary in Sébikhotane, not far from Dakar, for my last two years as a seminarian, from October 1967 to June 1969. Even there, one could sense the wind of the revolutionary movement of May 1968.

During my stay in Sébikhotane I was ordained a sub-deacon. The ceremony took place in January 1969 in the cathedral in Dakar and was presided over by Hyacinthe Cardinal Thiandoum. Diaconal ordination was then conferred upon me by Bishop Augustin Sagna in April 1969 in Brin, Senegal, in the Diocese of Ziguinchor. There were a dozen of us deacons, happy and resolved to love God. Most of the young deacons came from the dioceses of Dakar, Thiès, and Ziguinchor. There were two of us from Guinea, Father Augustin Tounkara and I. The mood at

Sébikhotane was very warm and studious, in an African environment that benefited from the spiritual proximity and liturgical quality of the Benedictine abbey of Keur Moussa, which was part of the Solesmes Congregation.

In fact, the year of my diaconate was full of emotion and inner fear and trembling. I could already see the hour of my priestly ordination coming and the special moment of my First Mass. How could I not tremble at the thought of being a priest, being like Christ, pronouncing the same words as he? During this same period, Archbishop Tchidimbo informed me that immediately after my ordination he would send me to Rome to study the Sacred Scriptures.

You can imagine my joy and happiness upon hearing this news. Never would I have dreamed that one day I would be in Rome, near the tomb of Peter, and that I would see the pope with my own eyes! The little boy in Ourous who watched the priests gather in the village church seemed so far away ... and yet nothing about me had really changed.

II

THE STAR OF THE MAGI

Luck, they say. But luck is like us.
Real humility is first and foremost decency.

—Georges Bernanos, *Sous le soleil de Satan*

NICOLAS DIAT : *After your ordination as a priest, did you leave immediately for Rome to finish your studies?*

ROBERT CARDINAL SARAH: Inasmuch as Archbishop Tchidimbo approved of my desire to study Scripture, first I had to get a degree in dogmatic theology. So I arrived in Rome in September 1969 to enroll in the Gregorian University.

Instruction was in Latin. At the same time I took courses in Hebrew, biblical Greek, and Aramaic at the Pontificium Institutum Biblicum. These courses were marvelous because they gave me the opportunity to have more direct access to the Word of God and to the Church Fathers who wrote commentaries on it.

I stayed in Rome until 1974, with a side trip of one year in Jerusalem.

Archbishop Tchidimbo had sent two other seminarians to Rome at the same time as me, André Mamadouba Camara and Jérôme Téa, as well as two Guinean novices, Marie-Renée Boiro and Eugénie Kadouna. He was anxious for us to get a solid human, intellectual, and spiritual formation there. This is the last letter he wrote to us on December 14, 1970, ten days before his arrest and imprisonment: "I have so little free time that I will not be able to send Christmas greetings to you individually this year; be so kind as to excuse me. But I am sure you will be able to discover in these lines the deepest of my sentiments for each of you, with regard to your formation for effective ministry in this dear country of Guinea. My concern for the formation of each one of you personally is a problem that haunts me every day; I know you are helping me to resolve this problem by the generous efforts that you make daily to acquire all you are capable of assimilating, both intellectually and spiritually; and for that I am infinitely grateful to you. May 1971 be a year of still greater effort for the sake of the Church of Guinea; these are my most ardent wishes for each of you. May the Child in the Manger receive these wishes and grant them in the near future. I know that I can count on your prayers; mine are with you daily, along with the affection that I have for each of you."

This letter-testament accompanied me throughout my studies in Rome.

However, while I was preparing to write my doctoral thesis in biblical exegesis on the subject of "Isaiah, Chapters 9–11, in Light of Northwestern Semitic Linguistics: Ugaritic, Phoenecian, and Punic" under the direction of my professor, Father Mitchell Dahood, Father Louis Barry, who had become the apostolic administrator of the Archdiocese of Conakry, asked me to return to Guinea because of the shortage of priests.

The objective of my research was to propose a new critical examination of certain textual difficulties in the Masoretic text of the Book of Isaiah, in terms of Ugaritic literature and Phoenecian and Punic inscriptions. In order to elucidate difficult texts, the methodology of modern exegesis insists on syntactic, lexicographic, and stylistic considerations offered by comparative studies of Northwestern Semitic literature. I want to emphasize how valuable Father Dahood's method was. He succeeded in convincing a large part of the scholarly community that the copyists of the Hebrew text of the Old Testament were scrupulously faithful to the original text, at least in its consonantal form.

Today, certainly it is important for us to show that same respect and fidelity to the Word of God, so as not to manipulate it to fit historical, political, or ideological circumstances, for the purpose of pleasing men and acquiring a reputation as a scholar or avant-garde theologian.... As Saint Paul says, "We are not like so many [who] practice cunning or ... tamper with God's word" (cf. 2 Cor 2:17; 4:2). This scrupulous concern about respecting the Word of God and its application in our lives reminds me of an exhortation by Johannes Albrecht Bengel (1687–1752), a Protestant theologian who tried to summarize the care that we must give to the Sacred Scriptures: "Te totum applica ad textum, rem totam applica ad te" (Apply yourself entirely to the text, and apply everything it says to yourself).

The true servant of the Bible, the true theologian, is the one who exemplifies each day, by his life and by his actions, the words of the Psalmist: "Oh, how I love your law! It is my meditation all the day.... I have more understanding than all my teachers, for your testimonies are my meditation. I understand more than the aged, for I keep your precepts. I hold back my feet from every evil way, in order to keep your word. I do not turn aside from your ordinances, for you have taught me" (Ps 119:97, 99–102).

Did this study of the Scriptures seem difficult for you?

Those years of biblical studies can seem long and demanding. Indeed, they require the knowledge of numerous languages and complex work to place the Sacred Scriptures back into the context of the major cultures that influenced the people of Israel, particularly the Sumerian, Egyptian, Babylonian, Canaanite, Greek, and Roman cultures, without neglecting the geopolitical setting of Israel's history. But those years are necessary in order to let the Word of God penetrate us like a two-edged sword. It takes time for our stony hearts to receive the Word of God so that it might really become the Word of the Covenant. We can then experience, as Baudouin de Fort says in one of his homilies, that "the Word of God, which is also the wisdom of God, truly becomes more penetrating when it is received with faith and love. Indeed, what could be impossible for someone who believes? And what could be difficult for those who love? When the voice of the Word speaks up, it sinks into the heart like arrows in battle that tear, like nails driven deeply, and it penetrates so far that it reaches the most secret recesses. Yes, this Word goes much farther than a two-edged sword, because there is no power or force that can deal such considerable blows, and the human mind cannot conceive of a point so subtle and so penetrating. All human wisdom, all the subtlety of natural knowledge, falls short of its keenness."

One must humbly acknowledge that a whole lifetime is necessary to study the Word of God and to acquire the wisdom that leads to love.

Was living in Rome an extraordinary experience for you?

When I was in Africa I imagined that Rome was something like paradise.... To me, the city of the pope seemed far off and inaccessible.

My arrival in the *urbs aeterna* (eternal city) is engraved into my memory. Each step was a marvel. I was staying on the viale delle Mura Aurelie, at the Collegio San Pietro, not far from the Vatican. When I entered the majestic Saint Peter's Basilica for the first time, how could I have imagined that one day I would celebrate Mass in that sacred place as a cardinal? I remember perfectly my first prayer at the tomb of the Prince of the Apostles. I had a very intense feeling of deep faith, of love for God, and of the heavenly inspiration that I could see in all those works of art. During that time, I discovered ancient Rome, the Coliseum, the Forum, the catacombs, and all the memories of the first Christian martyrs. Often, I told myself that I was walking in the footsteps of the saints, of whom I was supposed to be a humble pupil.

But our studies took up the main part of our days.... We had great professors, who were often the best specialists in their fields. At that time, Carlo Maria Martini was rector of the Biblicum. I remember in particular the courses given by Ignace de La Potterie, Stanislas Lyonnet, Etienne Vogt, and Albert Vanhoye, who was also created a cardinal later on. These competent academics were imbued with a radiant interior life. They communicated to us their knowledge and their faith in God.

Upon arriving in Rome in 1969, you witnessed the beginning of the liturgical reform in the pope's own city....

Yes, but I was ordained in the old rite in July 1969 because the new one was not yet in force. From the time of my arrival in Rome, however, I celebrated with the new Missal of Paul VI. In those days, at the Collegio of San Pietro, each of us still had his own altar. The practice of concelebration was rare.

Personally, I really tried to celebrate my daily Mass with great care. I could not help noticing around me that some priests were having difficulty finding a balance between their use of their free time, their personal life with the Lord, and their obligation to attend to their communal life as priests. For others, the important thing was their studies, while slackening somewhat in their spiritual life. I recall very well that the African priest who drove me to my apartment told me: "This is your room: you come and go as you please!" It was very edifying for a young priest to hear such an exhortation....

In the morning, I chose to get up early so as to be able to celebrate without hurrying. I was aware that Mass was the most important moment of my day, because without the Eucharist, my relationship with Christ could not achieve the great intimacy that every Christian desires. I was no longer at the seminary; it was up to me, therefore, to structure my days quite freely and to arrange my moments of meeting the Lord in order to deepen my union with God. The priest who neglects his Mass can no longer see how much God loves us, to the point of giving us his life.

During that time, I realized that the liturgy was the most precious sacred moment in which the Church allows us to encounter God in a unique way. We must never forget to unite the liturgy with the tragic event of the death of Jesus on the Cross.

Where do you get the lively and precocious liturgical sensitivity that you seem to have?

Thank you for that fine compliment. I am sure the example of the Holy Ghost Fathers was decisive. When I was an altar boy, I observed very attentively the sensitivity and fervor with which the priests in my village celebrated their daily Masses. In this sense, it is not wrong to say that from a young age I was able to understand the need to offer spiritual worship that was holy and pleasing to God. At Mass we are present first and foremost to God. If we do not turn our attention radically toward God, our faith becomes lukewarm, distracted, and uncertain. At Ourous, as an altar boy, I gradually learned to enter into the eucharistic mystery and to understand that the Mass was a unique moment in the life of the priests and of the faithful. Divine worship lifted us out of the ordinary. Seeing things with the eyes of a child, I had the feeling that the priest was literally absorbed by Christ at the moment when, facing East, he lifted the consecrated Host toward heaven.

I was also able to understand the importance of moments of silence during the liturgy. A priest ought to make a great deal of room for silence in his life, because that is fundamental if he is to remain attentive to God and to the souls that are entrusted to him. For a priest it is terribly important to learn, from the example of the monks, never to speak without reason. Because preaching involves silence. In noise, the priest wastes his time; chatter is an acid rain that can ruin our meditation. The silence of God should teach us when to speak and when to remain silent.

This silence that ushers us into the real liturgy is a moment in which to praise God, to confess him before others, and to proclaim his glory. I remember that on Sundays all the villagers were very fond of spending a long time in personal prayer. We were in the presence of the Presence.

Finally, my sense of liturgy acquired a maturity and a depth as I matured, particularly during my years at seminary. As an African, I certainly inherited our joyful fear of everything sacred. In pagan religious celebrations, after the dances and the sounds of rejoicing came the sacred moments of sacrificial libations, which required absolute silence.

During my years as a seminarian, and then after my ordination, my certainty was strengthened. I understood that the greatest way to be with the Son of God made man was still the liturgy. At Mass the priest is face to face with God. The Mass is the most important thing in our lives. And the Divine Office, the breviary, prepares us for it.

During my youth I did not have the chance to become acquainted with the rich liturgy that can be found in monasteries. It may be that many Christians in Europe do not appreciate the fact that abbeys are a unique treasure. However, the Holy Ghost Fathers' slow liturgical pace and their sense of the sacred did enable me during my childhood to anticipate the incomparable beauty of the Benedictine celebrations.

In the Old Testament the Hebrews always approached God with fear and veneration. Ultimately, I sought to imitate them. The best way to do this is through the liturgy.

Sometimes there is the sense that there was a sort of miracle in your journey.

I was fortunate to be mentored by spiritual fathers of great quality. In Nancy or in Senegal, the priests who accompanied me insisted a great deal on the importance of the interior life. Archbishop Tchidimbo, who was confined and tortured in a prison for many years, was always in my heart. A seminarian is first and foremost the work of the priests who have accompanied him. God gave me the gift of being mentored by pastors who were truly connected to Christ.

On July 20, 1969, the day of my ordination by Archbishop Tchidimbo at the Cathedral of the Immaculate Conception in Conakry, I was the only ordinand. Over the years, all my fellow seminarians from Guinea who were with me in Bingerville, Nancy, and Sébikhotane gradually left the seminary.

On that summer day in 1969, after so many accidents and tribulations, political upheavals in my country, travels, sorrows, and joys, I was the sole "survivor" of this adventure. Why did God pay so much attention to me? Why had God pampered me by giving me the supernatural strength to stay the course? Why did God want me to be the last priest ordained before the arrest of Archbishop Tchidimbo in December 1970? It is very difficult for me to answer these questions. One after the other, my companions left, and I found myself alone before the altar of the cathedral.

In fact, I have never doubted my vocation. Although there were events that made me sad, they were never anything but small wounds that never shook my love for God. I remained faithful because I truly loved God as much as a poor sinner can love him, given his own limitations. In my heart I always had the assurance that God loved me. In our lives, everything is the gift of his Love. How then could I remain indifferent to such a great mystery? How could I not respond to the Love of the heavenly Father by dedicating my whole life to him?

On July 21, 1969, I said my first Mass in the Cathedral of Conakry. Not until the following Sunday, July 27, was I able to celebrate my first Eucharist in the parish of Saint Rose of Ourous. You can easily imagine my emotion and that of my parents and of all the residents of my village. The joy was extraordinary. I had the feeling that this was a just reward for all the Holy Ghost Fathers who had suffered so much for us. However, it was the will of Providence that they could not participate that day because of the persecutions by Sékou Touré.

The Holy Ghost Fathers who gave their lives in Guinea, under such difficult conditions, did not die in vain. On that July morning, we began the day with a procession from the cemetery to the church, after a long time of prayer before the graves of the first missionaries.

During the weeks afterward, following a program established by Archbishop Tchidimbo, I had the joy of celebrating several Masses in various parishes in the Archdiocese of Conakry, and then I left for Rome.

In 1971, during your courses in Rome, you left for Jerusalem to study the Bible in greater depth. . . .

Yes, I stayed a whole year in the Holy City. At the Biblical Institute in Jerusalem, I had the sense that my devotion to Christ was becoming even stronger. It was not only an emotion. My prayer became palpable, because the places that had witnessed the presence of the Son of God were still so eloquent. In the Holy Land, the memory of Jesus is indelible.

The privilege of walking in the Holy Land, God's land, the land where Jesus was born, created an indescribable emotion in me and the sense of living in God's house on earth. Like Jacob, anyone who treads the Holy Land can say: "Surely the LORD is in this place, and I did not know: [...] This is none other than the house of God, and this is the gate of heaven" (Gen 28:16–17). Jerusalem is truly the place of his rest but also the place of Golgotha and of tears.

Why is the life of this city so complicated? In Jerusalem there is never an instant when someone is not praying, because here all monotheistic religions are represented. And yet the violence remains continuous.

On the morning of December 25, 1971, I participated in the Mass in the basilica in Bethlehem. The ceremonies of the various Christian traditions overlapped, and some celebrated simultaneously according to their own rite, language, and style of chant. This could produce tremendous chaos, which was not very conducive to prayer. The Christians are not able to pray together; on the contrary, they interfere with each other. The liturgies become obstacles that seem insurmountable. Why is it so hard for people to understand that in God's eyes these obstacles cause his Fatherly Heart to bleed painfully?

During that year I stayed as a guest with the Jesuits in a large house where Fathers Ludovicus Semkowski, R. M. Mackwoski, James Kelly, and some excellent professors of exegesis were also living. This human and intellectual experience was very rich, lively, and especially stimulating.

At that time, I wondered whether my vocation might not be to join a contemplative order. For a long time I thought about entering a Benedictine monastery. But I did not want to abandon my country, which so desperately lacked priests.

After spending time in Jerusalem and Rome, you returned to Guinea to become a parish priest....

After earning my degrees in theology and exegesis, I was appointed curate of Boké, which is located on the seacoast of Guinea. This ministry was the most beautiful priestly experience of my life. The parish was immense; the most distant parishioners lived on the Senegalese border. My vicar, Jean-David Soumah, and I had no car....

I remembered the missionaries of my childhood who set out almost every day on foot to evangelize the most remote populations. From now on, I could imitate them in every way. I walked long hours, always accompanied by two or three catechists, with a traveling Mass kit on my head, under a blazing sun; sometimes I would run into a cargo truck, and the driver would offer me a ride. When I went to marshy areas in the middle of lagoons, I would take a canoe. Often we had to cross very dangerous torrents, like that of Kakoulkoul. We held our breath for fear of being engulfed by a whirlpool....

Often I chose to travel to the most remote villages because I knew those inhabitants had not had a visit from a priest since the expulsion of the missionaries in 1967. After almost a decade without a priest, the villagers continued to teach the catechism to their children themselves, to recite daily prayers, to pray the rosary with great filial devotion to the Virgin Mary, and to listen to the Word of God on Sundays. I had the grace of fortifying those people who had kept the faith without any sacramental support because of the lack of priests. I will never forget their unimaginable joy when I celebrated Mass, which they had not experienced for so long. How could I not feel tremendous gratitude as I observed the catechists who kept this flickering flame alive by walking long hours from village to village? Their sacrifice has always remained in my heart.

Very quickly I determined that most of my missionary work should focus on strengthening the formation of the catechists. They were the real builders of our parishes.

Very soon I understood, too, that I had been put under close surveillance by the men of Sékou Touré's regime. For example, my homilies and those of other priests were systematically listened to by spies who reported all of our public statements to the regional cadres of the revolutionary party. I had to be careful not to question the doctrine of the State Party openly. At that time, Archbishop Tchidimbo had been in prison for four years, and the dictatorship was becoming increasingly harsh.

Thousands of Guineans tried every day to leave the country. All religious properties had been confiscated and nationalized; we lived in great poverty. In the name of national independence, following drastic orders from Sékou Touré, the Church in Guinea was totally cut off from the Catholic world, thus preventing the Holy See from providing any aid at all. This situation made our daily life difficult, but I considered that these sufferings allowed us, as priests, to live in the same destitution as the faithful. My meals were very frugal, as I had to count almost exclusively on the aid of the parishioners, who themselves lacked everything.

One day, while I was leaving for Zéroun, one of the most remote "Bassari" villages in the parish of Ourous not far from the border with Senegal, in order to celebrate Mass, I met a man who seemed to know the area. I asked him if he could give us directions. He offered to come with us. He turned out to be a militiaman disguised as a simple farmer who thought I was trying to leave Guinea. While letting me think he would help me find my destination, he made me walk for an entire afternoon, only to lead me to a military camp in Négaré. I had to spend a lot of time explaining myself, because the camp commander, too, thought that I intended to cross the border in secrecy! Little by little, I was able to appease his fears. But night fell, and I had no idea where I was. The commander finally ordered two soldiers to drive me into the village for which I was looking. Toward midnight, I arrived at the destination with my catechists.

The joy of the residents was indescribable. According to their customs, the sheep, goat, or any other animal that is going to be served is not killed until it has been presented alive to the foreigner. Only after the welcome and this rite of presentation did the women begin to make the meal. When the dinner and the dancing were done, I slept in the hut that was reserved for me, but the two soldiers who accompanied me stayed crouched in front of the door because they continued to have doubts.... The next day I was able to bless the small chapel that the Christian community had built as well as the hut in which I had spent the night, which they had named the "rectory". From then on, this hut would be reserved for the priest who was visiting the village. After breakfast, the two soldiers went back to the military camp. With the catechists we walked for three days in the brush to meet those who were most isolated. When we returned, I insisted on returning to the military camp to prove that I was not trying to leave the country. The soldiers apologized and offered me a chicken as a sign of reconciliation!

How could anyone ever forget these men and women who had almost nothing, who dressed, ate, and lived according to local customs, but who showed, in the midst of their fellow citizens who were still animists, the radical witness of their faith in Jesus? They are still in my heart, as they are role models for the faithfulness and perseverance that Christ requires of us on this earth.

During those two years, I was able to observe how much Guinea was suffering under a dictatorial regime that offered it no hope. Lies and violence were the favorite weapons of a system that was based on a destructive Marxist ideology. The economy of the country had collapsed, and the inhabitants of the villages experienced extreme poverty. In the countryside, the mutual assistance between the villagers allowed them to provide for their most basic needs. Sékou Touré was obsessed with carrying out his messianic plan, but he increasingly fell into a paranoia that saw enemies of the revolution everywhere planning his demise. Guinea was battered, drained, and destroyed. Its very soul was being reduced little by little to a shell of its former self.

In 1976, you were named professor then rector of John XXIII minor seminary in Conakry.

Yes, and the seminarians were numerous, almost a hundred of them; but the formators and educators who had preceded me certainly lacked discipline. A sort of moral disintegration prevailed. Moreover, it was an institution where we could merely house the seminarians outside of classes, because Sékou Touré had required that all young people pursue their studies in public institutions.

I wanted to establish true discipline very quickly. Unfortunately, the students, who had been left to their own devices for months, did not accept the strict rules that I wished to introduce. At first I had to face a small rebellion. But the absence of spiritual formation was much deeper than I could have imagined.

One night a student or group of students set fire to the chapel.... Therefore I asked those who were guilty to confess publicly. No one wanted to admit responsibility. As a second step, I appealed to those who knew to accuse the ones who had committed this serious offense. I even went so far as to say that if this abominable act had targeted my own room I could have forgiven it. But the chapel was the house of the Lord. Despite my insistence that the guilty party courageously take responsibility, no one would say anything. Therefore, I said that if this silence about the origin of the fire continued, I would make the decision to close the seminary. I thought of the formation that I had received from Archbishop Tchidimbo, and I knew that he would have made the same decision.

The prefecture of Kindia summoned me, ordering me to reverse my decision, because only a counter-revolutionary act would have authorized me to close the seminary. But I did not give in because I considered that a desecration committed by a seminarian could not remain unpunished. The government officials insisted that I reopen the doors of the seminary with all possible speed. Once again I explained that I would not go back on my decision. How could we allow future priests, men of God, to indulge in acts of sacrilege? Given my determination and my explanations, the prefect of Kindia understood better that the reasons for my decision were nonnegotiable. He finally backed my decision. During the year that had just begun, the minor seminary therefore remained closed.

At the beginning of the next school year, I asked the priests to send me a certificate of good conduct for each student who entered the seminary. The number of students was cut in half, but I was certain that these young men were fit to begin a life of service to God.

Despite this incident, I have good memories of my life as rector of John XXIII seminary. I had the sense that I was passing on the knowledge that so many professors had imparted to me with discipline, courage, and selflessness.

Was the year 1978 a radical turning point in your life?

On the night of April 18, 1978, Monsignor Louis Barry, who was then serving as the apostolic administrator since the imprisonment of Archbishop Tchidimbo, arrived unexpectedly at the seminary in Kindia. During the meal he told us about the surprising adventure that he had had that same morning.

By a most unusual coincidence, he had met emissaries from the Holy See. In fact, Louis Barry was scheduled to travel to Kissidougou, and while going past the airport in Conakry, he had seen a small private airplane from which "purple belts" were getting off. Surprised, he stopped and made a U-turn to follow the car into which two bishops had climbed. Monsignor Barry had then seen the vehicle enter the palace of the president of the Republic. Increasingly astonished, he decided to stop by the Sisters of Saint Joseph of Cluny, whose house was a few dozen yards from the presidential palace. A little later, the emissaries left President Sékou Touré's residence to call on the Sisters. Monsignor

Barry welcomed the two bishops, telling them of his joy and surprise at seeing them in Conakry. The two bishops were Archbishop Simon D. Lourdusamy, secretary of the Congregation for the Evangelization of Peoples, and Archbishop Luigi Barbarito, apostolic nuncio of Dakar. They came to take Archbishop Tchidimbo with them. But some journalists who were too well informed had anticipated the news of his release. And so President Sékou Touré, furious with this indiscretion, decided to postpone the release indefinitely. This was a new failure in the negotiations between the Holy See and the Guinean government.

Even more serious, the president had vehemently opposed the Holy See's choice of the new archbishop of Conakry. In spite of the Guinean government's position, Archbishop Lourdusamy secretly gave Monsignor Barry a mission; he was supposed to ask Father Robert Sarah if he would agree to become the next archbishop of Conakry....

When he told us his story at dinner, Louis Barry said nothing about the mission that had been given to him, because my two assistants from the seminary, Désiré Roland Bangoura and Apollinaire Cécé Kolié, were present. After dinner he asked to speak with me privately; we went to my room. Louis Barry then told me that Pope Paul VI had appointed me archbishop of Conakry and that I must give my response as quickly as possible. I was utterly frightened by this news. At first I protested by refusing the appointment, aware of my obvious inability to assume such a responsibility. The difficulties in the diocese were immense, and tensions between the Church of Guinea and the State were almost constant. My pastoral experience was truly inadequate, and most importantly I had not yet reached the age of thirty-three.

But Monsignor Barry immediately retorted, "I will be back for your written response in three days. In any case, if you refuse, Archbishop Raymond-Marie Tchidimbo will remain in prison, because Sékou Touré set as a condition for his release his immediate replacement in the Episcopal See of Conakry through the appointment of a new archbishop." Archbishop Tchidimbo had already submitted his letter of his resignation from the office of archbishop of Conakry. Therefore, the archiepiscopal see of Conakry was now vacant.

Monsignor Barry's second argument was as follows: "You cannot refuse to obey the pope, who trusts in you. He speaks in God's name; you absolutely must obey him as a son obeys his father." He then ended our conversation by saying to me: "The service and the mission that

God is entrusting to you through this office necessarily involve the cross. But God will be with you to support you." Needless to say, I was completely dejected.

I could not understand why Paul VI chose a simple, unknown young man like me. Why did the Holy See not nominate Monsignor Barry, who had all the requisite maturity? I felt as though I had been caught up in an unbelievable tempest, and I understood nothing about this decision. I was willing to suffer for my Church, but still I was petrified by this choice which seemed to me particularly grave.

Although I could understand that Monsignor Barry wanted to forward a rapid response to the nunciature, I was literally crushed by the short time that he gave me to reflect. I remained prostrate for three long days. Finally, I wrote a letter to the pope telling him that I was unworthy and incapable but that I accepted his decision. That same day I chose my episcopal motto: "Sufficit tibi gratia mea" (My grace is sufficient for you), from the Second Letter to the Corinthians (12:9). The apostolic administrator came to get my letter, and, for an entire year, negotiations were pursued between the Holy See and Sékou Touré.

In September 1978, Monsignor Barry asked me to leave the seminary and become his private secretary. He intended to help prepare me in this way for my heavy responsibility and to allow me to experience the ambiance of the city of Conakry, with which I was not well acquainted.

For me the year 1978–1979 at the archbishop's chancery was like a long retreat in the desert, a time of prayer, silent tears, and study. I wanted to place everything in God's hands. At the same time that I served as Monsignor Barry's private secretary, I also assumed the responsibilities of curate of the parish of Saint Joseph the Worker and chaplain of Saint Thérèse of the Child Jesus boarding school run by the Congregation of the Little Sisters of Our Lady of Guinea.

For a year and four months, I was alone with Monsignor Barry, carrying the weight of the papal secret and the terrible anguish it caused me. I could speak of it to no one, not even to my parents.

Then, as if by a miracle, Archbishop Tchidimbo was released and deported on August 7, 1979....

On August 18 and 19, 1979, a papal delegation came to meet once again with the president. Sékou Touré finally accepted my appointment, and time began to pass quickly. The Roman prelates asked me to organize within a few days a Mass of thanksgiving in the cathedral for

Thursday, August 23, with no other explanation than the joy of having a ceremony on the occasion of the presence among us of a special envoy from the Holy See....

I was living as if in a strange dream! God wanted me to become archbishop at the age of thirty-four, while the country was going through an unprecedented crisis and all the property of the Church had been confiscated. The Mass was celebrated at 10:00 A.M. in the cathedral, and the appointment of Bishop Philippe Kourouma, as bishop of N'Zérékoré, was made public at the same time as mine. On that occasion I was also named apostolic administrator of the Diocese of Kankan.

On that day in August, the few faithful who had gathered in haste wept with joy and emotion. Since that terrible day in December 1970, we no longer had a bishop in any of the dioceses in Guinea. I knew that the trials of Archbishop Tchidimbo were immense. During those long years in the camp where he lived, one of his cousins, Mother Louis Curtis, would come and bring to him, in total secrecy, some hosts that allowed him to consecrate clandestinely and consume the Body of Christ, before his cell companions had awakened. In his book-length testament, *Noviciat d'un évêque* (A bishop's novitiate), he wrote with the modesty so characteristic of him that "these brief Masses, celebrated in the utmost silence, around five o'clock in the morning, would be among the most moving ones of my priestly life."

On August 7, 1979, Archbishop Tchidimbo was released and immediately driven to the airport to leave for Rome. I heard the news on the radio, and no one had obtained permission to greet him before he left the country. It was an indescribable emotion.

When my appointment was made public on August 23, 1979, two Holy Ghost Fathers, Robert Haffmans and Michel Legrain, were in Ourous. They heard the news on the radio by chance and ran to announce my appointment to my parents. Instead of joy and enthusiasm, they found that my parents were anguished: "You should be so happy that your son is called to such a high position of responsibility in the Church! Why are you sad?" the two missionaries asked. And my father and mother replied: "Do you know where his predecessor was?" They feared I would very soon have the same fate as Archbishop Tchidimbo.

After the Mass of thanksgiving, we asked to have an audience with the president, who agreed to receive us. At that time it was important to give the impression that we respected the work of the revolution. Sékou Touré did want us to be able to invite bishops from Africa and Europe to the occasion of our episcopal consecration, which was major news for the regime. On December 8, 1979, the day of my ordination, some bishops, priests, and clergymen returned for the first time to Guinea; Giovanni Cardinal Benelli, assisted by Archbishop Luc Sangaré of Bamako and Bishop Jean Orchampt of Angers and accompanied by twenty-seven other bishops, ordained me in the gardens of the archbishop's residence in the presence of seven Guinean ministers led by the prime minister, Lansana Béavogui, and Andrée Touré, the president's wife.

Sékou Touré had done all that he could to oppose my nomination, but from then on he seemed to accept my episcopate; the mobilization of the Vatican, of Liberia, and of numerous international organizations on behalf of the release of Archbishop Tchidimbo had greatly offended the regime. Moreover, the leader of the revolution did not want to open a new breach by continuing to reject Rome's decisions. For me, however, it was the calm before the storm.

Very quickly I came to understand that the big problem of my ministry would be the relationships with my priests. The priesthood, families, young people, and the evangelizing influence of the Church were the four priorities for the beginning of my episcopal ministry.

In the beginning, I asked to be able to share my meals with all the priests of the diocese who worked in the offices of the archdiocese. I wanted to create a family atmosphere. But some laymen came to see me to warn me: everything I said was being reported to Sékou Touré's cabinet. With sadness I resigned myself to taking all my meals alone.

Your life as a bishop is in some ways parallel to that in Krakow of Karol Wojtyła, who fought against Communism, is it not?

I would not dare compare myself to Saint John Paul II, but it was in fact both an enriching and a trying time. Until his death on March 26, 1984, Sékou Touré never stopped watching my least actions and gestures. Several months before his death, he had even planned in minute detail my arrest and execution, according to secret intelligence that was revealed to me after his burial.

After the consecration, Monsignor Barry advised me to set out immediately on the roads of the archdiocese to meet the faithful. For two

years, therefore, I crisscrossed my ecclesiastical territory so as not to be
cut off from reality. I understood that the State Party revolution was literally destroying all the mainstays of the country. In particular, the educational system was in a chaotic state; the only thing that mattered was
the dissemination of official propaganda, inspired by Soviet Marxism-
Leninism. Clinics and hospitals had all but disappeared or were appalling
in their lack of hygiene. The weakest, in particular the children and the
elderly, were left to fend for themselves in terrible suffering.

Political opponents had no rights as citizens. The mere act of voicing
a simple criticism about the poverty of the people could lead to imprisonment at the Boiro camp, where the soldiers committed indescribable
tortures of which I would prefer not to speak.

In fact, the country was sinking into a hellish spiral, and nothing
seemed to be able to stop the ideological frenzy of Sékou Touré. Despite
the risks, I decided to speak. I could not remain silent faced with such
a tragic situation. Repeatedly, I explained my point of view about the
poverty of the people, the fear or the lies of the leaders, and the disastrous
political and economic management of our country. In a public speech,
I even launched the remark for which Sékou Touré never forgave me:
"Power consumes those who do not have the wisdom to share it!"

Thinking to myself, I reasoned: "I am thirty-five years old. In Africa,
that is much more than half a lifetime. There are many children who
die at birth and a multitude of people who have finished their life at
age fifty or even before reaching the age of twenty. I should consider
myself blessed by the Lord to have reached my age. Now, it is important that I dedicate myself totally to God and to his people. What more
could I hope for than a death for the glory of God and for the defense of
truth, for the dignity of the human person and freedom of conscience!
We must agree to leave this earth for the sake of the Gospel. Jesus died
because he testified to the truth: 'For this I was born, and for this I have
come into the world, to bear witness to the truth. Every one who is of
the truth hears my voice'(Jn 18:37) ".

After hundreds of hours of prayer, I came to the conclusion that the
worst that could happen to me was death; my life was nothing compared
to the blatant injustices, the horrible poverty, and the unspeakable horrors that I saw each day. Terror reigned even in families, where a father
might fear that his children would side with the dictatorship for the sake
of expediency. I had to speak, even if my life was at stake.

I therefore decided to use my homilies at the cathedral and the ceremonies on January 1, when the archbishop traditionally presented his greetings to the president, to make some remarks about the degradation of the country. Without any provocative comments and with great respect, I formulated several proposals so the people might benefit from less trying conditions. Similarly, I called on the regime to grant greater freedom to the Guineans. The Catholics and many Muslims no longer knew what to do to convince me to take fewer risks. I was not afraid, and if I had to be arrested, it would be for a worthwhile reason.

Of course, no one wants to be tortured in a concentration camp. Nor was I unaware of the fact that Sékou Touré was capable of the worst against an opponent. However, I continued to consider my battle more important than my own survival. If God preferred to have me in heaven, I felt ready to meet him after defending my people against oppression.

Moreover, I sought to organize programs for youth. Sékou Touré in fact refused to allow anyone to work with young people. The State Party alone was in charge of education. Back in 1959, Sékou Touré had created the "Youth for the African Democratic Revolution", which was supposed to promote all artistic, cultural, and athletic activities for young people. Any other youth movement was forbidden.

I wanted young people to have available a different point of view from that of the forces of the revolution. Therefore, I started a survey, asking the priests to approach young people and to ask them to write to me and tell me their grievances. In the overwhelming majority of the letters that I received, there was a thirst for spiritual and human formation. From then on, each year, in late August, I decided to gather young people who wished to participate for two-week courses on the Bible and human formation. I took care of the religious questions, and some experts came to answer their questions, which were often very specific, about work, management, marriage, and family. The human and financial investment was burdensome, because my diocese was not rich. Quickly I saw that the desires of these young people were profound. Needless to say, Sékou Touré took a very dim view of my initiative.

I also tried to help families; I saw how harmful Communism could be to them. Often inside the same home was a fear of what one of the spouses might do. The children literally escaped from education by their parents.

Generally speaking, the most important measures taken by revolutionary governments always affect the family. In addition, during the first five years of my episcopate, my pastoral letters were all dedicated to the defense of the Christian family.

Did you know what Sékou Touré thought of you?

At first he was very surprised by my freedom of speech. He also knew that I respected the protocol of the regime. For example, I never missed the long ceremonies on the national holiday or any other public manifestation organized by the State Party, and if Sékou Touré invited me to the presidential palace, I did not decline.

On several occasions, he had me sit beside him, among his ministers, presenting me as an example of faithfulness to the policies of the State Party. He proclaimed that he placed all his trust in me.... Several people came to see me to warn me about the trap that the president would not fail to set for me.

During our one-on-one meetings, he listened attentively to my observations, and the tone of our conversations was cordial. However, he must have known my opinions, because I knew that secret service agents listened to a great number of my conversations.

In fact, I was very worried by the depression that was poisoning the entire country. The moral conscience of the Guineans in particular had changed. Terror reigned everywhere, and a small minority of Guineans were drunk on deceptive revolutionary slogans and commitments. Sékou Touré instilled in the hearts of men such a deep fear that it took years before the people found the courage to stand up again. Unfortunately, it is easier to destroy a country than to rebuild it.

In January 1984, when Omar Bongo, president of the Republic of Gabon, was visiting our country, Sékou Touré wanted to honor me by introducing me to his guest. He once again warmly congratulated me on my adherence to the principles of the revolution.... The dictator's strategy became obvious. By encouraging me and publicly manifesting his high esteem for me, Sékou Touré could more easily accuse me later of betraying his confidence along with the ideals of the regime.

A few weeks later, several European ambassadors, as well as my vicar general, Father André Mamadouba Camara, came to warn me about confidential remarks by ministers close to the president. These dignitaries of the regime claimed that the Church no longer had the same ideology as the State Party. In fact, Sékou Touré intended to prepare their minds for my arrest. But God placed his hand on me to protect me and keep me.

In December 1983, an earthquake struck Guinea; the damage was very extensive.

Those in charge of international aid in response to this natural disaster were welcomed by Commander Siake Touré, the leader of the Boiro camp. While he was at the airport in Conakry waiting for the arrival of a plane, he slipped, fell, and broke his leg. He was immediately evacuated to Morocco. According to the plans of Sékou Touré, that man was supposed to have arrested me a few weeks later....

Then, in March 1984, on the occasion of the first World Youth Day organized in Rome, I asked the government for permission to go to Italy in response to the pope's invitation. Usually, only a notification from the minister of the interior and national security was required. This visa was almost a mere formality. For this trip, the minister also asked for the president's approval. He telephoned Sékou Touré, who asked about the date of my return, and upon hearing that I would be returning in April, gave his authorization for the trip. Joseph Hyzazi, who takes care of the finances of the diocese and my trips, reported to me the president's discussion with the minister. These arrangements seemed strange and ominous!

But a few days later, Sékou Touré had a stroke. Saudi Arabia quickly dispatched an air ambulance. When it arrived in Conakry, the control tower, following procedures, tried to contact the president to obtain his authorization. Unable to reach Sékou Touré, since his critical condition was being kept secret, the tower refused to let the plane land, and it then headed for Dakar. Not until the next day, when the prime minister—a physician by profession—inquired about the arrival of the air ambulance, did the plane finally return to Conakry. Sékou Touré was evacuated to Morocco, then to the United States.

Thus the president, who had planned to have me arrested, and Siaka Touré, who was to carry out the plan, were both rendered incapable of doing any harm!

Despite the intensive care that he received, the dictator died on March 26, 1984, in Cleveland, in the United States, during heart surgery.

Prime Minister Lansana Beavogui became interim president, as the country waited for the elections that were supposed to be held within forty-five days. But on April 3, the armed forces seized power, denouncing the last years of the regime as a "bloody and merciless" oligarchy. The constitution was suspended, and the national assembly was dissolved, along with the one party. The leader of the coup, Colonel Lansana Conté, assumed the presidency on April 5, as the head of the Military Committee of National Recovery, the CMRN. As a pledge of goodwill, more than two thousand political prisoners were released from the sinister Boiro camp. The people were overjoyed.

Several days after Lansana Conté came into power, the ambassador from the Federal Republic of Germany, Bernard Zimmermann, informed me that documents containing a list of public figures who were to be executed had been found on Sékou Touré's desk. I was at the top of the list.... This document planned my secret arrest and assassination for the month of April. God had been quicker than Sékou Touré! The Savior wanted me to stay a little longer on earth.

How did your country react to the death of Sékou Touré?

In fact, I think that the military forces were unprepared to assume the highest responsibilities of the State, which is not their job anyway. They were unable to reform the country so as to restart the economy and fight poverty. Public freedoms improved, but the political opposition was unfairly persecuted. We went from a Marxist regime to a military junta. Certainly, the country was less cut off from the world than it could ever have been under Sékou Touré. But, in fact, the framework of the country had not changed. The same rusty machine continued to run. How was it possible to put the new wine of truth and freedom into the old wineskins of the revolution?

As for me, even though I got along cordially at first with the new president, our relations quickly became strained because I continued to speak very freely. One day, I publicly protested against the fact that Guinea was the water reservoir of Africa, while its capital, Conakry, had practically no access to electricity and drinkable water was scarce.

Were you involved in the political life of Guinea?

No, but I felt that it was important to raise my voice to defend the dignity of the human person and respect for the life of the people of this country. I was the only one capable of protesting against the downward spiral of a military regime that could be guilty of actual murders. I was certainly never afraid to defend the rights and political positions of the main opposition figure of that period, Dr. Alpha Condé, the current president of the Republic. When he was in exile in Paris, I came to visit him in his apartment on the Place d'Italie, which the CMRN did not like at all.

The Catholic Church was a minority, but she was the only truly free institution. I knew that Christians as well as Muslims were waiting impatiently for me to speak out on the everyday concerns of the life of the people. After the failed coup by Colonel Diarra Traoré, violence, arrests, and murders were once again unleashed.

The Italian ambassador, Mr. Roberto Rosellini, informed by one of his compatriots that Colonel Diarra Traoré and three other persons were hiding in the house of an Italian national, was obliged to intervene to avoid implicating Italy in any way. He went and found Diarra Traoré in his hiding place. Traoré asked him for gas and a 4x4 in order to escape to Mali. The ambassador refused his request, because such an act would run the risk of implicating Italy in the attempted coup. The ambassador therefore decided to entrust Diarra Traoré and the three other wanted men to the minister of foreign affairs, Monsieur Facinet Touré. He wanted international law to be applied so as to avoid bloodshed.

Mr. Rosellini then came to see me, not in his official capacity as ambassador, but as a Catholic, so that we could combine our efforts and save human lives. Diarra Traoré himself wrote me a hasty, misspelled letter dated July 7, 1985: "Archbishop, it is with a broken heart that I write this letter to you today to ask you to be so kind as to intervene in the name of the Catholic Church on my behalf to the Head of State to ask him for an exceptional pardon. I have committed the worst mistake of my life, but I know that it had to be inscribed in my life, because as a believer, all destiny is inevitable. I ask you to do this for me, and you are quite capable of doing it; for I know of your legendary humanitarianism. Do not let me die, because as a human I think that I can still be redeemed. I am not telling you anything that you do not already know, but spare my brother from making the final decision. I am the father of a very large family made up of fourteen children who are still very young. I have complete confidence in you, and I count on your goodness of heart. May God provide you with vigorous health and long life. Amen. Diarra."

He entrusted the letter to Lieutenant Bangoura Panival Sama, who delivered it to me on July 11, 1985, at 10:30 P.M. Before we went our separate ways, Lieutenant Bangoura Panival said to me: "You know, Archbishop, that I am Catholic, and a Catholic never lies or cheats anyone. I promised Diarra Traore that I would deliver this letter to you. How can I prove to him that I kept my promise?" I gave him the souvenir photo of my episcopal ordination; and on the back of the photo I then wrote, above my signature: "I did receive your letter. I pray for you and give you my blessing. Have courage, I commend you to God."

On July 28, 1985, another letter arrived bearing the signatures of twenty-one people, with those of Commanders Kabassan Abraham Keita and Abdourahamane Kaba heading the list, along with the signatures of Captains Karifa Traoré, Fodé Sangare, et Ahmadou Kouyaté. The letter read: "We, the undersigned, respectfully convey to you our sentiments of profound gratitude and our utmost appreciation for your noble task of national reconciliation, in which you were one of the undisputed heroes. As a Man of God, be assured that from the depths of our prison cell, we have been very moved by the results of your actions as a pilgrim of peace and humanitarianism to help keep this country from reliving the tragedy of recent memory."

In order to try to save the soldiers who had been arrested at the time of the failed conspiracy, I requested a meeting with the president, General Lansana Conté, and also with Madame Henriette Conté, his wife, in order to remind them of God's commandment: "Thou shalt not kill!" Since I was unable to obtain a meeting as requested, I decided to write them a letter so that Guinea would not experience again the hell of the Sékou Touré regime, which so often had resorted to bloodshed. Much later, some dignitaries of the regime replied, saying that military law demands that traitors be shot. And so the leaders or the assumed perpetrators of the July 1985 coup as well as some members of the former government of Sékou Touré were all put to death. I was dismayed but helpless.

Without getting involved in politics, the Church in Guinea has always been firmly committed to proclaiming the rights of God and of man, in defense of human and moral values. Without truth, a country walks in darkness and causes the worst of misfortunes to befall its people. The Church must be involved in the daily life of people. No Christian can be cut off from the human condition or from the history of his contemporaries.

Even after the coup, it seems your life was not calm and peaceful every day....

Of course, there were some very difficult moments. I, too, had to carry what Saint Augustine called the *sarcina episcopalis*. This popular military term denotes the baggage of a soldier, the *barda*, the cumbersome, heavy gear that he carried. Quite often, it is a particularly heavy *barda* that the bishop must carry each day on his shoulders, and it gradually becomes heavier and heavier as his ministry meets with obstacles—especially if they come from within the Church and from his closest collaborators.

I had moments of discouragement and even collapse. So it was that in February 1990, at the point of exhaustion, I drafted a letter to the pope, resigning from my position as archbishop of Conakry. I wanted to retire to a small parish to serve as a simple priest. Before sending it to the Holy Father, I wanted to inform Father Barry so that he could give me his advice and help me to think with discernment. I had also written this short cover letter that had a touch of bitterness about it: "Why have I written to you to tell you of my decision? It is not to flaunt my troubles or to complain. No! It is simply because eleven years ago, in April 1978, you were the one to whom I gave my affirmative response to Pope John Paul II, who asked me to assume the office of pastor of the Archdiocese of Conakry. It is also because I have always considered you a father, a guide, and an adviser. I can say, as St. Paul said, 'What we are is known to God, and I hope it is known also to your conscience.... [We have spoken to you frankly]; our heart is wide [open to you]' (2 Cor 5:11; 6:11)."

He reacted negatively, retorting that the Cross is not the business of a day or a week but of a whole lifetime. He strongly dissuaded me from sending my letter to the pope.... And he kept it. Not until 2010, after my Mass of thanksgiving for the cardinalate, did he give it back to me, in Ourous!

The almost constant underground struggle with the political authorities, from the dictatorship of Sékou Touré to the military regime of Lansana Conté, was undoubtedly trying. But these external difficulties were not what was gnawing away at my courage and determination to serve the Lord. Instead, it was the internal struggles that I had to face, that shattered me by showing me with increasing clarity that I was objectively incapable of leading the Church of Conakry.

In order to address the situation, I established a program of regular spiritual retreats. Every two months, I would leave, alone, for a completely isolated spot. I would subject myself to an absolute fast, with no food or water for three days. I wanted to be with God, to speak with him in private. When I left Conakry, I would take nothing with me except a Bible, a small traveling Mass kit, and a book of spiritual reading. The Eucharist was my only food and my sole companion. This life of solitude and prayer helped me to recharge and to return to battle.

I think that a bishop, in order to fulfill his role, must do penance, fast, listen to the Lord, and pray for long periods of time in silence and solitude. Christ withdrew for forty days in the desert; the successors to the apostles must imitate Christ as faithfully as possible.

My Christian experience and conviction were born through contact with the Holy Ghost Fathers of my village. When they encountered difficulties, the missionaries took refuge in prayer. The process of human birth takes a long time and is not a single act. It happens moment by moment. There were stages that gave my life a decisive orientation. But these turning points were the hours, the moments of the day when, one-on-one with the Lord, I became aware of his will for me. The most important moments in life are the hours of prayer and adoration. They give birth to a human being, fashion our true identity; they root our existence in mystery. My daily encounters with the Lord, in supplication and prayer, are the basis for my life. I began to be attentive to these moments even as a child, in my family, and through contact with the Holy Ghost Fathers in Ourous. When we must live the Passion, we have to retreat to the Garden of Gethsemane, in the solitude of the night.

Therefore I prayed once again, and I decided not to send my letter of resignation.

Two years later Pope John Paul II traveled to Guinea. Was this a historic visit for your country?

Originally John Paul II was supposed to visit Sierra Leone, Liberia, and Guinea. The war in Sierra Leone changed his itinerary. The Holy See therefore chose to organize an apostolic visit, this time selecting Senegal, Gambia, and Guinea. At that time the archbishop still did not have his own residence; therefore, the organizers of the papal visit did not know how to put up the Holy Father, especially since he was determined to visit Guinea. He knew that the country had gone through tremendous difficulties under the revolutionary Communist regime.

In fact, the residence had been confiscated by Sékou Touré after the arrest of Archbishop Tchidimbo. It had become the home of the governor of Conakry, then the residence of the prime minister, Colonel Diarra Traoré. It was from this house that Diarra Traoré had organized his failed coup.

The house was then ransacked, destroyed, and set ablaze by soldiers who were loyal to President Conté.

Given this situation, the pope's collaborators could see only one solution: John Paul II would come from Dakar, in Senegal, would spend the day in Conakry, and would return to Dakar for the night.

Frustrated and disappointed, I requested an audience with President Conté to explain to him that Guinea would be seen in a poor light if it could not offer the pope a house because of a lack of goodwill on the part of the State, which was never willing to return property to the Church. The head of State then decided to return the house, after a complete renovation. Then we learned that the pope himself wanted to stay for three days in Guinea in order to console us for all the sufferings we had experienced under the dictatorship of Sékou Touré.

John Paul II arrived on February 24, 1992. I feared that the crowds would be sparse, since Guinea is a mostly Muslim country. Contrary to my fears, the Catholics and many Muslims came to express their joy in welcoming the successor of Peter. Muslim believers told me very seriously: "During the revolution, we were forced to welcome leaders of the USSR; there is no reason why we would not got out into the streets to see a great believer and a man of God!"

From the airport to the center of Conakry, there was not one empty street. During the first Mass at the cathedral, the joy of the faithful was immense. In the afternoon, at the college of Saint Mary of Dixinn, there was a meeting with the catechists and the parish councils that had kept the Christian communities alive for a long time when they were deprived of any priestly presence. The day culminated with the dedication of the hospital that today bears the name of the Supreme Pontiff. The next day, during a second Mass at the large "September 28" stadium, John Paul II ordained three priests. After lunch, he met some young Guineans at the People's Palace. Several hours later, I wanted him to be able to speak also with the representatives of the Muslims. Finally, in the evening, we had planned some time for prayer at the grotto of Our Lady of Lourdes in the gardens of the archbishop's residence. The recollection of the faithful was very impressive.

After crowning the Blessed Virgin, the pope knelt down and recollected himself for some time. The depth and length of his prayer, which seemed endless, greatly impressed the crowds gathered there. Then, after he got up, he slowly approached me and put the beautiful stole that he was wearing on my shoulders. I was quite shocked, because I did not understand the reason for his gesture, which was unplanned. While going back to the residence, he took me in his arms and said firmly: "This is a very beautiful ending." The following day, on the last day of his visit, he celebrated a private Mass in the chapel of the Stella Maris residence.

Several days later, I knew he had been really very impressed by the simplicity of the welcome by the people. To thank us, he asked Francis Cardinal Arinze, president of the Pontifical Council for Interreligious Dialogue, to go to the countries he had visited to thank the Christian and Muslim people as well as the governments.

The mobilization of the laity was exceptional. Without them, I would have never been able to prepare so effectively for the pope's journey.

Your farewell speech in Guinea, in November 2001, as you were about to leave for Rome, has remained a significant moment in the country's history. The remarkable part of it was an especially harsh indictment of the regime of General Lansana Conté. . . . How did you decide to give such a speech?

The situation was paradoxical. The president was proud of my appointment to Rome, and he insisted on organizing a great banquet in my honor with all the State leaders. I did not want to fall into the trap of that worldly atmosphere. On November 17, 2001, I therefore decided to take advantage of this platform to communicate my concern.

My speech was not broadcast on national television, since the recording of it was seized by the minister of information. President Conté was represented at the ceremony by his prime minister, Lamine Sidimé, accompanied by many members of his government. But during my speech, several of them dashed out of the banquet hall. . . .

Inasmuch as the prime minister had just bestowed on me the highest honor of the State of Guinea, I could make a long speech. And so

I was able to say: "I am worried about Guinean society, which is built on the oppression of the insignificant by the powerful, on contempt for the poor and the weak, on the cleverness of poor stewards of the public good, on the bribery and corruption of the administration and the institutions of the republic.... I am speaking to you, Mister President of the Republic, even though you are not here. Endowed by the Lord with all sorts of natural and culture resources, Guinea, paradoxically, stagnates in poverty.... I am concerned about the young people; they have no future because they are paralyzed by chronic unemployment. I am also concerned about national unity, cohesion, and harmony, which are greatly compromised by the lack of political dialogue and the refusal to accept differences. In Guinea, the law, justice, ethics, and human values no longer provide a frame of reference and a safeguard to regulate social, economic, and political life. Democratic freedoms are taken hostage by ideological trends that can lead to intolerance and dictatorship. In the past, giving your word was something sacred. It is true that a person's merit is measured by his ability to be faithful to his word. Today, the media, demagoguery, mind conditioning, and all sorts of other methods are used to sway public opinion and manipulate minds, giving the impression of a collective rape of consciences and a serious confiscation of freedoms and of thought."

The minister of information was furious. He decreed an embargo on my entire speech. The next day, during the farewell Mass in the gardens of the archbishop's residence, one lone member of the government was present, the minister of energy, Mr. Niankoye Fassou Sagno, who is now the prime minister's chief of staff. The wife of the president, Henriette Conté, and Élisabeth Sidimé, the wife of the prime minister, also attended. But I was very disappointed because not one Christian minister was present at this farewell Mass.

I again decided to speak loudly and forcefully. As I finished my homily, I could not hide the truth: "I know that the people of Guinea have great esteem and respect for me. But I leave Guinea with the impression that I am hated by my government because I speak the truth."

At the end of the Mass, the prime minister arrived very hastily.... He assured me that the government paid great attention to my point of view. In fact, I knew perfectly well that the minister for national security was doing all that he could to discourage people from coming to say goodbye to me the next day when I departed at the airport.

Even so, the streets were lined with an indescribable crowd who were determined to meet me before my departure. The police tried to disperse the crowd, but it was wasted effort.... In the great hall of the airport, I made a final brief impromptu speech calling for calm, while many had tears in their eyes. With a heavy heart, I boarded the plane, and from the window I continued to look for a long time at this gigantic crowd of people who were waving to me. I remembered Archbishop Tchidimbo and that night in April 1978 when Monisgnor Barry came to tell me that the pope had thought of the most unknown priest in Guinea as the next archbishop.

What memories do you have of your first moments in Rome as secretary of the Congregation for the Evangelization of Peoples?

I arrived in Rome on November 19, 2001. When Bernardin Gantin, who like me had also been named secretary of the congregation, had first stepped onto Roman soil, he was hurt that no one came to welcome him at the airport. He wanted to make sure that I did not suffer the same fate.... With his usual tact with regard to me, the cardinal sent to Fiumicino Airport the nuns who kept house in his apartment, with his own car, to provide me with transportation to my new residence. But Crescenzio Cardinal Sepe, who then headed the dicastery to which I was called, had also sent his representative in the person of the undersecretary. Thus, I had a special entourage!

It is important to understand that the competencies of the Congregation for the Evangelization of Peoples are vast. This dicastery has the responsibility for nominating all the bishops of Africa, Asia, Oceania, a number of important apostolic vicariates in Latin America, and several dioceses in Northern Canada. It was an extraordinary experience, because I had the opportunity of being in contact with all those peoples, all those mission countries, all those cultures and had so many edifying pastoral experiences. Every day I could consult with missionary congregations and institutions throughout the world. The work of preparing episcopal nominations was absolutely immense. During those years, I was able to understand both the strengths and the weaknesses of most of the dioceses in the world.

In Europe, we still have the impression that Catholicism is now near its last gasp. It is enough to spend a week at the congregation to understand that, on the contrary, the Church has an extraordinary vitality. We are experiencing a "new springtime of Christianity", as John Paul II liked to say. In 1900 there were two million African Catholics; today there are 185 million. In Asia, Catholicism, prompted and stimulated by the tradition of different forms of mysticism, is the embodiment of modernity. I would add that the beauty of the Church does not lie in the number of her faithful but in their holiness.

I have been able to follow the work of more than a thousand dioceses and of countless missionaries who give themselves generously to others in the most arid, remote regions of this earth; with ridiculous resources, they bring all of God's goodness to mankind. Often the missionary institutions are the only ones to care for the poor and the sick, whom no one wants to look at. When irresponsible governments, cruel armies, or lobbies hungry for profits have sown terror or despair, there is nothing left but the open hands of God, who, through the courage of his messengers of the Gospel, comes to console the poorest of the poor. Among these missionaries there are saints. Many will remain unknown, and yet their sanctity is impressive.

Finally, I always took special care in following up the aid that we were able to provide for the formation of seminarians in disadvantaged countries. In this major dicastery, I had the sense that I understood the fundamental insights of John Paul II. In the West, where everything seems to be dying and Christianity appears to be evaporating inexorably, there are nevertheless extraordinary hidden flowers. For the true springtime of the Church consists of the saints! How could we forget John Paul II, Mother Teresa, and all the saints of the modern era?

Certainly, the job of secretary of a congregation is not easy, but it is a fine apprenticeship. I liked very much working with the two men who succeeded one another at the head of the congregation during my time there: Cardinal Sepe, who has an especially impressive gift for organization, and then with Ivan Cardinal Dias, who displayed such fine spiritual qualities. They were quite different, and I received much from those years.

From 2008 on, I gradually replaced Cardinal Dias in a number of meetings because he suffered from an illness that increasingly disabled him. In those circumstances, I had the chance to have many working meetings with Pope Benedict XVI, in particular concerning his appointment of bishops. His humility, his ability to listen, and his intelligence always struck me.

In 2010, after nine years at the Propaganda fide, *you were appointed president of the Pontifical Council* Cor unum. *Was that the beginning of a new stage in your life?*

Yes, indeed, on the morning of October 7, 2010, Tarcisio Cardinal Bertone telephoned me to tell me that Pope Benedict XVI was thinking of having me take the position of president of the Pontifical Council *Cor unum*. I was astonished because I had not asked for anything at all. Cardinal Dias was happy about my appointment, and at the same time I felt that he was sad to see me leave. The next day I left Rome for a trip to India that had been planned long before.

On October 20, when I finished my stay in India with a visit to Goa, Cardinal Bertone came to join me. We finally managed to speak to one another. So it was that the secretary of state told me that the Holy Father was planning a consistory to create new cardinals. Tarcisio Bertone then revealed to me that I would be raised to the cardinalatial dignity on that occasion.

I cannot say that I was proud. The confidence of Benedict XVI touched me because I had the feeling that this promotion was undeserved. Right away I thought of my parents, who would have been so happy about it! I prayed that God would help me to assume this responsibility, not as an honor, but as a weighty, difficult trial in defense of Christ. My parents would never have dreamed of such a surprising appointment. I thought also of Archbishop Tchidimbo, who would have deserved that dignity more than I.

I do not know why; God has always come to hold my hand and accompany me along more important paths. In my life, God has done everything; for my part, I just wanted to pray. I am sure that the red of my cardinalate is really the reflection of the blood of the suffering missionaries who came to the remotest parts of Africa to evangelize my village.

When I returned to Rome, Benedict XVI granted me a private audience. During that meeting, the pope made this remark, which I will never forget: "Your Excellency, I appointed you to *Cor unum* because I know that of all people you have the experience of suffering and of the face of poverty. You will be most capable of expressing tactfully the Church's compassion and closeness to those who are poorest."

The ceremony in which Benedict XVI created you a cardinal must have been a great moment.

On November 20, 2010, God crowned many trials and sacrifices. Indeed, I really cared about one thing: I wanted the Holy Ghost Fathers of my childhood to be present in Saint Peter's Basilica in Rome on the day of my elevation to the cardinalatial dignity. God caused many fine fruits to mature in my life, but the Holy Ghost Fathers witnessed the first breath of God on my heart. At a time when I had no merit, God always put his trust in me. Similarly, although I am far from having succeeded in everything that the Church might have expected of me, the different popes, from Paul VI on, have always given me important responsibilities. Although we are the product of a human heritage, more profoundly we are the work of God in the first place.

The honors that the Church may bestow on some of her sons are first of all a grace of God so that faith, hope, and charity might be more radiant. The temptation of worldliness is a plague. There is no human promotion in the Church, but merely an imitation of the Son of God. The good fortunes of ecclesiastical offices are just petty deceptive tinsel. Francis often correctly recalls the worldliness of Satan.

Even today, when I enjoy privileges due to my position, I strive to remain in union with God through profound mental prayer. If we refer everything back to God, there will be plenty of humility. The honor given to a cardinal can only be for the glory of God. Nothing will ever be too fine for Him.

What did your daily work consist of in the Cor unum *council?*

My mission was to be able to express as well as possible the compassion and the spiritual and material closeness of the Church for people who are suffering from all the most difficult trials in this world. As I traveled to the most afflicted countries in our time, I very quickly understood that the greatest misery is not necessarily material poverty. The most profound misery is the lack of God. He can be absent because people are too much imprisoned in their materialism and profoundly desperate; they have abandoned him or reject him. Often there is a hunger for bread, but also a hunger for God.

Cor unum, as a representative of the charity of the successor of Peter, was systematically present at all the sites of war, natural catastrophes, famines, and epidemics. Often, behind these immeasurable tragedies, there is an abandonment of God by men. And so *Cor unum* always tried to bring emergency material aid, without forgetting divine consolation. Charity is service to man, but it is not possible to serve mankind without telling people about God. In this respect, the Church will never be able to conduct work comparable to some humanitarian organizations that are often guided and dominated by ideologies.

In his encyclical *Deus caritas est*, Benedict XVI correctly recalls that "Christian charitable activity must be independent of parties and ideologies. It is not a means of changing the world ideologically, and it is not at the service of worldly stratagems, but it is a way of making present here and now the love which man always needs" (DCE 31). And the source of this love is God himself. We must reflect theologically on charity so as to prevent Catholic charitable agencies from falling into secularism.

The nature of the Church is in the love of God, and the charity of the Church is in the first place the charity of God.

True charity is neither almsgiving nor humanistic solidarity nor a form of philanthropy: charity is the expression of God and an extension of Christ's presence in our world. Charity is not an ad hoc function but the inmost nature of the Church, *intima Ecclesiae natura*.

It urges us to evangelize; to put it simply, the Church reveals the Love of God. Often the absence of God is the deepest root of human suffering. And so the Church gives the Love of God to all. Consequently, a Christian cannot perform acts of charity only for his brethren in Christ, but must do so for all men without any distinction.

What are your most striking memories of those four years?

The trip to Japan was an extraordinary time. On March 11, 2011, a severe earthquake of magnitude 9, followed by a tsunami, struck the eastern part of Tohoku, around Sendai, causing the deaths of several thousand persons, very serious damage in the entire northeastern part of Honshu, and the nuclear accident in Fukushima.

I arrived in the country on May 13, 2011. Two months after the catastrophe, everything needed to be rebuilt. I was struck by the welcome that I received from the population, which was predominantly

Buddhist, who were helpless but strong at the same time. During those days I understood that the people whom I was visiting expected from me not just material relief; despite the difference in our religious beliefs, they wanted me to give them the hope that comes from God. And so, after distributing the pope's logistical and financial aid, the most important thing that I had to do was to pray at length in the midst of that whole populace which was so sorely tried. It became essential for me to turn to God for those orphaned children whose eyes were so sad, for those men and women who were trying to rebuild their houses, for those old people exhausted from fatigue. I was distressed when I left, because I knew that God alone could truly come to the aid of all the Japanese by entering into the depths of their hearts. Money is a necessity, but there is a tenderness that can come from God alone.

A letter from a young Buddhist woman, who wrote to me two months after my return from Japan, moved me profoundly. She told me: "After the terrible tsunami in which we lost many members of our family, and almost all our belongings, I wanted to commit suicide. But after hearing you on television, with the peace and serenity that I rediscovered while watching you pray for the survivors and for the dead, after the effect in me of your recollection and your silent prayer on the seacoast, and, finally, after the moving gesture that you made by throwing flowers into the ocean in memory of all who were engulfed by the waves, I gave up the idea of killing myself. Thanks to you, I understood, and now I know that, despite this disaster, someone loves us, lives beside me, and shares my sufferings, because we must certainly be of great price in his sight. This someone is God. I felt his Presence and his compassion through the Holy Father the Pope and through you. I am not Catholic, but I write you these lines to thank you and to thank the Holy Father Pope Benedict XVI for this immense comfort that you have given me. I know that other persons have received, as I did, this precious spiritual aid that we all need, especially at a time of great, terrible trials."

I had never seen the person who wrote me that letter. She did not receive any concrete material relief from me. Nevertheless, this Buddhist woman helped me to understand better that charity has a value in itself, as a testimony to God, above and beyond its technological, economic, political, or sociological effectiveness. It is part of the Church's mission, which consists of revealing God's love and tenderness and helping people to rediscover the presence, the compassion, and the merciful love of our Father in the midst of our sufferings. That Japanese woman helped me profoundly to grasp my mission as president of the Pontifical Council *Cor unum*.

The real relief that we must bring to the poor and to afflicted people is not just material but spiritual. It is necessary to reveal to them the love, the compassion, and the closeness of God. God is with us in the trial. He walks with us along the road to Emmaus, the road of disappointment, suffering, and discouragement.

Some Catholic organizations are ashamed and refuse to manifest their faith. They no longer want to talk about God in their charitable activities; their excuse is that they do not want to proselytize. Nevertheless, Pope Francis writes even more strongly in *Evangelii gaudium*: "Since this Exhortation is addressed to members of the Catholic Church, I want to say, with regret, that the worst discrimination which the poor suffer is the lack of spiritual care. The great majority of the poor have a special openness to the faith; they need God, and we must not fail to offer them his friendship, his blessing, his word, the celebration of the sacraments, and a journey of growth and maturity in the faith. Our preferential option for the poor must mainly translate into a privileged and preferential religious care" (EG 200).

Several months ago, in Jordan, in the Syrian refugee camps, a little seven-year-old Muslim boy shouted at me: "Does Allah exist? Does Allah exist? Why did he allow my father to be killed?" Indeed, his father had had his throat cut by the Islamist rebels, in his presence, and he was profoundly shocked. We attempted to talk to him about the good Lord, God the Father and Creator of all wonderful things, who detests evil, to try to help the boy get over his traumatic experience. How could anyone ever forget such suffering, which is a direct result of the barbarity of men who have perverted religion? This child had all the necessary material aid, he lacked nothing, neither clothing nor food nor sanitary facilities nor housing. That was not enough to console him. Only the closeness of God and the experience that he loves us and suffers with us, in us, reveal the mystery of suffering and bring consolation, comfort, and interior peace.

In Haiti, in 2010, after the earthquakes, the population had to face very violent hurricanes. Over the course of my life, I have witnessed many situations of great poverty. In Africa, I remember so many tragedies that followed one after the other with terrible regularity. But I can say that I never saw such sufferings as in Haiti. I had the feeling that an entire population was overwhelmed by the natural catastrophes that pummeled it. The sadness seemed to pervade the soul of a whole nation. I worked a great deal to make our aid as effective as possible. I also discovered a people with immense faith and absolute confidence in God in the midst of its numerous sufferings.

If we know how to practice charity, we will know how to revere God and we will be able to journey toward eternity. Through charity, we allow God to accomplish his work in us. Through charity, we abandon ourselves entirely to God. And he is the one who acts in us, and we act in him and through him and with him.

There is never any more authentic relation with God than in an encounter with the poor. For this is the source of life in God: poverty.

Our Father is poor. This is perhaps an image of God that eludes us and repels us, because we have not really met "the Son of man [who] has nowhere to lay his head" (Mt 8:20).

III

FROM PIUS XII TO FRANCIS,
THE POPES OF A LIFETIME

Tu es Petrus, et super hanc petram aedificabo Ecclesiam meam, et portae inferi non praevalebunt adversus eam. Et tibi dabo claves Regni coelorum.
(You are Peter, and on this rock I will build my Church, and the gates of Hades shall not prevail against it. I will give you the keys of the kingdom of heaven.)

—Matthew 16:18–19

NICOLAS DIAT: *In 1945 you came into the world during the pontificate of Pope Pius XII.*

ROBERT CARDINAL SARAH: When I was a child, I knew that there was a pope at the head of the Church, because I used to hear his name at Mass. I was convinced that I would never see that unreachable summit. I imagined the successor of Peter as a man living in some sort of paradise, and all those who worked with him, too. I considered them saints and true models of Christian life. Far-off Rome appeared to be a bit of heaven.…

At the minor seminary in Bingerville, I began to understand better the significance of the papal office. That was where I learned about the death of the pope, on October 9, 1958, when we had just begun the school year. I was afraid because I understood that it was an important moment for the Church. Furthermore, Pius XII was very popular in Africa.

That pope was a very dignified man. The accusations concerning his role during the war seem to me to be a terrible injustice. Far from the ideological polemics, the historians have begun their work of research. Recently I appreciated very much the studies published by the Englishman Gordon Thomas and by the Frenchman Pierre Milza. The testimonies of thousands of Jews, who were protected in the monasteries of Rome at his personal orders, even in the papal apartments of the Vatican and in the summer residence at Castel Gandolfo, are extraordinary. Pius XII wanted to save people who were doomed to death. His diplomatic silence was motivated by the desire not to aggravate the awful tragedy that was playing out at that time. In dealing with mad and dangerous dictators, words can sometimes prove counterproductive.

In another setting, I myself was able to experience persecution in Guinea during the reign of Sékou Touré. I therefore know from experience that bloody, repressive regimes are complex problems and that it is not enough to speak out publicly in order to fight against a dictatorship.

Indeed, the pope feared that Hitler's policy against the Jews might become even more barbaric and that the Polish and German Christians would suffer the consequences of that horrible violence.

Of course I am not an expert on this matter, nor do I claim to summarize such a difficult subject. The horror of the Holocaust is still a mystery of iniquity.

At the ecclesial level, as soon as he was elected, Pius XII decided to recall, through his first encyclical, *Summi pontificatus*, dated October 20, 1939, that his first duty was to bear witness to the truth: "The present age, Venerable Brethren, by adding new errors to the doctrinal aberrations of the past, has pushed these to extremes which lead inevitably to a drift towards chaos. Before all else, it is certain that the radical and ultimate cause of the evils which We deplore in modern society is the denial and rejection of a universal norm of morality as well for individual and social life as for international relations; We mean the disregard, so common nowadays, and the forgetfulness of the natural law itself, which has its foundation in God, Almighty Creator and Father of all, supreme and absolute Lawgiver, all-wise and just Judge of human actions. When God is hated, every basis of morality is undermined" (SP 28). Pius XII was already confronted with the beginnings of the problems with which we are familiar: the denial of God and moral relativism.

I can also say that Pius XII was more of an innovator than the superficial critics of his conservatism would have you believe. His encyclical *Fidei donum*, published in April 1957, on the renewal of the missions, inspired in part by the example of Archbishop Marcel Lefebvre, then archbishop of Dakar and apostolic delegate for French Africa, was very important for the development of evangelization. The Supreme Pontiff wished to reawaken the Bride of Christ by inviting the most ancient Church of the East to become involved in a missionary effort and by encouraging European priests to go and serve for a time in a mission diocese. The encyclical was written especially with a view to Africa. At that time, there was a dire lack of apostles and evangelizers on that continent. Thanks to Pius XII, priests were able to leave their dioceses of origin to help regions of the world that lacked clergy. In Guinea, after the foundational work of the Holy Ghost Fathers, the priests whom we have called since then *fidei donum* (the gift of faith) made possible a remarkable development of the Catholic faith.

For my continent, the figure of this pope remains even more historical because he was the first to consecrate African bishops, in particular, Bernardin Gantin. His interest in a native episcopal hierarchy was real.

In 1958, therefore, you were at the seminary when John XXIII was elected pope?

I was very young on the day when Angelo Roncalli ascended to the throne of Peter. Nevertheless, I noticed rather quickly the occasional difference between his style and that of his predecessor. I had loved the noble, thoughtful figure of Pius XII, and now I appreciated the almost naïve simplicity of John XXIII. Commentators everywhere said that he was kindly and close to the people, like the father of a family.

On the other hand, I still lacked the maturity needed to understand the scope of the council desired by that pope. I knew, however, that Archbishop Tchidimbo represented my country and that he traveled regularly to Rome for discussions with the bishops from the other countries of the world. Although he did not really speak to us about the content of the debates, I must nevertheless relate an event that impressed the Catholic faithful of Conakry.

The cathedral in Conakry had an elegant, ornate choir, with a beautiful replica of the Bernini baldachin, surrounded by very beautiful angels. At the time of the first discussions about liturgical reform, Archbishop Tchidimbo returned to Conakry and ordered the destruction of the baldachin and the main altar. We were angry, incredulous at this hasty decision. Rather violently, we passed without any preparation from one liturgy to another. I can attest to the fact that the botched preparation for the liturgical reform had devastating effects on the Catholic population, particularly on the simpler people, who scarcely understood the swiftness of these changes or even the reason for them.

No doubt it is regrettable that some priests allowed themselves to be so carried away by personal ideologies. They claimed to be democratizing the liturgy, and the people were the first victims of their actions. The liturgy is not a political object that we can make more egalitarian according to social demands. How could such a strange movement produce in the life of the Church anything but great confusion among the people?

Nevertheless, the idea of John XXIII was extraordinary. Calling the Council truly responded to the new needs of an era. At the major seminary, as we studied the various constitutions, we were awestruck by the work of the Council Fathers. Our emotion was understandable, because many conciliar documents are particularly edifying. I am convinced that Pope John wished that the faithful of the Church could experience great intimacy with God. He wanted believers to enter into a deeper spirituality. Indeed, the spiritual vision of man is the source of his program for reform. His concern about adapting to modern times never caused him to forget the transcendental necessity of evangelization work.

And so his denunciation of the "prophets of doom" is correct. A certain pessimism could prevail in the Church in those days. The fight against Soviet Communism and its expansion throughout the world was so difficult that it gave rise to a form of defeatism. Some circles perhaps did not believe sufficiently in the power of Christ, who has never abandoned his disciples. John XXIII appealed for realism, and two decades later God sent John Paul II, who saw the fall of the Berlin Wall....

The Council wanted to emphasize what was beautiful and dignified in this world. We should not regret this manner in which the Council Fathers worked. The recognition of great accomplishments, when they exist, has never implied the renunciation of the truth. How could the Church fail to praise the technological and scientific advances of that era? However, he also noted the Petrine duty to continue the Church's magisterial teaching. John XXIII, and later Paul VI, remained faithful to both aspects. A positive view of the world did not prevent John XXIII from noting with uneasiness the signs of God's eclipse.

So how do you understand the word aggiornamento *used by the pope since the opening of the Council?*

Aggiornamento is a tool for reflection used to situate the Church in a changing world, in which some economic, media, or political sectors were abandoning God by sinking into a dreamlike, liberal, relativistic materialism. How could the Church better bring the Gospel to countries that were showing signs of a crisis of faith? The insight of John XXIII was therefore prophetic. This pope never intended to abandon tradition; some fantasized about a revolution, and they sought, with the aid of the media, to popularize the image of a revolutionary pontiff. This was a political mistake that would not be without consequence.

Benedict XVI never stopped reminding us that the work of the Council Fathers may have been diminished by the media interpretations of Vatican II. Thus, the intention of John XXIII was not made known but instead was commented on and interpreted in an ideological way. Nevertheless, the documents of the Council Fathers are the faithful reflection of Pope John's original insight. We possess a precious treasure that it is important to consult faithfully.

Do your memories become much more precise with Paul VI, who is ultimately the pope of your youth?

Yes, indeed, I arrived in Rome in September 1969. I was able to see Paul VI when he came to dedicate one of the buildings of the Collegio San Pietro, where I resided. For the first time, I had contact with a pope! The child of Guinea experienced a kind of miracle....

Paul VI had to cope with extraordinarily difficult upheavals. The world was changing very quickly, and the Council did not bring the much-awaited in-depth understanding. The progressive hermeneutic was even leading the faithful into dead ends. Many priests left the priesthood. Convents emptied out, and many nuns started to put aside their habits. Little by little, the spirit of the age caused the disappearance of the signs indicating that God's hand had been placed on those who had devoted their lives to the Lord. There was a widespread impression that, even among consecrated persons, the presence of God was forbidden! For the pope, this meant terrible suffering.

His sorrow did not prevent him from standing firm. He knew better than anyone that the Council had been created by the Holy Spirit. In directing the work of the Council Fathers, Paul VI showed authority and theological reliability that were particularly well rooted in the faith. The pope intended to preserve the deposit of revelation from the reformist or revolutionary aberrations of the ideologues in attendance. He did all he could to fend off very violent attacks.

Thus, in June 1967, in his encyclical *Sacerdotalis caelibatus* on priestly celibacy, he rigorously confronted the arguments challenging the chastity expected of ministers of worship. He wrote: "Priestly celibacy has been guarded by the Church for centuries as a brilliant jewel and retains its value undiminished even in our time when the outlook of men and the state of the world have undergone such profound changes. Amid the modern stirrings of opinion, a tendency has also been manifested, and even a desire expressed, to ask the Church to re-examine this characteristic institution. It is said that in the world of our time the observance of celibacy has come to be difficult or even impossible. This state of affairs is troubling consciences, perplexing some priests and young aspirants to the priesthood; it is a cause for alarm in many of the faithful and constrains Us to fulfill the promise We made to the Council Fathers. We told them that it was Our intention to give new luster and strength to priestly celibacy in the world of today" (SC 1–2).

In fact, Paul VI issued a decree confirming the Council of Carthage in 390 as well as the ancient tradition of the Catholic Church with regard to consecrated celibacy. The law of celibacy promulgated by the assembly of African bishops has always remained in force, and it would be officially included in the major legislative anthology of the Church of Africa, the *Codex Canonum Ecclesiae Africanae*, which was compiled and promulgated in 401, during the time of Saint Augustine.

There are many who think that priestly celibacy is a merely disciplinary matter. What is your position?

Jesuit Father Christian Cochini, the author of a remarkable book, *Apostolic Origins of Priestly Celibacy*, correctly writes: "When, after hesitating for a long time, Pius IV finally decided to give his answer to the German princes asking Rome to authorize the marriage of priests, his first word on the matter would be a quotation from the decree of Carthage. Here then is the document that was to play such a part in the history of ecclesiastical celibacy. 'Epigonius, Bishop of the Royal Region of Bulla, says: The rule of continence and chastity had been discussed in a previous council. Let it [now] be taught with more emphasis what are the three ranks that, by virtue of their consecration, are under the same obligation of chastity, i.e., the bishop, the priest, and the deacon, and let them be instructed to keep their purity. Bishop Genethlius says: As was previously said, it is fitting that the holy bishops and priests of God as well as the Levites, i.e., those who are in the service of the divine sacraments, observe perfect continence, so that they may obtain in all simplicity what they are asking from God, what the apostles taught and what antiquity itself observed, let us also endeavor to keep. The bishops declared unanimously: It pleases us all that bishop, priest, and deacon, guardians of purity, abstain from [conjugal intercourse] with their wives, so that those who serve at the altar may keep a perfect chastity.' This text is interesting in many respects. Mention is made of the clerics' wives, and particularly, the wives of the hierarchy's high-ranking members: bishops, priests, and deacons. Most of those—or at least a large number—were thus bound by marriage. Such men are being asked by the African synod to give up no less than all conjugal intercourse and to observe perfect chastity.... Moreover, we are assured that such a discipline is not a new one: the Fathers of Carthage are only stressing the obligation of something that was 'taught by the apostles and observed by antiquity itself.' "[1] This law is unanimously accepted and confirmed by the whole Church, in fidelity to the teaching of Jesus, who rewards those who leave everything in order to serve him: "Truly, I say to you, there is no man who has left house or wife or brothers or parents or children, for the sake of the kingdom of God, who will not receive manifold more in this time, and in the age to come eternal life" (Lk 18:29–30). And John Paul II insists: "The Latin Church has wished, and continues to wish, referring to the example of Christ the Lord himself, to the apostolic teaching and to the whole Tradition that is proper to her, that *all those who receive the sacrament of Orders should embrace this renunciation 'for the sake of the kingdom of heaven'*. This tradition, however, is linked with respect for different traditions of other Churches. In fact, this tradition constitutes a characteristic, a peculiarity, and a heritage of the Latin Catholic Church, a tradition to which she owes much and in which she is resolved to persevere, in spite of all the difficulties to which such fidelity could be exposed, and also in spite of the various symptoms of weakness and crisis in individual priests. We are all aware that 'we have this treasure in earthen vessels' (cf. 2 Cor 4:7); yet we know very well that it is precisely a treasure."[2]

[1] Christian Cochini, S.J., *Apostolic Origins of Priestly Celibacy*, trans. Nelly Marans (San Francisco: Ignatius Press, 1990), 4–5.
[2] John Paul II, *Letter to Priests on the Occasion of Holy Thursday 1979*, 8.

No, priestly celibacy is not responsible for the dearth of vocations in some countries of the world.

In this particular case, and in others, the ordination of married men would be a sad lure, an illusion, a confusing concession.

In addition, Paul VI had to deal with a subject that Pius XII had mentioned in a famous address to midwives. And that was Humanae vitae....

Yes, in 1968 the publication of the encyclical *Humanae vitae* caused a surge of bitter criticism against the teaching of Paul VI on marriage and the regulation of births. This pope, with great intelligence and perfect fidelity to Church teaching, intended above all to emphasize two inseparable aspects of the conjugal act, union and procreation. He wrote: "This particular doctrine, often expounded by the magisterium of the Church, is based on the inseparable connection, established by God, which man on his own initiative may not break, between the unitive significance and the procreative significance which are both inherent to the marriage act. The reason is that the fundamental nature of the marriage act, while uniting husband and wife in the closest intimacy, also renders them capable of generating new life—and this as a result of laws written into the actual nature of man and of woman. And if each of these essential qualities, the unitive and the procreative, is preserved, the use of marriage fully retains its sense of true mutual love and its ordination to the supreme responsibility of parenthood to which man is called. We believe that our contemporaries are particularly capable of seeing that this teaching is in harmony with human reason" (HV 12).

Despite the challenges, the pope never intended to get involved in a debate that was distorted by libertarian thinking. Paul VI published his document; then he remained silent, bearing with all the difficulties in prayer. Until his death, on August 6, 1978, he never wrote another encyclical.

The successor of Peter knew that he was faithful to the truth. I think that Giovanni Battista Montini had infinite confidence in the wisdom of Church teaching; as he saw it, despite the temporary sufferings, trends would pass. This pontiff's battle was all the more meaningful in that he had great respect for freedom of conscience. In completing his document, he chose to address priests specifically by writing: "And now, beloved sons, you who are priests, you who in virtue of your sacred office act as counselors and spiritual leaders both of individual men and women and of families—We turn to you filled with great confidence. For it is your principal duty—We are speaking especially to you who teach moral theology—to spell out clearly and completely the Church's teaching on marriage. In the performance of your ministry you must be the first to give an example of that sincere obedience, inward as well as outward, which is due to the magisterium of the Church. For, as you know, the pastors of the Church enjoy a special light of the Holy Spirit in teaching the truth. And this, rather than the arguments they put forward, is why you are bound to such obedience. Nor will it escape you that if men's peace of soul and the unity of the Christian people are to be preserved, then it is of the utmost importance that in moral as well as in dogmatic theology all should obey the magisterium of the Church and should speak as with one voice. Therefore We make Our own the anxious words of the great Apostle Paul and with all Our heart We renew Our appeal to you: 'I appeal to you, brethren, by the name of our Lord Jesus Christ, that all of you agree and that there be no dissensions among you, but that you be united in the same mind and the same judgment.' Now it is an outstanding manifestation of charity toward souls to omit nothing from the saving doctrine of Christ; but this must always be joined with tolerance and charity, as Christ Himself showed in His conversations and dealings with men. For when He came, not to judge, but to save the world, was He not bitterly severe toward sin, but patient and abounding in mercy toward sinners? Husbands and wives, therefore, when deeply distressed by reason of the difficulties of their life, must find stamped in the heart and voice of their priest the likeness of the voice and the love of our Redeemer. So speak with full confidence, beloved sons, convinced that while the Holy Spirit of God is present to the magisterium proclaiming sound doctrine, He also illumines from within the hearts of the faithful and invites their assent. Teach married couples the necessary way of prayer and prepare them to approach more often with great faith the Sacraments of the Eucharist and of Penance. Let them never lose heart because of their weakness" (HV 28–29).

On April 18, 1978, a few months before his death, Paul VI made you the youngest bishop in the world. You were less than thirty-three years old. . . .

Yes, indeed, and John Paul II confirmed my appointment in August 1979. I felt a sorrowful joy, but I was at peace. Nevertheless, I did not forget Paul VI; indeed, I was a little sad that he was not able to see me become an archbishop.

When the government informed the Holy See that I was too young to hold an episcopal office, the Secretariat of State replied, essentially, to get around their argument: "Certainly, he is young, but he was formed by the revolution, and he will understand better the political directions of your government!"

As a priest in a parish, and then in charge of the seminary, I was almost unknown in the Archdiocese of Conakry. I made no noise, and I was not looking for anything in particular. For Sékou Touré, I was an enigma....

In 1969, Paul VI was the first pope to take a major trip to Africa.

For us it was unforgettable. In Uganda, he made this defining statement: "The new homeland of Christ is Africa." Then he added: "You Africans are now your own missionaries!"

Paul VI considered us now the ones primarily responsible for the evangelization of our continent, and he encouraged us to take bolder initiatives. I think that he consecrated our vocation. Certainly, Africa was evangelized late. But if we read carefully the documents on revelation, we observe that the continent was always associated with the salvation of the world. How can anyone forget that Africa welcomed and saved the Infant Jesus from the hands of Herod, who wanted to kill him? How can we forget that the man who helped Christ to carry his Cross to Golgotha was an African, Simon of Cyrene?

"Nova Patria Christi Africa...." By this historic statement, Paul VI intended to indicate in a striking manner how inseparable Africa was from salvation history. Later on, in his 1995 post-synodal apostolic exhortation *Ecclesia in Africa*, John Paul II made a statement that commits us to remain crucified with Christ for the salvation of the world: "'I have written your names on the palms of my hands' (Is 49:16). Yes, on the palms of Christ, pierced by the nails of the Crucifixion. The names of each one of you [Africans] is written on those palms" (EA 143).

These two popes called Africa to be a contribution to the spiritual life of the whole world. God does not abandon Africans, just as he does not abandon mankind. I think that Africa can, in the time of crisis through which we are going, modestly offer the religious sense that dwells in it. Africa can remind the Church of what the Lord expects of us; God always counts on the poor to stand up to the powerful. The African people, who preserve their innocence, can help societies in crisis to be humbler, more reasonable, more respectful of human life and of the meaning of nature. For God wants us to rediscover wisdom and humility. Africa knows that God always forgives, man sometimes forgives, but nature never forgives.

For the former president of the Pontifical Council Cor unum, *is Paul VI therefore the pope of the encyclical* Populorum progressio*?*

Paul VI hoped that the world could become better. In that year, 1967, he wrote: "Some would regard these hopes as vain flights of fancy. It may be that these people are not realistic enough and that they have not noticed the world is moving rapidly in a certain direction. Men are growing more anxious to establish closer ties of brotherhood; despite their ignorance, their mistakes, their offenses, and even their lapses into barbarism and their wanderings from the path of salvation, they are slowly making their way to the Creator, even without adverting to it" (PP 79).

Pope Montini believed in the importance of the development of peoples in order for them to end their destitution.

In a rich country, this sort of reflection may seem superfluous. As an African, I can assure you that I see the problem quite differently....

In the sorrow of Paul VI there was also great disappointment with the indifference of the Western countries. The beatification of this pope seems to me a resounding response to the suffering that he endured on this earth.

Paul VI was a prophet.

What precise memories do you have of John Paul I?

On the day of his death, I was sad and was unable to understand. Why had God chosen this man whom he then called to himself so swiftly? Indeed, I had the greatest difficulty in formulating any sort of answer to this question. But I allowed myself to be enveloped in the mysterious wisdom of the Eternal.

How can God make such a short Petrine ministry fruitful in the Church's growth and influence? The true value of a life does not depend solely on its length. Similarly, a very short pontificate can be a defining moment in the life of the Church. God gave those few weeks in the summer of 1978 a marvelous brilliance because John Paul I had the smile, the simplicity, and the radiance of children. His gentleness was so profound that it became a dazzling purity. Given the impurity of some, even in the Church, I think that he did not die in vain.

How are we to understand the election of John Paul II?

This pope shows the glory of suffering. His pontificate was prodigious and at the same time crucified. John Paul II experienced great triumphs for the Church on the international, political, and media scene. On the pastoral level, his contribution was essential, particularly his dialogue with youth, whom he set back on the path of Jesus. And yet, he remained a pontiff closely associated with the Passion and suffering of Christ. For, in union with the Son of God, the successes always brought trials with them. This pope lived fully the glorious mystery of Christ, the mystery of the Cross, in which victory triumphs in suffering.

John Paul II combated the forces of evil with unequaled fervor. Since he defended human life, the hidden powers could only unleash torrents of hatred against him. The assassination attempt on May 13, 1981, so soon after his election, and the serious consequences of his injuries were the response of the forces of evil to the extraordinary election of that man.

But God had a plan that the enemies of the Church could not thwart. John Paul II thought that the Blessed Virgin had deflected the bullet that was supposed to kill him. With the rare strength that was characteristic of him, he was a warrior chosen by heaven to defend life, the dignity of every human person, and the family.

During an Angelus message on May 29, 1994, when John Paul II was very weak because of a troublesome hospitalization at the Gemelli Hospital, he said these extraordinary words: "Precisely because the family is threatened, because the family is attacked, the pope must suffer, so that all families and the whole world might see that there is a Gospel of suffering, through which we must prepare the future, the third millennium of families, of every family and of all families."

John Paul II had an acute awareness of the ministry of Christ that he had to bear. God conformed this pope to the suffering of his Son. The lance that pierced Christ and the nails of his crucifixion went to the heart of John Paul II. The Polish pope showed that there is no pastoral success without sharing in Christ's suffering.

What do you find most touching about this pope?

I admire his extreme courage in facing all the storms he weathered throughout his life. His last struggle with the illness that was consuming him was heroic. In refusing to hide himself or to deny the progressive destruction of his body, John Paul II intended to help all sick people, who could look to him as an example. For the pope, people who suffer are worthy of being honored.

I think that his last moments on earth were a sort of unwritten encyclical. The pope was carrying the Gospel in his broken body, which was more luminous than ever. While his sickness was leading him to the gates of eternity, he had to make his last Way of the Cross, on that Good Friday in 2005, in his private chapel. We could see him only from the back. Deprived of all physical strength, he was literally fastened to the Cross, as though to invite us to focus, no longer on him, but on the "sign" that reveals God and his love. That Good Friday summed up the whole life of John Paul II, who wanted to be totally configured to Christ and to live in profound communion with his sufferings, to be conformed to him in his death, so as to arrive one day, if possible, at the resurrection from the dead with him. He actualized what Saint Paul wrote to the Corinthians: "And we all, with unveiled face, beholding the glory of the Lord, are being changed into his likeness from one degree of glory to another; for this comes from the Lord who is the Spirit" (2 Cor 3:18). On Sunday, March 27, 2005, he had already entered into the silence of the "passage" that prepares for the rising of new life. That day he wanted to speak a few final words to us from his window, but not a word came out of his mouth. He had entered into the silence of God. At that painful moment, we got the impression that we could hear John Paul II murmuring: "I am happy to be nailed to the Cross with Christ, my side against his side, my hands against his hands, my feet against his feet, the same nails pass through him and through me, our blood mixed into one blood." And despite so many sufferings, a long and painful agony, the mystery of the apostolic tenacity of John Paul II and of his serene death reminds us of this remark by Saint Bernard: "The faithful soldier does not feel his wounds when he lovingly contemplates the wounds of his King."

The words that he could no longer manage to express during those final hours of his life, at the time of the Angelus on Easter Sunday, should not sadden us. God willed that his own Word should now be read in the tormented body of the pope.

Sometimes we are such a bookish, academic Church that it is not easy for us to understand the truth of this testimony of bodily suffering. The Cross of Christ is not a theory but a dreadful ordeal and a sign of love. The message is given not only thanks to the Word of God, but also through the Incarnation. The body of John Paul II bore Christ's message for mankind.

The pope who had written so much about the human body was now fastened to the tormented body of Christ.

What do you remember about your first audience with John Paul II?

My appointment took place in August 1979. In the following weeks, I came to Rome to greet John Paul II and to express to him my gratitude for his confidence. Together with the bishop of the third diocese of Guinea, I asked for an audience. Inasmuch as Sékou Touré did not look favorably on my appointment, this meeting with the pope was very important. Upon our arrival at the Vatican, in September 1979, the officials at the Secretariat of State told us that the pope could not receive us in a private audience because of an overcrowded agenda.... For us, considering the Guinean government, that was unthinkable. We absolutely had to return to Guinea with a photo of our conversation with the pontiff! Without a meeting with John Paul II, Sékou Touré would have scorned our episcopal authority since the pope himself did not take the trouble to meet with us.... I begged the pope's staff, but there seemed to be no possibility. By chance, the nuncio stationed in Dakar, Bishop Giovanni Mariani, was in Rome. I was able to talk with him to explain my problem. As someone well acquainted with the authoritarian regime of Sékou Touré, he quickly understood the full extent of the misunderstanding. The situation was serious because Sékou Touré was perfectly capable of throwing us into prison if the pope did not give us some recognition.

The nuncio then advised me to write immediately to the pope, explaining to him the details of my dangerous situation. He personally guaranteed that my letter would be delivered into the hands of the

Holy Father. One day later, when I was with the Marianist Sisters in Monteverde Nuovo, the pope's secretary telephoned me to inform me that John Paul II expected us, Bishop Philippe Kourouma and myself, to celebrate Mass with him the following day. You can imagine my astonishment and my excitement.... At seven o'clock in the morning, we found him in his private chapel. I was seized with unimaginable emotion. I prayed a great deal for the men and women who had made me the Christian, the priest, and the bishop who found himself, contrary to all expectations, in the pope's chapel, in particular for my family in Ourous, the Holy Ghost Fathers, and Archbishop Tchidimbo, who had been ruined by nine years in prison.

Then, after the service, the pope asked us to have breakfast with him. As we were about to leave, he decided that we could take all the necessary photos. On that September morning I spent more than an hour with John Paul II. During the meal he asked me my age. I told him that I was thirty-four years old. He then let out a great burst of laughter and exclaimed: "But then you are a baby bishop! *Un vescovo Bambino!*" There was no arguing with that; I was at that time the youngest bishop in the world....

In your opinion, what would be the best way of summarizing the long pontificate of John Paul II?

All those very productive years can be traced back to the three pillars of his interior life, which were the Cross, the Eucharist, and the Blessed Virgin, *Crux, Hostia, et Virgo*. His extraordinary faith sought the foundations for its strength only in the most ordinary tools of the Christian life.

Before he was elected pope, whenever he came to Rome, Karol Wojtyła used to stay with his great friend Cardinal Deskur. At night, the latter often found his friend lying on the cold marble floor of his private chapel. He remained in adoration until dawn, without sleeping. Worried about his friend, Andrzej Deskur had the marble removed so as to install a wooden floor that would be less uncomfortable....

In his everyday routine, the simplicity of this pope was disarming. Let us not suppose that the virtues of godly men are unattainable. John Paul II lived in intimacy with God without leaving the men with whom he dealt. The relation of trust that he had with Cardinal Ratzinger was immense, while at the same time these two giants remained disarmingly humble.

Without really being aware of it, we walked with a saint who is now a protector of the Church in heaven.

How would you describe the relationship between John Paul II and Joseph Ratzinger, his prefect of the Congregation for the Doctrine of the Faith?

I think that there was such harmony between the two men that it had become impossible for them to be separated from each other.

John Paul II was always amazed by the intellectual depth and obvious theological genius of Joseph Ratzinger. For his part, the cardinal was fascinated by John Paul's immersion in God.

These two successors of Peter had the same vision of the challenges facing the Church: the need for a new evangelization, the dialogue between faith and reason, the battle against the "culture of death", to use the expression of John Paul II, and resistance against various forms of ideological oppression, from Communism to liberal relativism. Above all, they wanted to lead each of us to develop a true interior life.

The cultures of the Polish philosopher and the German theologian, the athletic ascetic and the "Benedictine" professor, were different. Yet the popes met in the depths of their spiritualities. Indeed, they had one and the same mystique: God himself no doubt wanted his two sons to be similar.

The great bond uniting Paul VI, John Paul I, John Paul II, and Benedict XVI is still suffering. John XXIII also suffered a great deal. He used to say, with arms outstretched, "I suffer painfully, but with love." When his friends questioned him, at the time of the opening of the Council, he replied, "My portion will be suffering."

There is no Petrine ministry without a share in the Cross of Christ.

How do you interpret all the difficulties that Benedict XVI had to face?

During the long years when he remained at the Congregation for the Doctrine of the Faith, Joseph Ratzinger always intended to defend the truth revealed by God, as it was preserved and transmitted by tradition and the Magisterium. Hence, some in the media sought relentlessly to categorize him as an inflexible, old-fashioned, intolerant conservative.

I remember that on the very day of his election, some voices spoke up expressing their disapproval of the election of Cardinal Ratzinger.

They forgot how swiftly the college of cardinal electors had lined up in support of John Paul II's right-hand man.... The election of a pope is always an act of faith.

Often, in thinking about Benedict XVI, I hear these words from Saint Paul to Timothy: "I have fought the good fight, I have finished the race, I have kept the faith" (2 Tim 4:7). I think that this successor of Peter had reached the end of many battles, of all that he could give to the Church and to the faithful in the spiritual, human, theological, or intellectual order. Basically, this pontificate was like a magnificent book open toward heaven, a marvelous intellect turned toward God alone. Joseph Ratzinger has always had the humility of the sons of Saint Benedict, which is summed up in their motto, *Ora et labora. Quarere deum*, to search for God, is the true synthesis of the pontificate of Benedict XVI.

Maybe some people—inside and outside the Church—never accepted the fundamental insights of Benedict XVI, the battle against the spirit of relativism, the denunciation of the possible dictatorial currents of secularism, the fight against anthropological reversals, a deeper appreciation of the liturgy. Benedict XVI suffered when the wolves were unleashed, in Regensburg, during the Williamson affair, all through the so-called "Vatileaks" crisis. Nevertheless, as early as 2005, he was lucidly aware of the situation. During the Mass of his inauguration, did he not ask: "Pray for me, that I may not flee for fear of the wolves"? In particular, he was wounded when his thought was twisted and distorted by the newspapers, to the point where it became the exact opposite of his own argument. Maybe that gentle, humble man never wanted to defend himself. But did Christ defend himself even once against his detractors and against the wolves that surrounded him in the Garden of Olives?

How could anyone imagine that the text that he read aloud during the Way of the Cross in the Coliseum, in March 2005, would leave people indifferent? Benedict XVI never feared the truth. And in return, there was no end to the violence of the worldly attacks.

If we are seeking the truth, Benedict XVI is an exceptional guide. If we prefer lies, silence, and omissions, Benedict XVI becomes an unacceptable problem....

In your opinion, who is Benedict XVI the man?

Joseph Ratzinger did not change after his election. He remained a very sensitive, modest, and reserved man. If he got the impression that he had offended his interlocutor, Benedict XVI always sought to explain to him the reasons for his position. This pope was incapable of an authoritarian or peremptory act. He was the embodiment of gentleness, meekness, humility, and God-fearing kindness.

The authority of a pope is spiritual, theological, pastoral, but also political. The Vatican is a State, which maintains diplomatic relations with many countries throughout the world, and the pope must necessarily show great administrative rigor and true firmness in managing personnel.

Nevertheless, I do not think that his respect for others and his spiritual wealth prevented this pope from living up to the political demands of his office.

Indeed, his vision of God and man is so profound that I am certain—and I hope—that one day, by the grace of God, he will be canonized, venerated as a great saint, and proclaimed a Doctor of the Church.

Was Benedict XVI right to resign from the See of Peter?

When I heard about the decision of Benedict XVI, I was in Congo-Kinshasa, where I was preaching a retreat for bishops. For me, the pope's decision was very distressing, a terrible earthquake. I cannot hide the extent of the disappointment that I felt. After a few days, I accepted his resignation with confidence and serenity, because I knew, in the light of faith, that the pope had reached that decision on his knees before the Cross. Benedict XVI resigned from his office with the conviction that this was in keeping with God's will. All his life he had sought God; once again God showed him the way.

The Pope Emeritus took up residence in a house that John Paul II had allotted to contemplative nuns who prayed for the Holy Father.

Today Benedict XVI is the one praying for the Church.

Do you think that there is a big difference between Benedict XVI and Francis?

Proud intellectuals are fond of rewriting the 2005 conclave, depicting Cardinal Bergoglio as the challenger of Joseph Ratzinger. Certainly, some cardinals had had high hopes of seeing the archbishop of Buenos Aires succeed the Polish pope. But Cardinal Bergoglio absolutely did not want to get into a confrontation with the former right-hand man of John Paul II. He had genuine admiration for Ratzinger's intellect and honesty. No doubt there are major stylistic differences between these two men: on the one hand, a reserved man with the sensibility of a Benedictine monk and, on the other, a seasoned pastor, a Jesuit, but it is possible for their fundamental visions of the Church to converge.

Today Pope Francis is aware of the complexity of his task and unceasingly begs for our prayers.

What do you think about the name Francis that he took as pope?

Pope Francis thinks that the founder of the Franciscans can help us to begin a profound reform of our spiritual life. Saint Francis loved Jesus so much that he had the privilege of being absolutely identified with him, to the point of bearing the stigmata of his Passion. In drawing our attention to Saint Francis, the pope invites us to imitate the *Poverello* of Assisi so that we, too, might bear, always and everywhere, the sufferings of Jesus' death (2 Cor 4:10; Gal 6:17). So it is that Saint Paul, seeking to be identified with Christ, could say: "Now I rejoice in my sufferings for your sake, and in my flesh I complete what is lacking in Christ's afflictions for the sake of his body, that is, the Church" (Col 1:24). For the Holy Father, Christians can never hope for anything but the demanding, arid way of Jesus, which is lined with pitfalls.

Saint Francis, too, experienced an era of moral, spiritual, and political crisis. The Church seemed to be crumbling. Jesus asked Francis to repair his Church; this was not about the little church in San Damiano, but about the whole Church of Christ, which was in ruins, symbolized and represented by the Basilica of Saint John Lateran, which Pope Innocent III saw in a dream, ready to collapse, while a little monk supported it with his shoulders to prevent it from falling.

Today how can anyone deny the fact that some men of the Church are in a state of moral ruin? The careerism and the temptation to worldliness, of which the successor to Peter speaks so often, are very real evils. Some people imagine they are products of the pope's imagination. Alas, clerical narcissism is not just a literary theme. The sickness can be deep-seated.

In order to turn the tide, we must first reform our interior life. The Church depends on the purity of our souls.

Finally, Saint Francis was a great evangelizer. He went as far as Morocco and Egypt to try to convert the Muslims. Missionary work was written in golden letters in the depth of his memory. He wanted the Gospel to be his only light. The Word of God is at the heart of his Rule.

Francis follows in the footsteps of that great pioneer. I find again in him the true missionary impulse of Saint Ignatius of Loyola. The founder of the Society of Jesus never balked at discerning between good and evil, nor does Pope Francis hesitate to do so.

IV

IN SEARCH OF THE CHURCH

Since in seeking you, my God, I seek a happy life, let me seek you so that my soul may live, for my body draws life from my soul and my soul draws life from you.

—Saint Augustine, *Confessions* 10, 20

NICOLAS DIAT: *At the end of his pontificate, in 2012, Benedict XVI insisted on celebrating the fiftieth anniversary of the opening of Vatican II. Why are there so many divisions over the last Council, even today?*

ROBERT CARDINAL SARAH: Indeed, on the subject of Vatican Council II, we will never be able to thank Pope Benedict XVI enough for his hermeneutical work and his authentic interpretation of the will of the Council Fathers. The fact that I refer to his analysis goes to show that the intention of the Council has not been understood fully.

Joseph Ratzinger grasped quite accurately the fact that John XXIII wanted first of all to respond to a major challenge for the modern world: receiving God as he manifested himself in Jesus Christ. Here are the words of Pope John at the opening of Vatican Council II: "The serious problems confronting the world after almost two thousand years remain unchanged. Jesus Christ is ever resplendent as the center of history and of life. Men are either with Him and His Church, and then they enjoy light, goodness, order, and peace. Or else they are without Him, or against Him, and deliberately opposed to His Church, and then they experience confusion, bitterness in human relations, and the danger of fratricidal wars."

From the start of Vatican II, although concerned about *aggiornamento*, the renewal of the Church, and the reunion of Christians, the pope had strongly emphasized that the Council's chief task was to reveal God to the world, to defend and promote doctrine. That is why the Church, while rejoicing in the admirable inventions of human genius and in the progress of science and technology, had to remind mankind that beyond the visible aspect of things the primordial duty remains to turn to God. For John XXIII, the Council was first of all an encounter with God in prayer, with Mary, like the apostles in the upper room on the eve of Pentecost.

As he announced in that same opening speech, the Holy Father also wanted to determine what place was still reserved for God in the hearts of men and to "examine more fully and in greater depth the modern conditions of faith and religious practice and of Christian and Catholic vitality".

At the end of the Council, on December 7, 1965, Paul VI also declared: "And so this council can be summed up in its ultimate religious meaning, which is none other than a pressing and friendly invitation to mankind of today to rediscover in fraternal love the God 'to turn away from whom is to fall, to turn to whom is to rise again, to remain in whom is to be secure ... to return to whom is to be born again, in whom to dwell is to live.'"

God therefore came first in all the conciliar reflection. This view of the Council remained central to the concerns of Benedict XVI until the final days of his pontificate. On February 14, 2013, he presented to the clergy of Rome a *lectio divina* (spiritual reading) that will always be one of the fundamental documents of his theological and pastoral legacy. In it he distinguished the true Council of the Fathers from that of the journalists and media. Now what does it mean to implement the Council if not to show that the Church's first preoccupation was to restore God's primacy in the hearts of men and of societies? Benedict's first encyclical, *Deus caritas est*, has no other explanation than that.

Given the worldwide economic and financial crisis, Benedict XVI wrote in *Caritas in veritate*, his second encyclical: "Without God man neither knows which way to go, nor even understands who he is" (78). The crisis involves not just the economy, but mankind. The social question has become a radically anthropological question; it also touches on the serious question of "the eclipse of God".

In order to help us see that everything at the heart of the conciliar documents was centered on and oriented toward God, Benedict XVI invited us to focus our attention on the way in which they are ordered. He says that the architecture of these documents has an essentially theocentric orientation. Let us begin with the Constitution on the Sacred Liturgy *Sacrosanctum concilium*. The fact that it is the first document to be published indicates that there were dogmatic and pastoral reasons of the utmost importance. Before all else, in the Church, there is adoration; and therefore God. This beginning, says Benedict XVI, corresponds to the first and chief concern of the Rule of Saint Benedict: "Nihil operi Dei praeponatur" (Nothing should be preferred to the work of God). Now, if there is one reality too often left out of consideration, it is certainly the consubstantial relation between the liturgy and God. The foundation of the liturgy must remain the search for God. We can only be dismayed by the fact that this intention of Popes John XXIII and Paul VI, and of the Council Fathers as well, is often obscured and, worse yet, betrayed....

And does the same go for the documents that follow?

Yes, because the Dogmatic Constitution on the Church, the second document of the Council, begins with these words: "Lumen gentium cum sit Christus" (Christ is the Light of nations). The first sentence of the constitution clearly presents a theological vision of the Church. Benedict XVI always tried to demonstrate that the heart of the ecclesiology of the Second Vatican Council is a fundamentally theological ecclesiology.

During a talk on the ecclesiology of the constitution *Lumen gentium*, at the International Congress on the implementation of the Second Vatican Ecumenical Council organized by the Committee for the Great Jubilee of the Year 2000, quoting a conference given in 1933 by Father Johann Baptist Metz, he said: "The crisis reached by European Christianity is no longer primarily or at least exclusively an ecclesial crisis.... The crisis is more profound: it is not only rooted in the situation of the Church: the crisis has become a crisis of God." Joseph Ratzinger recalled that the Second Vatican Council was not only an ecclesiological council but, much more than that, a discourse about God, and not just within the Christian world, but directed to the whole world. The Council spoke to mankind about this God who is the God of all, who saves all and is accessible to all. Vatican II intended to subordinate its discourse about the Church to its discourse about God and to propose an ecclesiology along theological lines. The Council does not consider the Church as a self-enclosed reality but sees her in terms of Christ.

The Church is like the moon. She does not shine with her own light but reflects the light of Christ. Indeed, just as the moon without the sun is dark, opaque, and invisible, so too is the Church if she separates herself from Christ, true God and true man. Ecclesiology shows that it depends on Christology and is connected to it.

It is likewise easy to see the close connection between the two constitutions that follow and support one another. The Church allows herself to be led by an intense life of prayer, praise, and adoration and by her mission of glorifying God in the midst of nations. Ecclesiology is thus inseparable from the liturgy. The Church is made to praise and adore God; she is nothing without God.

It is understandable that right after that comes the third dogmatic constitution, *Dei Verbum*, on the Word of God, who calls the Church together to nourish and renew her and to enlighten her path. For the Word of God is the heart of the message that the Church must reveal and transmit to the world.

The fourth document, the pastoral constitution *Gaudium et spes*, on the Church in the Modern World, shows how the glorification of God appears in the active life of the Church. The Word of God is like a light that the Church receives and brings to the world so that it might emerge from the darkness and become a glorification of God.

Unfortunately, right after the Council, the Constitution on the Sacred Liturgy was understood, not in terms of the fundamental primacy of adoration, of the Church humbly kneeling before the greatness of God, but rather as a book of formulas.... We have seen all sorts of "creative" liturgical planners who sought to find tricks to make the liturgy attractive, more communicative, by involving more and more people, but all the while forgetting that the liturgy is made for God. If you make God the Great Absent One, then all sorts of downward spirals are possible, from the most trivial to the most contemptible.

Benedict XVI often recalled that the liturgy is not supposed to be a work of personal creativity. If we make the liturgy for ourselves, it moves away from the divine; it becomes a ridiculous, vulgar, boring theatrical game. We end up with liturgies that resemble variety shows, an amusing Sunday party at which to relax together after a week of work and cares of all sorts. Once that happens, the faithful go back home, after the celebration of the Eucharist, without having encountered God personally or having heard him in the inmost depths of their heart. What is missing is this silent, contemplative, face-to-face meeting with God that transforms us and restores our energies, which allows us to reveal him to a world that is increasingly indifferent to spiritual questions. The heart of the eucharistic mystery is the celebration of the Passion and tragic death of Christ and of his Resurrection; if this mystery is submerged in long, noisy, elaborate ceremonies, we have to fear the worst. Some Masses are so hectic that they are no different from a county fair. We have to rediscover the fact that the essence of the liturgy will eternally be characterized by care in seeking God as his sons and daughters.

Finally, do you, like Benedict XVI, consider that the absence of God from society was at the heart of the reform intended by the Council Fathers?

Absolutely! Although the religious crisis of the West was less visible at the beginning of the Council than it is today, many Fathers sensed the urgent need to bring their faithful back to God, who for them was becoming a more and more distant reality. During his various missions as apostolic nuncio, John XXIII had come to understand how distant contemporary societies were from God. In France, where he had represented the Holy See, he was able to observe how the "Eldest Daughter" of the Church, and many other Western countries, were little by little turning away from Christian ideals. Pope Roncalli wanted to go back to the basics so as to combat this crisis by placing the relation between God and mankind at the center of the Council's work. In particular, he fostered a great devotion to the beauty of the liturgy. The successor of Pius XII knew that when man is in the presence of God, he enters into the mystery of what is sacred; then a relation is established that once again gives him a profoundly divine structure. Finally, John XXIII wanted to restore to man his dignity, so that he might attain the unfathomable grandeur of God. He wished to offer the contemporary world the possibility of rediscovering its capacity for praise, adoration, and wonder in the presence of God. The major message of the Council remains that of affirming in a new way that God dwells among us.

With deep bitterness, Pope John deplored the fact that much of the world's population was distant from the Church and indifferent toward her. In his address at the opening of the Council, he said: "It is a source of considerable sorrow to see that the greater part of the human race—although all men who are born were redeemed by the Blood of

Christ—does not yet participate in those sources of divine grace which exist in the Catholic Church." Fifty years later, how right Benedict XVI and Francis are to insist on the tragedy of societies that want to get rid of God so as to live without him! The elimination of God within Western cultures is a tragedy with unsuspected consequences. John Paul II was the first pope to experience the disaster of societies arbitrarily deprived of God, through the cynicism of atheistic Communism in Eastern Europe and then its brutal replacement by unfettered materialism. The lack of a connection with God has remained the major concern of all the popes since John XXIII, an abyss that continues to yawn ever deeper.

Can the "crisis of God", so to speak, cause a crisis in the very notion of Church? In The Ratzinger Report,[1] *Joseph Ratzinger saw at the root of the crisis of faith a defective understanding of the idea of Church.*

If the tie between God and Christians is weakened, the Church becomes simply a human structure, one society among others. With that, the Church becomes trivial; she makes herself worldly and is corrupted to the point of losing her original nature. Indeed, without God we create a Church in our own image, for our little needs, likes, and dislikes. Fashion takes hold of the Church, and the illusion of sacredness becomes perishable, a sort of outdated medication. To return to our earlier discussion, the same goes for the liturgy. If man claims to adapt the liturgy to his era, to transform it to suit the circumstances, divine worship dies. The development of some liturgical symbols is necessary sometimes; however, if man goes so far as to confuse the temporal and the eternal, he turns his back on the essential justification for the liturgy. The Church is the people of God that becomes the Body of Christ. She is born from the opened side of Christ, for our salvation. Christ is the Alpha and the Omega of the Church. Without God, the Church is nothing but a storm-tossed boat. History shows that the crisis of the Church can never be separated from a crisis of God. Without God, she is eclipsed, like a body separated from the light that illuminates it. Today there is a serious problem because we are no longer aware of the supernatural bond that exists between Christ and his Church. For

[1] Joseph Ratzinger with Vittorio Messori, *The Ratzinger Report: An Exclusive Interview on the State of the Church*, trans. Salvator Attanasio and Graham Harrison (San Francisco: Ignatius Press, 1985).

example, those who are so bold as to criticize the bishops or to pit some of them against others just because they do not agree with their own petty, more or less opportunistic inspirations forget that they are the successors of the apostles chosen by Christ. We must continue to build up the Church willed by the Son of God, and not a Church modeled on our incidental desires ...

Consequently, is it a crisis of the Church or a "crisis of God"?

Contrary to what we may think, the greatest difficulty of men is not in believing what the Church teaches at the moral level; the most difficult thing for the postmodern world is to believe in God and in his only Son.

This is why Benedict XVI defends the thesis of the "crisis of God". The absence of God from our lives is more and more tragic. The Council's intention—not the "spirit" of those who misinterpret it—was to give back to God all his primacy. This is why the Council Fathers wished for a deepening of the faith, which was losing its savor in the ever-changing society of the postwar era. In this sense, the problem of the Council remains entirely unsolved in some regions of the world where the absence of God has unceasingly widened.

I wonder sometimes whether even we clerics are really living in the presence of God.... Can we speak about the "Treason of the Intellectuals"? My reflection may seem severe, but I could mention many examples of priests who seem to forget that their life is centered solely on God. They devote only a little time to him during the day because they are swamped in what I would call the "heresy of activism". How can we not be deeply moved, then, by the final message of Benedict XVI? Here is a pope who, like Jesus in the Garden of Olives, after praying for a long time and trying to discern God's will, decides to renounce the "office and authority of Peter". He retires into solitude, silent adoration, so as to pass the rest of his earthly life as a monk, in a permanent face-to-face meeting and intimate union with God. He stays close to the Cross, as he said during one of his last catecheses.

His decision reminds me of one by an eighty-year-old African prelate, Bishop Silas Silvius Njiru, Bishop Emeritus of Meru, in Kenya, who wanted to enter the Trappist Monastery of Tre Fontane in Rome. Because of his episcopal status, he could be accepted only as a permanent guest, yet with the privilege of sharing the same life and the rigors of the Rule of the Trappist brothers. He told me: "I spent my whole life speaking about God. Now I will spend the rest of my life speaking with God, doing penance for the glory of God and the salvation of souls." The service of prayer that Benedict XVI is now performing is an exceptional example to the world. For his whole life he spoke about God; now he devotes his time to speaking with God and staying constantly before his face. It is not possible to believe the Church unless we fix our hearts on God.

Well, then, in such a complex era, where is the best path for the Church?

I am repeating myself, but I think that the major concern must continue to be God. The circumstances and developments in the world surely do not help us to give God his proper place. Western societies are organized and live as though God did not exist. Christians themselves, on many occasions, have settled down to a silent apostasy. If the concerns of contemporary man are centered almost exclusively on the economy, technology, and the immediacy of material happiness that has been wrongly sentimentalized, God becomes distant; often in the West the last things and eternity have unnecessarily become a sort of psychological burden. . . .

Well, then, given this existential abyss, the Church has only one option left: she must radiate Christ exclusively, his glory and his hope. She must immerse herself more deeply in the grace of the sacraments, which are the manifestation and the continuation of God's salvific presence in our midst. Only then will God be able to find his place again. The Church proclaims the Word of God and celebrates the sacraments in the world. She must do this with the utmost honesty, a genuine rigor, a merciful respect for human miseries that she has the duty to lead toward the "splendor of truth", to quote the opening words of an encyclical by John Paul II.

Some commentators speak up often, calling for a new and authentic application of collegiality in the Church. How do you see this problem?

The social changes in the world caused by progress and technological advances, the many questions that concern the Church, such as the harmonization of her internal discipline, the transmission of Christian doctrine, the implementation of catechetical methods, the evangelization of an increasingly complex world, the crisis affecting the family and marriage, the formation of the laity and of future priests, the education of young people, today go beyond the limits of any one diocese. No merely diocesan solution is sufficient. In order to respond to the development of a globalized society, it is necessary to analyze phenomena together and to offer solutions that enlighten and involve the episcopate of a nation or of several countries or even of a continent.

This is nothing new. In the Church there has always been a willingness to consult with one another at the hierarchical level to examine important questions with a view to arriving at a common position of the bishops. Today such measures are taken with regard to everyday situations and questions.

The competencies and the validity of the decisions of episcopal conferences are surely defined by canon law or by a special mandate of the Holy See. Nevertheless, the doctrinal responsibility is incumbent on each bishop in his diocese and on the See of Peter for the whole Church, while at the same time each successor of the apostles bears some responsibility with regard to the whole Church.

Necessary collegial consultation therefore does not abolish the autonomy and responsibility of the bishop in his own diocese. No one should feel obliged or forced by the collegial decision of the episcopate, especially when pressures and campaigns are organized to exert influence on certain persons for the purpose of imposing a point of view that is not spiritual but ideological. Episcopal collaboration becomes deficient if it is biased because of political aims. Each bishop is responsible before God for the way in which he fulfills his episcopal responsibilities toward the flock that the Holy Spirit has entrusted to his protection.

Collegiality ought to be affective and effective at the same time. Certainly the worst thing is indifference to the advice of others, when a bishop shuts himself up in his diocese without taking into account the expertise of his brother bishops. Synods, which are a highly successful form of implementing collegiality, are great moments in the life of the Church. But the various forums must not demobilize the bishops or give them the sense that their powers of evaluation are diminished. Nor can the major assemblies listen to the fine speakers only, the more "intelligent" ones, the experts who impress, stifle, and impose. The fear of the possibility of seeing ideological ideas and positions being imposed has rather ironically caused opponents of collegiality to say that the apostles never acted in a collegial fashion. The one and only time when they practiced collegiality was in Gethsemane.... The Gospels tell us that "then all the disciples deserted [Jesus] and fled" (Mt 26:56). Nevertheless, the Acts of the Apostles describe for us their consultative activity, especially after Pentecost. They go to prison together; they remain in Jerusalem during the persecution. Similarly, they convoke the first council of Jerusalem to examine the question about circumcision for pagans who have become Christians (Acts 15:6).

Pope Francis would like to increase collegiality, and I think that he is right. Roman centrality has made important achievements possible, but it can also lead to a form of sclerosis. For if the bishop's responsibility is weakened, there is a problem of trust. Trust is essential but fragile, and it must be preserved like a treasure.

Although it is necessary to promote the responsibility of the bishops and the episcopal conferences, Rome absolutely must keep the management of the apostolate as a whole. Of course, as the Council recalls, every baptized person may participate in the apostolate without any need of a hierarchical mandate. Yet because of the diversity of opinions on some serious questions and the loss of values and the disorientation caused by relativism, we would commit a grave sin against the unity of the Body of Christ and of the doctrine of the Church by giving episcopal conferences any authority or decision-making ability concerning doctrinal, disciplinary, or moral questions. During an address to cardinals and bishops on November 2, 1954, Pius XII called for policies whereby Church "government is made more uniform, the wonder of the faithful is avoided, for often they do not understand why in one diocese a certain policy is followed, while in another, which is perhaps adjacent, a different or even a quite contrary policy is followed." In addition to consultation among brother bishops, "there should be added close union and frequent communication with this Apostolic See. The custom of consulting the Holy See not only in doctrinal matters, but also in affairs of government and discipline, has flourished from the earliest days of Christianity." Pius XII concluded: "This union and harmonious communication with the Holy See arises, not from a kind of desire to centralize and unify everything, but by divine right and by reason of an essential element of the constitution of the Church of Christ. The result of this is not detrimental but advantageous to the Bishops to whom is entrusted the governing of individual flocks." John Paul II clearly gave his opinion on these points in his apostolic letter *Apostolos suos*, in the form of a *Motu proprio*, dated May 21, 1998, while spelling out certain norms concerning bishops' conferences.

In your opinion, would Francis like to make the government of the Church more flexible?

I think that Francis wants to give on-the-ground pastoral experiences a fair place in the reflection by the central government of the Church. And so, in choosing a cardinal from each continent for his council for the reform of curial operations, the pope intends to gather in all the riches of the Catholic world. Similarly, the pope's desire to foster synodal reflection is a fortunate initiative. Indeed, the synod should become a new Emmaus experience during which the heart of the Church is burning with the fire of the Scriptures. For in each one of our synodal assemblies, Jesus joins us and walks with us toward the inn and the breaking of the bread. There, he reveals his risen face and sends us back so that we can find the other apostles and rebuild the Church *in terris* [in many lands] where she has been abandoned or disfigured by our disappointed ambitions and frustrated hopes. Once we reach the Cenacle again, the place of the first Eucharist, Jesus then breathes on us so that we can announce to the world that he is alive. The "little hope", as Charles Péguy used to say, then revives in us.

What are the most worrisome signs today, in your opinion, for the future of the Church?

As I see it, the current difficulty is threefold and one at the same time: the lack of priests, gaps in the formation of the clergy, and an often erroneous idea about the meaning of mission.

There is a missionary trend that emphasizes political involvement or struggle and socio-economic development; this approach offers a diluted interpretation of the Gospel and of the proclamation of Jesus. The shortage of priests, the defects in their missionary activities, and a troubling absence of interior life, for lack of a prayer life and frequent reception of the sacraments can eventually cut the Christian faithful off from the wellsprings from which they ought to quench their thirst.

I sometimes have the sense that seminarians and priests are not doing enough to nourish their interior life by founding it on the Word of God, the example of the saints, on a life of prayer and contemplation, all rooted in God alone. There is a form of impoverishment or aridity that comes right from the interior of the Lord's ministers. Very often Benedict XVI and Francis have denounced careerism among the clergy. Recently, in speaking to various university communities, Pope Francis spoke these strong words: "Your intellectual commitment, in teaching and in research, in study and in the most comprehensive formation, will be all the more fruitful and effective the more fully it is animated by love for Christ and for the Church, the more the relationship between study and prayer is strengthened and made more harmonious. This is not outdated, this is the center! This is one of the challenges of our time: transmitting knowledge and offering a key for vital comprehension, not a heap of notions unconnected to one another."

The adequate formation of seminarians, revolving around the maturation of faith and leading to personal adherence to Christ, remains fundamental. Today's world and our egocentric, ever-changing societies scatter us by their turbulence. We are too weighed down with possessions; if we wish to create for the seminarians an atmosphere conducive to an encounter with Christ, silence and the edification of the interior man are indispensable. The fact that the issue is almost invisible makes it all the more serious. We might very well look into the seminaries that, in a number of countries, particularly in the West, are insufficiently provided for. But although this problem is indisputable, the crucial point is elsewhere.

Indeed, a true seminary must be a school that leads to the "brook Cherith" (1 Kings 17:1–6), to the source of the Word of God, a place where one learns to develop a genuine interior life. A man formed by that school to become a priest prepares to pray well so as to speak about God better, for one can find words about God only after having encountered him and established personal ties with him.... Prayer is always the first thing. Without the vitality of prayer, the priest's motor and that of the Church idles as a result.

We must combine prayer with ongoing work on ourselves. The Church is made solely to adore and pray. Those who are the blood and the heart of the Church must pray or else they will dry up the whole body of the institution willed by Christ. This is why seminarians, priests, and bishops have no alternative but to maintain a personal relationship with God. If this intimate relationship with Jesus is not firmly established from the beginning and all through the years of seminary formation, the seminarians run the risk of becoming mere functionaries; and on the day of their ordination they will not be struck to the very core, they will not perceive the seriousness and the consequences of the words that Jesus speaks to them: "Non jam dicam servos, sed amicos" (No longer do I call you servants ... but I have called you friends) (Jn 15:15). What is at stake is simple: it is about identification with and configuration to Christ. And so our priestly intentions and God's will must coincide more and more perfectly. We will be able to say, as Christ said to his Father: "Not my will, but yours, be done" (Lk 22:42; Mk 14:36).

Of course intellectual, theological, philosophical, exegetical formation and diplomas are important, but the treasure does not lie in knowledge.... The real treasure is our friendship with God. Without a priesthood according to God's Heart, cleansed of human ways, the Church has no future. I am not minimizing the role of the baptized people, the people of God. But by the will of God, these souls are entrusted to priests. If the latter obey merely human rules, without heavenly charity, the Church will lose her sense of mission. The crises in the Church, as serious as they may be, always have their origins in a crisis of the priesthood.

Does that mean that there are books on the one side and prayer on the other?

Certainly not. But the interior life is without a doubt the light and the salt of priestly life. It is not a question of neglecting the intellectual preparation of seminarians. Nevertheless, this aspect must not be the sole concern.

A priest who has interiorized his priestly life is careful to communicate his encounter with God in a comprehensible way. He will be capable of speaking simply. Some have intellectualized and complicated the Christian message so much that a great number of people are no longer touched by or interested in the teaching of the Church. God is not a rational argument, for the Father is in the heart of every man. That is where he waits to reveal himself to us: "You were within me, but I was outside, and it was there that I searched for you. In my unloveliness I plunged into the lovely things which you created. You were with me, but I was not with you", Saint Augustine writes in his *Confessions*. The

Fathers of the Church knew how to express themselves in a moving way and succeeded in converting whole populations to Christ. Through vivid expressions and beautiful images, they merely communicated their own spiritual experiences.

Even today, pastors must speak in a way that their sheep can understand. We are insistently invited to follow the great example given to us by Pope Francis, with his simple, concise, direct language. A hermetic Christianity that claims to be "scientific" would be an aberrant Christianity. And yet, how many self-assured, empty, and arrogant formulas do we hear so often in our churches. . . .

Nowadays the unity of the Church is threatened at the level of revealed doctrine, for there are many who consider their own opinion to be the real doctrine!

One of the major difficulties at present is found in ambiguities or personal statements about important doctrinal points, which can lead to erroneous and dangerous opinions. These bad habits disorient many of the faithful. Sometimes contradictory answers to very serious questions are given by the clergy and the theologians. How can the people of God help but be disturbed by such behavior? How can the baptized be certain of what is good or bad? Confusion about the right direction to take is the worst malady of our era.

The Church is holy in her mystery. But if she resembles a tower of Babel, there is no chance that she will manage to meet the major challenge of contemporary relativism. We can thank Benedict XVI for his keen discernment of what he named "the dictatorship of relativism". Contrary to the surrounding subjectivism, the Church must know how to tell the truth, with humility, respect, and clarity. I think that men, like trees, need roots that can be nourished by the best soil, which is quite simply the heritage and millennial tradition of Christianity. The variety of opinions in a society that is flooded with news ought not to make us forget the centuries-old tradition of the Church. The best way to understand and transmit it is the interior life in God!

The men who have received a responsibility from God himself through their vocations must not lose their souls, for that would be an incalculable betrayal. God did not ask us to create personal projects but to transmit the faith. Men of God are conveyors, not interpreters; they are faithful messengers and stewards of the Christian mysteries. Much will be demanded of those who have received much.

Do you sometimes have the sense that the faithful are disoriented?

If I take the example of the new evangelization desired by John Paul II, I see that we all agree on the need to give fresh impetus to our missionary life. On the other hand, when it is a question of understanding how the Gospel applies in everyday life, then disagreements loom on the horizon. We Catholics are divided on what is or is not a moral good.

God alone should be our point of reference. However, there is great discontent. Concerning internal Church questions, we have different concepts of the liturgy that go so far as to cause mutual rejection, hostility, or even a cold war. But this is about giving worship to God. So we ought to be especially united.

Too often we are opposed, each one enclosed in his little chapel. When ideology replaces adoration, how can we not detect the worrisome symptom of a crisis of unsuspected depth? If we are torn apart, then what about the new evangelization to which we all seem so attached? If the new evangelization means an authentic return to Christ, why so much scattered effort, so many divergent opinions, so many politicized views?

Do you think, then, about the Holy Ghost Fathers with whom you were acquainted in your youth?

The first missionaries never separated the proclamation of the Word of God, the celebration of the sacraments, and charitable service. These three tasks call for one another and are closely united. Today, we have the tendency to emphasize socio-political involvement and economic development, while excluding evangelization.

We are misusing the social doctrine of the Church without understanding it correctly. It becomes a tool for political action. Benedict XVI perfectly spelled out the place and the role of social doctrine; in *Deus caritas est*, he wrote: "Catholic social doctrine ... has no intention of giving the Church power over the State. Even less is it an attempt to impose on those who do not share the faith ways of thinking and modes of conduct proper to faith. Its aim is simply to help purify reason and to contribute, here and now, to the acknowledgment and attainment of what is just. The Church's social teaching argues on the basis of reason and natural law, namely, on the basis of what is in accord with the nature of every human being. It recognizes that it is not the

Church's responsibility to make this teaching prevail in political life. Rather, the Church wishes to help form consciences in political life and to stimulate greater insight into the authentic requirements of justice as well as greater readiness to act accordingly, even when this might involve conflict with situations of personal interest" (DCE 28). In other words, the Church must never abandon her mission of teaching, sanctification, and government, which consists of enlightening minds and purifying consciences and hearts by the light of the Gospel. The Church would betray Jesus by becoming actively involved in political life. We can tell that the vision of Benedict XVI is correct just by looking at and meditating on the life of Jesus.

The Holy Ghost Fathers of my parish had this unique assurance; they were giving their life and their health for the cause of Jesus, devoting themselves as much to evangelization as to education, charitable service, and health care. My parents believed in God because they were dazzled by the strength of the testimony of the French missionaries. Today, when a Jesuit remains in Syria, in spite of all opposition, what a magnificent, concrete image it is of fidelity to Christ alone! Ultimately, one question matters: What do we want to say about God? What do we want to hand on as God's love? It is necessary to proclaim God in season and out of season, by finding the most human methods, the most respectful language, but without stinting on the truth.

The place of women in the Church is a very important subject. How are their roles to be understood?

It is necessary to respect women, which is not the case in some countries. The dignity and the rights of women can be put seriously at risk by dangerous practices. In Africa, girls ought to be able to pursue their studies as far as boys. Similarly, it is necessary to fight vigorously against forced marriages. When I travel to the four corners of the world, I realize that the real problem is not an illusory equality, but respect for the dignity and the very freedom of women. The images of women that the Western media present are too often degrading and humiliating. A woman's body is treated as merchandise for the depraved pleasure of certain men. Through organized prostitution, women become objects with commercial value. Yet the West falsely claims to champion and defend women's rights. . . .

There are small groups of women who demand ordination to the priesthood and the episcopate. Along this line, aberrations have been perpetrated in some Protestant communities. People accuse the Catholic Church of insufficiently respecting the place of women. If I may make a remark, it seems to me that the relevance of this question is very restricted geographically.... Unfortunately, I have the sense that the West is still trying to influence other cultures. In many regions of the world, I do not think that ideological egalitarianism in relations between men and women is the model being sought.

The extravagance of the feminist ideology goes so far as to try to eradicate some words from the vocabulary: father and mother, husband and wife. God created us as complementary and different. If I look in the Gospels at how Jesus treated women, I see that he had great respect for them. The Church's only model must be this gentle, respectful way that Christ had of associating women with his mission. In this regard, it is a shame that some are trying to blame the pope, the cardinals, or the bishops by suggesting that their positions are reactionary.

The idea of a woman cardinal is as ridiculous as the idea of a priest who wanted to become a nun! The Church's point of reference remains Christ, who behaved justly toward women and men, giving to each person his or her appropriate role. Jesus was followed by some women from Galilee who were happy to be at his service. At the foot of the Cross, he had Mary Magdalen and some other sorely wounded women who watched the terrible scene of the crucifixion. According to the Gospels, Mary Magdalen was the first person to see the risen Jesus on Easter morning. She asked for nothing else but to serve the Lord in her specific role as a woman, in the purity that she had regained and consecrated.

In the world there are societies that are matriarchal or patriarchal. In them everyone plays his role, in terms of his nature. Following God's plan, the woman is mother and the man is father. Women ought to fight so that their bodies, which are sacred, will not be utilized and commercialized, because they are God's temple and the sanctuary of new life. In the Church, women can have a very important role, starting with the most prestigious ideal, aspiring to sanctity.

How can we not mention the endless host of daughters of God, starting with the Most Blessed Virgin Mary, the *Theotokos*, the Mother of God, and then Saint Monica, mother of Saint Augustine, Jeanne de Chantal, Teresa of Avila, Thérèse of Lisieux, Maria Goretti, Mother

Teresa of Calcutta, Blessed Clementine Anwarite, virgin and martyr, or Josephine Bakhita. For a long time the Church has known how to exalt and appreciate the specific genius of women. Saint John Paul II spoke about them as sentinels of the invisible; he was quite right. The Church must not allow herself to be impressed by that ideological feminism that can be seemingly generous in its intentions yet false in its deeper aims. Above all, we must not consider these problems in terms of function. God asks us to place ourselves at the service of the Church. It is not a question of making a career for oneself. Careerism already affects too much of the clergy; therefore we must not spread that virus to women!

The idea of reserved positions may be a political objective, but it does not seem to be a criterion of the Holy Spirit. I understand what a big trap it would be to entrust a dicastery of the Roman government to a woman just because she is a woman. The first criterion must not be a person's sex, but fidelity to the will of Jesus as it has always been understood by the Church's tradition. Then, if a woman theologian is in close union with the Magisterium and she wishes to place herself at the service of Christ, like the Virgin Mary or Mary Magdalen, there is no problem with her offering her full collaboration to the mission of a given dicastery, provided that it is in keeping with her competence.

In Africa there are many catechists, both men and women; the Christian communities praise them and are grateful for their great work of evangelization. Women carry out this mission with their own sensitivity and maternal sensibility, just like the specific presence that is reserved to them in our families. It would never occur to any man with common sense to try to accomplish this maternal task or to acquire a woman's prodigious power of transmitting life.... Likewise, how can we imagine that the Church lived for centuries according to erroneous anthropological paradigms? I see in these feminist demands great arrogance and a rigid form of status-seeking. In the Gospel, Mary holds one of the highest positions. There is our true model.

Our world is familiar with spiritualities that are easy and sometimes fashionable. How should we characterize these trends, which may enter into direct competition with Catholicism?

Actually there are many people who have a tendency to take from each spirituality the part that suits them, syncretically, so as to devise a comfortable subjective religion; that leaves us far from the truth in its totality as promoted by the Church. In Africa I see also that the traditional cults are still very much alive. Likewise, in Latin America, the evangelical groups have launched a merciless war of competition against the Catholic Church, with the idea of winning some of the "market share".

Man's natural tendency is always to look for places and ideas in which he can find health, wealth, and satisfaction in an almost miraculous way. In the ancient world, the Jewish authorities, or the priests among the early Christians, had to fight against the temptation to go over to the idols and enjoy sweet dreams. The major heresies of the Low Middle Ages often corresponded to a similar logic, exploiting fears, passions, and fantasies. Even today it is still about a search for immediate happiness. Modern man observes more or less correctly the limits of materialism, and to him Christianity seems exhausted or sometimes paralyzed. Here we see the lack of depth to our faith: often a Christian no longer knows what he believes in and is not sufficiently fastened to the Cross. Now, if we move away from God, the snare is never far. The catechetical, biblical, and spiritual formation of the faithful, the priests, and the religious remains the main response to such threatening lack of commitment.

Yes, the Church has only one method: the search for God in prayer and an in-depth, contemplative knowledge of his Word. Without a personal connection with God, there is neither constancy nor perspective.

Spiritual drifting is also encouraged by the surrounding relativism. In the winds of passing fashions, having no spiritual roots and without the nourishment of prayer, every Christian is in danger. When I see young African Catholics going back to the traditional cults, which still have the practice of offering sacrifices, I can tell that the priests have been unable to quench a great thirst. Weakness in the life of faith can lead to trends that are sometimes difficult to stop. What breaks my heart is the deep wound caused by the African Catholic priests who have abandoned the grace of their priesthood to enter the sects and to perform in them a sort of sacrilegious priestly ministry. What a loss! What a dagger in the Heart of Jesus! My only response is still prayer.

How would you describe this life of prayer that you speak about so often?

Each one of us absolutely must schedule time for prayer each day and build up his prayer life. How? I will tell you a little story that offers food for thought.

One day an elderly professor was hired to provide training in efficient time management to a group of fifteen heads of major businesses. This course was one of the five workshops of their training day. The elderly professor therefore had only one hour. While standing, he looked at them one by one, slowly, and then told them: "We are going to do an experiment." From beneath the table, the professor brought an enormous pot holding several gallons, which he gently placed in front of him. Then he held up a dozen rocks, each about the size of a tennis ball, and gently placed them one by one into the big pot. When the pot was filled to the brim and it was impossible to add another rock, he looked up at his students and asked them, "Is the pot full?" They all answered, "Yes." He waited a few seconds and added: "Really?" Then he bent down again and brought out from under the table a container filled with gravel. He meticulously poured this gravel onto the big rocks and then gently stirred the pot. The bits of gravel filtered between the rocks down to the bottom of the pot. The old professor looked up again at his listeners and repeated his question: "Is the pot full?" This time his brilliant students were beginning to understand his scheme. One of them answered: "Probably not!" "Right!" the old professor replied. Again he bent down and this time brought some sand from under the table. He poured it into the pot. The sand settled into the spaces between the big rocks and the gravel. Once again he asked: "Is the pot full?" This time, in chorus and without hesitating, the students answered: "No!" "Right!" the old professor replied. And as the students expected, he took the pitcher of water that was on the table and filled the pot to the very brim. Then the old professor said: "What important truth does this experiment demonstrate for us?" The boldest of the students, who was no slouch, thought of the subject of the course and answered: "It demonstrates that even when we think that our agenda is completely full, we can always add more meetings and more things to do if we really want to." "No," the old professor replied, "that is not it! The important truth that this experiment demonstrates for us is the following: if you do not put the big rocks into the pot first, you will never be able to make them all fit later." There was a profound silence, each one becoming aware of the obvious truth of these remarks. The old professor then told them: "What are the big rocks in your life? Your health, your family, your friends, your dreams, your professional career? What you need to remember is the importance of putting the big rocks into your life first; otherwise you run the risk of failing to do so. If we give priority to junk—the gravel, the sand—we will fill our life with futility, with unimportant, worthless things, and we will no longer have the time to devote to the important things. So do not forget to ask yourself the question: What are the big rocks in my life? Then, put them first into the pot of your daily routine." With a friendly gesture of his hand, the old professor saluted his listeners and slowly left the room.

Is prayer one of the big rocks in my life? I answer without hesitation: Prayer truly must be the big rock that has to fill the pot of our life. It is the time when we do nothing else but be with God. It is the precious time in which everything is done, everything is regenerated, and God acts to configure us to himself.

Saint Paul often exhorts us to live in prayer and supplication: "Pray at all times in the Spirit ...," he says, "keep alert with all perseverance, making supplication for all the saints" (Eph 6:18). But at the same time he insists on our inability to know what to ask for in order to pray as we ought; nevertheless, the Holy Spirit comes to our aid and intercedes for us himself "with sighs too deep for words" (Rom 8:26).

Prayer is, in the first place, the work of the Holy Spirit, who prays in us, reshapes us interiorly, and plunges us into the depths of the One and Triune God. This is why it is essential to keep silence and to listen, to agree to be stripped of our possessions and to give ourselves up to God, who is present in us. Prayer is not a magical moment in which we present some grievance or other so as to improve our well-being. Interior silence allows us to hear the prayer of the Holy Spirit, which becomes our own prayer. The Spirit intercedes in place of us. What matters in prayer is not our talking but managing to be silent so as to let the Holy Spirit speak, to listen to him sighing and interceding on our behalf. If we enter into the mysterious silence of the Holy Spirit, our prayers will certainly be heard because we have a listening heart. God does not respond as we would have liked insofar as we often ask for impossible things, like children who wish for thousands of presents. Nonetheless, that must not turn us away from God when we have real problems that torment us and we are experiencing the dark night of doubt. Indeed, prayer is not an extraordinary act but, rather, the silence of a child who turns his gaze completely toward God. Prayer is allowing God a bit of freedom within us. We have to be able to wait for him in silence, abandonment, and confidence, with steadfast perseverance, even when it is dark in our interior night.

Prayer, like all friendship, takes time to establish. Prayer is therefore a school that is sometimes difficult. To persist in silence can be like crossing a long, arid desert, without water or food, where we might happen to say with Saint Thérèse of Lisieux: "I do not even know any more whether I believe in what I am chanting." A believer who prays is one who walks in the dark and often remains like a pilgrim searching for light. To pray is to enter into God's will. Sometimes, when we are in the black night of suffering and confronted with hatred, we may shout as Jesus did: "Eloi, Eloi, lama sabachthani" (My God, my God, why have you forsaken me?) (Mk 15:34). No one will understand the meaning of our shout, because it is a prayer, a cry of faith to our God and Father: it is the cry of Jesus on the Cross, a cry of filial abandonment to the will of the Father alone, as though to confirm the total submission already made in the Garden of Gethsemane. While he was praying, seized with anguish, and his sweat became like big drops of blood that fell to the ground, he declared: "Abba, Father, all things are possible to you; remove this chalice from me; yet not what I will but what you will" (Mk 14:36).

God loved us first. To pray is to allow oneself to be loved and to love oneself. To pray is to look at God and to allow oneself to be looked at by him; it is truly knowing how to prepare to look at God, who dwells and lives within us in a trinitarian way. This is not just imagery; in truth, the Father, the Son, and the Holy Spirit live in us. They dwell in us in unity and trinitarian communion. One God in three distinct Persons—that is the heart of our baptismal faith. We really are God's dwelling place. Saint Athanasius explains this magnificently in his *Letter to Serapion*, bishop of Thmuis: "When the Spirit is in us, the Word who gives the Spirit is also in us, and the Father is in the Word. So it is that 'I and my Father will come and make our dwelling in him' (Jn 14:23), as it is said. For where the light is, there is the radiance; and where the radiance is, there is its active energy and luminous grace."

The soul is the place of prayer. However, in this sanctuary reserved for God, in this house of God, solitude and silence must reign. For in prayer it is essentially God who speaks and we who listen attentively, while seeking his will. To pray is to seek God and to allow him to unveil his face and to reveal his will to us. Certainly we believe that God dwells and lives in us, but very often we never allow him the freedom to live, act, move, and express himself. We occupy all the ground of our interior landscape, all day long and endlessly. We always persist in doing a lot of things, talking a lot, thinking a lot. We fill God's house with so much noise....

We have to learn that silence is the path to close personal encounter with the silent but living presence of God within us.

God is not in the storm, the earthquake, or the fire, but in the murmur of a light breeze. True prayer requires us to cultivate and preserve a certain virginity of the heart; in other words, we must not live and grow in interior or exterior commotion, in dissipation and worldly distractions; some pleasures divide, tear apart, separate, and scatter the center of our life. Spiritual virginity, interior silence, and a necessary solitude are the most suitable rocks on which to build a life with God, in an intimate face-to-face encounter with him.

We emerge from this encounter with the brilliant splendor of God's face on the skin of our face, like Moses when he came back down from the mountain after speaking with the Almighty.

Benedict XVI often insisted that the liturgy was a moment when divine realities descended into the life of men. How do you understand this perspective?

The liturgy is a moment when God, out of love, desires to be in profound union with men. If we truly experience these sacred moments, we can encounter God. We must not fall into the trap that tries to reduce the liturgy to a simple place of fraternal conviviality. There are plenty of other places in life in which to enjoy each other's company. The Mass is not a place where men meet in a trivial spirit of festivity. The liturgy is a great door that opens onto God and allows us symbolically to step beyond the walls of this world. The Holy Mass must be treated with dignity, beauty, and respect. The celebration of the Eucharist requires first a great silence, a silence inhabited by God. It is necessary to pay attention to the material circumstances in order for this encounter to take place fruitfully. I am thinking, for example, of the dignity and exemplary character of the liturgical vestments and furnishings. The place where Mass is celebrated must be marked with a beauty that can foster recollection and encounter with God. Benedict XVI contributed much to the Church in reflecting on the meaning of the liturgy. His book *The Spirit of the Liturgy*[2] is the fruit of mature theological thinking. If the liturgy becomes

---

[2] Joseph Ratzinger, *The Spirit of the Liturgy*, trans. John Saward (San Francisco: Ignatius Press, 2000).

impoverished and loses its sacred character, it becomes a sort of profane space. We live now in an era that is intensely seeking what is sacred; but because of a sort of dictatorship of subjectivism, man would like to confine the sacred to the realm of the profane. The best example of this is when we create new liturgies, the result of more or less artistic experiments, that do not allow any encounter with God. We claim somewhat arrogantly to remain in the human sphere so as to enter into the divine.

For many years now, it seems that the liturgy has been divided, so to speak, along the lines of two different schools that are even opposed: the classical and the modern. What do you think?

The liturgy is God's time, and it tends to become the heart of an ideological pitched battle between different concepts. It is sad to enter God's house with one's shoulders loaded with weapons of war and one's heart filled with hatred. If this division exists, do those who wage the battle really know what they are experiencing in the liturgy? Divine worship is an encounter with supernatural realities, through which a human being should be transformed and not reduced to vain, sterile endeavors. Does the God whom I encounter in the liturgy permit me to "cling" to one rite to the exclusion of the others? The liturgy can be nothing other than a relation with the divine. The lack of understanding between different ways of thinking about the liturgy can be explained by legitimate cultural factors, but nothing can justify its transformation into anathemas hurled by either side. Benedict XVI ardently wished to reconcile the different liturgical schools. He put a lot of energy and hope into that endeavor, and yet it has not arrived at its noble goal.

Indeed, beyond the rite, God looks first for human hearts. In the liturgy, Jesus gives us his Body and Blood to configure us to himself and to make us one with him. We become Christ, and his Blood makes us his kin, men and women immersed in his love, with the Holy Trinity dwelling in us. We become one family: God's family.

If a person respects the ancient rites of the Church but is not in love, that individual is perishing. I think that this is the situation of the most extremist adherents of the various liturgical schools. Strict, almost fundamentalist ritualism or the modernist-type deconstruction of the rite can cut people off from a true search for the love of God. There is no disputing the fact that this love is born and grows in respect for [liturgical] forms; but the tensions lead sooner or later to nothingness.

As I speak to you, I hear the voice of Saint Ambrose, who, in his commentary on Cain and Abel, warns us, saying: "The Lord Jesus asked you to pray attentively and frequently, not so as to prolong your prayer in boredom, but rather to renew it in regularity. When prayer goes on too long, it very often drifts into emptiness, but when it becomes rare, negligence invades our heart."

In Africa, when I attend Masses that last six hours, I see only a celebration that suits personal preferences. I strongly doubt that there is a true encounter with God in such moments of continual excitement and dances that are not very conducive to the encounter with the mystery. God is horrified by forms of ritualism in which man satisfies himself. Even though it is necessary to give thanks to God for the real vitality of our African liturgies and the full participation of the Christian people, when the mystery of the death and Resurrection is encumbered by additional elements that are foreign to the Eucharist, it gives the impression that we are celebrating ourselves. We absolutely must strive to do again what Jesus did. Let us remember his Word: "Do this in memory of me."

The Catholic Church should reflect and take action in response to scandalous liturgical phenomena. Other people of faith, especially Muslims, are shocked to see the debasement of some celebrations.

This can be the case with processions, which lead us to the celebration of the great mystery of our faith but are made without any recollection, without any sense of wonder, without any religious "awe" at being face to face with God. The celebrants chat and discuss all sorts of trifling things while walking up to the altar of the Lord!

This type of behavior cannot be observed in a mosque, because Muslims have more respect for the sacred than many Christians do.

How are we to understand the future of the priesthood?

The future of the priesthood can be found in the example of the saints. Its survival and fruitfulness are guaranteed by Jesus' promise to be with us always until the end of time. In the life of John Paul II, the Cross of Christ was absolutely central. From the first year of his pontificate, he believed it was essential to give a wooden cross to young people; he asked them to plant it throughout the world, in the hearts of men and in societies. I think that his example is all the more important given the fact that priests are bound up forever with the mystery of the crucifixion.

The priest is a man who is crucified with Christ; he celebrates Mass not only to perpetuate, commemorate, and make present the crucifixion, but also in order to experience his own crucifixion; then the priest is Christ himself.

The Curé of Ars always carried out his priestly ministry deep in prayer and lost in God. He was like a bridge that leads men to the Lord. For Saint John Vianney, the priest is the witness to the vertical dimension of existence; he puts others in communication with God and tirelessly repeats his message, so that it might be heard in the noise and commotion of the world. The priest possesses the divine power to bring God and his Word down among men. He used to say: "The priest is a man who takes the place of God, a man who is vested with all the powers of God."

The second central reality in the life of John Paul II was the Eucharist. Our configuration to Christ is accomplished through an intense life of prayer, adoration, and silent contemplation. Without prayer, a priest runs the risk of falling into activism, superficiality, or worldliness. It is by contemplating the face of Christ in prayer that a priest can acquire the generosity to give himself, body and soul, as Christ did, to his priestly ministry.

Before every apostolic appointment, every morning, the priest must enter into the mystery of the Eucharist. This little Host, which carries within it the entire universe and the history of mankind, must be the center of our life. As priests, we must become this white Host, allow ourselves to be "transubstantiated", and resemble Christ himself in every feature. In *The Spirit of the Liturgy*,[3] Joseph Cardinal Ratzinger writes that the Eucharist transforms us down to the inmost depths of our being: "Becoming contemporary with the Pasch of Christ in the liturgy of the Church is also, in fact, an anthropological reality. The celebration is not just a rite, not just a liturgical 'game'. It is meant to be indeed a *logikē latreia*, the 'logicizing' of my existence, my interior contemporaneity with the self-giving of Christ. His self-giving is meant to become mine, so that I become contemporary with the Pasch of Christ and assimilated unto God.... The liturgy does indeed have a bearing on everyday life, on me in my personal existence. Its aim, as St. Paul says in the text already referred to, is that 'our bodies' (that is, our bodily existence on

---

[3] Ibid., 58.

earth) become 'a living sacrifice', united to the Sacrifice of Christ (cf. Rom 12:1)."

This is why the priesthood has a future: it is the greatest gift that God gave to mankind. The Words of Jesus are eternal. In a supernatural order, the future of the priesthood is assured.

Nevertheless, doubts arise as to the receptiveness of many of our contemporaries and their willingness to respond wholeheartedly to God's call. Of course, situations vary from one continent to another; everyone knows that vocations are very plentiful in Africa, Asia, and many countries of Latin America. But how can we not be saddened by the sight of all the young men in Europe who hesitate to respond to the Lord's urgent appeal, "Come and follow me"?

God is still calling as many men as in the past; it is the men whose hearing is not what it used to be.

Finally, the priestly vocation is inseparable from the Virgin Mary. This is one great lesson from the life of John Paul II. The life of a priest is inconceivable without a filial bond with Mary. The Mother of Christ supports priests in their fidelity to their commitments. Thanks to the Blessed Virgin, I am convinced that the priesthood will never disappear.

At the risk of startling you, I think that the number of priests is not such a fundamental problem. Besides, Saint Gregory the Great says the same thing.... Paradoxically, the historical context of the late sixth century is rather similar to our era. In a homily given to the bishops gathered at the baptismal fonts of the Lateran Basilica on March 31, 591, Saint Gregory commented on Jesus' saying: "The harvest is plentiful, but the laborers are few; pray therefore the Lord of the harvest to send out laborers into his harvest." He wrote as follows: "We can speak only with a heavy heart of so few laborers for such a great harvest, for although there are many to hear the good news, there are only a few to preach it. Look about you and see how full the world is of priests, yet in God's harvest a laborer is rarely to be found; for although we have accepted the priestly office, we do not fulfill its demands.... We accept the duties of office, but by our actions we show that we are attentive to other things. We abandon the ministry of preaching and, in my opinion, are called bishops to our detriment, for we retain the honorable office but fail to practice the virtues proper to it. Those who have been entrusted to us abandon God, and we are silent. They fall into sin, and we do not extend a hand of rebuke. But how can we who neglect ourselves be able to correct someone else? We are wrapped up in worldly concerns, and the more we devote ourselves to external things, the more insensitive we become in spirit." We need priests who are men of the interior life, "God's watchmen" and pastors passionately committed to the evangelization of the world, and not social workers or politicians.

What matters most is the quality of a priest's heart, the strength of his faith, and the substance of his interior life. Intense and lasting fidelity requires a profoundly spiritual interior life and solid human maturity. Thanks to an authentic interior life and proven maturity, a priest can detach himself from what is merely superficial and transitory so as to be more fully present to what is essential. Fidelity often demands a long struggle.

When Christ inaugurated the priesthood, he had twelve apostles around him; they turned the whole world upside down. Today, there are more than four hundred thousand of us priests. Well, then, everything is possible.... We will never be more overwhelmed with work than the apostles were! The most important thing is the interior transformation of the men who have chosen to follow Christ.

We must not fear the shortage of priests but, rather, hope that there will be good, holy priests, men of God and men of prayer; on the other hand, the worst thing is the behavior of unfaithful priests, who are always agitated because they never take the time to be with God in prayer. Saint John of the Cross exhorts us to be constantly in prayer and adoration in the presence of God, so as to arm ourselves against activism, especially of the ideological sort, which produces nothing lasting that can raise us up to God. He wrote in his *Spiritual Canticle*: "Let those, then, who are singularly active, who think they can win the world with their preaching and exterior works, observe here that they would profit the Church and please God much more, not to mention the good example they would give, were they to spend at least half of this time with God in prayer, even though they may not have reached a prayer as sublime as this. They would then certainly accomplish more, with less labor, by one work than they otherwise would by a thousand. For their prayer they would merit this result, and themselves be spiritually strengthened. Without prayer, they would do a great deal of hammering but accomplish little, and sometimes nothing, and even at times cause harm."[4]

---

[4]John of the Cross, *The Spiritual Canticle* 29, 3, in *The Collected Works of St. John of the Cross*, trans. Kieran Kavanaugh, O.C.D., and Otilio Rodriguez, O.C.D. (Washington, D.C.: ICS Publications, Institute of Carmelite Studies, 1979), 524.

Are ideological façades and sources of division that important in the Church?

Benedict XVI used to say that ideologies will not save the world but, rather, the saints and their great, gentle insights. Ideologies coarsen, crush, and destroy men, because they are not intrinsically oriented to their advantage. In Guinea, I was personally acquainted with Communism, which was so full of generous promises. On fraudulent pretexts it put many of my compatriots to death. The ideological spirit is the opposite of the Gospel spirit. That is why priests who choose to follow or to propagate political ideas are necessarily on the wrong path, since they make sacred something that is not supposed to be. Ideology is by nature disconnected from reality, and it is necessarily a source of division, since it cannot win the lasting allegiance of people who are still anchored in reality, in good times and bad.

Following Vatican Council II, some tried with all their might to give a political reading to the work of the Council Fathers. That was a serious error. But, alas, that phenomenon was not new. Down through the centuries, the Church has always had to confront ideologies; the heresies themselves were of an ideological nature. There is always a combat between light and darkness, a confrontation between the Church, with her view of man and the world, and political fashions that soon grow dull. John Paul II dared to fight Communism; historians agree in saying that he had a preeminent role in the fall of the Soviet empire.

I am not afraid to say that the Church will always have to confront ideological lies. Today, she must address gender ideology, which John Paul II did not hesitate to describe as a "new ideology of evil". Moreover gender, the product of reflection by American structuralists, is a deformed child of Marxist thinking. In his last book, *Memory and Identity*,[5] John Paul II had already written: "I am thinking ... of the strong pressure from the European Parliament to recognise homosexual unions as an alternative type of family, with the right to adopt children. It is legitimate and even necessary to ask whether this is not the work of another ideology of evil, more subtle and hidden, perhaps, intent upon exploiting human rights themselves against man and against the family."

Gender ideology conveys a crude lie, since the reality of the human being as man and woman is denied. The lobbies and the feminist

---

[5] John Paul II, *Memory and Identity* (New York: Rizzoli, 2005), 11.

movements promote it with violence. It has rapidly been transformed into a battle against the social order and its values. Its objective does not stop just at the deconstruction of the [human] subject; it is interested above all in the deconstruction of the social order. It is about sowing discord over the legitimacy of social norms and introducing a suspicion over the model of heterosexuality; for [proponents of] *gender* [theory], it is necessary to abolish Christian civilization and construct a new world.

And so I think of the American sociologist Margaret Sanger, who admittedly engaged in an ongoing struggle for the moral deconstruction of the West. A woman, she said, must be able to control her body and her sexuality. Since she is its owner, she must be able to do as she likes with it, to enjoy the freedom of her body and of its rights, and to manage her life. She must freely choose to be a mother or not. Every child from now on must be "wanted", "chosen", "planned". No religious morality, no dogma, no cultural tradition can prevent women from achieving their goals. No one should prevent or forbid women from having access to contraception and abortion.

In the same way, Simone de Beauvoir, like Jean-Paul Sartre and atheistic existentialism, wanted to liberate the individual from the living conditions that God established. In order to exercise his rights, the individual must be committed to the denial of what exists outside of himself or of what is given by nature and divine revelation. A radical feminist, Simone de Beauvoir asserted: "One is not born a woman, one becomes so." Hence, if a woman remains passive and submits to traditions, she becomes a "wife" and "mother". This is what theoreticians of gender studies call the stereotype or the repressive social construct that must be "deconstructed". Conversely, if a woman is committed to constructing herself in a way that is radically autonomous with respect to others and to God, she "liberates" herself; the woman becomes herself and lives for herself. She can thus own herself and control her destiny.

In December 2012, during his last address on the occasion of Christmas greetings to the Roman Curia, Benedict XVI decided to reflect on Simone de Beauvoir's statement, "One is not born a woman, one becomes so": "These words lay the foundation for what is put forward today under the term 'gender' as a new philosophy of sexuality. According to this philosophy, sex is no longer a given element of nature, that man has to accept and personally make sense of: it is a social role that we choose for ourselves, while in the past it was chosen for us by society. The profound falsehood of this theory and of the anthropological revolution contained within it is obvious. People dispute the idea that they have a nature, given by their bodily identity, that serves as a defining element of the human being. They deny their nature and decide that it is not something previously given to them, but that they make it for themselves. According to the biblical creation account, being created by God as male and female pertains to the essence of the human creature. This duality is an essential aspect of what being human is all about, as ordained by God. This very duality as something previously given is what is now disputed. The words of the creation account: 'male and female he created them' (Gen 1:27) no longer apply. No, what applies now is this: it was not God who created them male and female—hitherto society did this, now we decide for ourselves. Man and woman as created realities, as the nature of the human being, no longer exist. Man calls his nature into question. From now on he is merely spirit and will. The manipulation of nature, which we deplore today where our environment is concerned, now becomes man's fundamental choice where he himself is concerned."

In a completely different area, what are we to think about the dialogue between the Church and the various Christian denominations and also the other religions?

This question is extremely important and delicate. There is a widespread idea today that religions have equal value and that the mission of evangelizing all nations is a thing of the past; that we should let everybody follow his own religion. After all, the argument goes, a person would be saved by following his own religious tradition.

John Paul II, wishing to study in greater depth the permanent meaning of mission, declared in his encyclical *Redemptoris missio* that although the Church recognizes the importance of other religions, she must consider it her priority to proclaim Christ as the one Savior of the world. The solemn introduction to that encyclical shows clearly that only an erroneous understanding of religious liberty and respect for other peoples can restrain the force of the missionary impulse.

A book by Father Jacques Dupuis, *Toward a Christian Theology of Religious Pluralism*,[6] and the philosophical study by the Presbyterian John Hick, who argues for relativizing various religious positions as a

---

[6] Jacques Dupuis, *Toward a Christian Theology of Religious Pluralism* (Maryknoll, N.Y.: Orbis Books, 1997).

prerequisite for any interreligious dialogue, led the Congregation for the Doctrine of the Faith to publish on January 24, 2001, the *Notification* on Father Dupuis' book. In this document, the congregation denounces "notable ambiguities and difficulties on important doctrinal points, which could lead a reader to erroneous or harmful opinions. These points concerned the interpretation of the sole and universal salvific mediation of Christ, the unicity and completeness of Christ's revelation, the universal salvific action of the Holy Spirit, the orientation of all people to the Church, and the value and significance of the salvific function of other religions."

The christological statement in the Acts of the Apostles that "there is no other name under heaven given among men by which we must be saved" (Acts 4:12) and the Vatican Council II, in its declaration on the relations of the Church with non-Christian religions, *Nostra aetate*, are clear. The Catholic Church rejects nothing of what is true in other religions; she considers with sincere respect ways of acting and living that may reflect a ray of the truth that enlightens all mankind. Nevertheless, she proclaims and is obliged to proclaim that Christ is "the way, and the truth, and the life" (Jn 14:6), in whom men and women must find the fullness of religious life.

The Spirit is the one who prompts us to proclaim the great works of God. I always feel the duty to repeat the exclamation of Saint Paul, in the name of the whole Church: "If I preach the gospel, that gives me no ground for boasting. For necessity is laid upon me. Woe to me if I do not preach the gospel!" (1 Cor 9:16).

How can we not feel a certain uneasiness, given the negative tendency manifested in the weakening of missionary efforts toward non-Christians? This decline is the sign of a crisis in faith and the result of the relativism that has very profoundly invaded the Church herself.

Could the desire to continue asserting the place of Christ and of the Church within mankind cause us to be described as intolerant fundamentalists? In the search for truth, I think that it is necessary to acquire the ability to come to terms with oneself as "intolerant", in other words, to have the courage to tell someone else that what he does is bad or wrong. Then we will be able to take someone else's criticism when it is meant to open our eyes to the truth. A little while ago I was struck by the remarks of the philosopher Thibaud Collin, who forcefully declared during a conference: "The guarantee of future progress in one's personal search for the truth is the keenness with which one assigns weight to what each person says about reality. All this presupposes that man is not the measure of reality and that he therefore has to receive the true and the good." Then, turning his attention to John Paul II and Benedict XVI, he added: "Because the last two popes are lucid about the depth of the crisis of postmodern civilization, they therefore invite Catholics to practice a downright Socratic boldness. Socrates, indeed, is the one who sought the truth his whole life long. He unceasingly questioned people about their custom so as to arouse in them the desire for the true and the good. But far from being undecided, he always subjected himself fully to the force of reason within him. It is necessary to reread his dialogue with Crito a few hours before his death in order to grasp the reasons for his death. So as to remain faithful to the end to the consistency of the divine calling that he had received, he refused to compromise with the Athenian people and with his childhood friend, who was nevertheless begging him to escape. Far from reveling in the Sophistical use of reason, Socrates bears witness to its enlivening freshness. Maybe that was why Cardinal Ratzinger, in commenting on the encyclical *Fides et ratio*, ventures to make this comparison: 'I would say that in it the pope [John Paul II] is attempting what Vatican II attempted also: to come to terms with the Socratic function of restlessness, the challenge not to be resigned to the weakness of reason, which no doubt exists, and to try to take a step farther toward the truth.'"

Finally, the great strength of contemporary nihilism comes from a certain political consensus that ceaselessly fosters it. We must not be conformed to this world but allow ourselves to be transformed by renewing our way of thinking, so as to be able to discern God's will. Often the media present speaking out against the Church's Magisterium as a form of courage. In reality, no courage is needed for that, because then we can always be sure of the applause of the public. It takes courage, rather, to adhere to the faith of the Church, even if that contradicts the scheme of the modern world. Following Saint Paul, Benedict XVI called for a "mature" faith. This is the faith of the Christians who die every day for Christ in Nigeria, in Pakistan, in the Middle East, and throughout the world.... It is the magnificent faith of Assia Bibi, a [Pakistani Christian] woman who is threatened with death for blasphemy and is fighting for her life.

In the name of truth, we must proclaim and announce Jesus Christ, the only Savior of the world, to all nations. This proclamation is in no way an obstacle to dialogue among the different religions.

Relations among various confessions must not be a stumbling block in mission work. On the contrary, it should reinforce it. John Paul II, then Benedict XVI, and now Francis are only reaffirming the faith of the Church. The missions are the diamond in the rough of the Bride of Christ. The Son of God is the Way, the Truth, and the Life; no one can go to God except by him. Jesus is the one gate to heaven: there is neither intolerance nor religious fundamentalism in this loving proclamation. In a commentary on Psalm 85, Saint Augustine made this clear statement about the Church: "Our Lord Jesus Christ alone, the Son of God, is the savior of his body; he prays for us, he prays in us, and we pray to him."

Again, as always, your reflections and your concerns go back to the absence of God in our world.

Again, as always, because man understands himself only through Jesus Christ! At another level, the absence of God is the result of an absence of the Church.

Inasmuch as God has lost his primacy among man's preoccupations, inasmuch as man himself gets in the way of God, we are experiencing an eclipse of God. Consequently, there is increasing obscurity and incomprehension as to the true nature of man, for he is defined only in relation to God.

We no longer know who man is once he detaches himself from his Creator. Man intends to recreate himself; he rejects the laws of his nature, which become contingent. Man's rupture with God obscures his way of looking at creation. Blinded by his technological successes, his world view disfigures the world: things no longer possess ontological truth or goodness but, rather, are neutral, and man is the one who must give them meaning. This is why it is urgent to emphasize that the abandonment of God by contemporary societies, especially in the West, affects not only the teaching of the Church but also the foundations of anthropology.

Do your travels, as well as your African roots, allow you to look differently at ecumenism?

You have to recognize that the emphasis on interreligious dialogue and ecumenism is very recent. The Second Vatican Council paid particular attention to these questions. Although the results seem meager, there is better understanding now between the different religions. Sometimes we can be very disappointed by the use of religion and of God to satisfy the violence that slumbers within every man.

Although there was real progress made with the Anglicans, some theological developments and the decision to go ahead and ordain women as priests and bishops are now an insurmountable obstacle. This mutation of Anglicanism has led a significant number of Protestant pastors to seek admission as priests in the Catholic Church.

Let us turn then to Orthodoxy. I know that Benedict XVI did great work to promote unity among Christians. Relations between the Orthodox and the Catholics are going forward; the question of the primacy and the jurisdiction of the pope could be accepted by Orthodoxy without great difficulty at the doctrinal level. Benedict XVI rightly recalled that Orthodoxy acknowledges that the bishop of Rome is the *Protos*, the First; this had already been enacted at the Council of Nicaea, in 325. It remains to be seen whether the bishop of Rome has specific functions and missions.

Certainly, the pontificate of Benedict XVI was too short to accomplish major progress. On March 14, 2010, he made a historic gesture of great ecumenical importance when he visited the Lutheran church in Rome that John Paul II himself had visited in 1983.

How can we forget, finally, that the Polish pope was the first successor of Peter to go into a synagogue? In the Holy Land, that man, who could not forget that many of his Ashkenazy friends from Wadowice had perished in the Nazi death camps, did not hesitate to declare that the Jews are our elder brothers in the faith. His successor, Benedict XVI, stressed in his Petrine ministry an appreciation for the spiritual heritage common to Jews and Christians. For they share much: both religions pray to the God of Abraham, Isaac, and Jacob, and they have the same roots. As a symbolic action, Benedict XVI decided to plant an olive tree at the residence of Shimon Peres, the president of the State of Israel. In his farewell speech at Ben Gurion Airport in Tel-Aviv, the pope mentioned this gesture and recalled that the apostle Paul, in his Letter to the Romans, had described the Church of the Gentiles as a branch "from a wild olive tree, grafted into a cultivated olive tree" that is, the People of the Covenant (see Rom 11:17–24). The pilgrimage of Francis to the Holy Land was then a magnificent witness promoting peace.

What about interreligious dialogue?

With Islam, there can be no theological dialogue, because the essential foundations of the Christian faith are very different from those of the Muslims: the Trinity, the Incarnation, namely, the fact that "Jesus Christ has come [among us] in the flesh" (1 Jn 4:1–10), the Cross, the death and Resurrection of Jesus, and consequently the Eucharist are rejected by the Muslims. But we can promote a dialogue that might lead to an effective collaboration at the national and international level, particularly in the context of defending human life, from conception to natural death. For example, like the Church, the various authorities of Islam vehemently reject the new gender ideology.

However, in Africa, with different accents depending on the country, for instance, Sudan, Kenya, or Nigeria, to mention a few, Christian-Muslim relations have recently become very difficult, almost impossible; in Sudan, a Christian is considered a slave by the Muslims. My remarks, however, ought to be nuanced; generally speaking, relations between Christians and Muslims, at least in West Africa, have always been harmonious and quite friendly.

But in the countries that were the cradle of Christianity, in the Near East and the Middle East, it distresses me to see the development of the relations between the different religious communities. In Iraq, for example, the results of Western and American policies are catastrophic for the Christians, who are being driven by Muslim extremists from the lands that their forefathers occupied since time immemorial. In the Syrian refugee camps that I visited, set up in Lebanon or in Jordan, how can one not be struck by the profound misfortune of the Christians who are condemned to a diaspora that will not speak its name? I heard the Syrian bishops, during our meeting in December 2013 in Beirut, voice their suffering and their fear that one day the Middle East will be devoid of any Christian presence. Their communities are undergoing considerable trials and are experiencing a demographic decline that is so significant that the future of Christianity in its cradle of origin is thereby threatened. According to leaders of the Churches of the various rites, the exodus of Christians has reached alarming proportions. Given the uncertainty that weighs heavily on their life as baptized believers, the kidnapping or assassination of priests, brothers, and nuns, and of bishops too, Christians easily give in to the temptation to emigrate—when they are not brutally driven from their homes, as has been the case in Iraq since the violent American military invasion in 2003.

I would like to report the anguished cry of a great pastor, Archbishop Basil Casmoussa, archbishop of the Syriac Catholics of Mosul, who during the Special Synod of Bishops for the Middle East in October 2010 deplored "the unjust accusation against Christians of being troops hired or led by and for the so-called Christian West and thus considered as a parasitical body in the nation". Continuing his speech, he added that Christians were "present and active here well before Islam, [but now] they feel undesired in their own home, which becomes more and more a *Dar el-Islam* [a house of Islam].... The Eastern Christian in Islamic countries is condemned be it to disappear or to go into exile. What is happening in Iraq today makes us think back to what happened in Turkey during the First World War. It is alarming!" This suffering of our brethren in faith breaks our heart and invites us to prayer and communion with the Churches of the Middle East, which today, to borrow the words of Saint Ignatius of Antioch, are "God's wheat, ground by the teeth of beasts, that [they] may become the pure bread of Christ". Yes, I can say emphatically that some Western powers will have perpetrated, directly or symbolically, a crime against humanity.

In the dicastery that I headed for several years, *Cor unum*, we promoted dialogue, to the extent we could, inasmuch as our aid was destined for all people, without distinction as to race or religion; material difficulties, wars, famines, droughts, and earthquakes can strike any human being, whether he is Christian, Muslim, Buddhist, animist, or atheist. I regarded projects designed to assist Muslims in the same way I did the requests submitted by Christians. For example, the John Paul II Foundation for the Sahel offers assistance mostly to countries where the population is overwhelmingly Muslim. To put it quite simply, our model is still God; he is the Father, and he is concerned about all his children.

It is necessary to believe in dialogue while thinking always about the example of God himself. Our Father never tires of engaging us in dialogue, of coming to us despite our oft-repeated infidelities. He comes again, as always. In the same way, despite the difficulties, which are often excruciating, we have to go back a hundred times to the drawing board in our dialogue with our brethren who profess another belief. But without personal conversion, without true union with God, reconciliation with other religions remains an empty exercise.

In our plan for interreligious dialogue, we can run several risks. Postmodern ideology, which is everywhere today, is fundamentally soft, fluid, indeterminate, and for that very reason receptive to all "truths" that have lost their vitality.... Therefore, we must never lose sight of the fact that dialogue has meaning and legitimacy only because of a more basic relation to the truth being sought and to an objective good, namely, the dignity of persons that is manifested precisely in this search for truth. There are no truths about God that are inconsistent with each other. There is only one truth that must be sought, attained, and proclaimed: it is Jesus Christ.

The second danger is that of a falsely happy syncretism, which comes precisely from our lack of faith in God. If we are sincerely in God's hand, we can be optimistic about ecumenism; if it does not make sufficient progress, it is because our sin is still great and our faith too tepid. The division of Christians remains a major scandal. We must be one body so that the world might believe.

Have there always been peaceful relations among the different religions in Guinea?

Yes, indeed, even in everyday life we have a long tradition of interreligious dialogue. The religions have always lived peacefully with each other. The Muslims are in the majority, but they respect the Christians. We stimulate each other in our fidelity to prayer, to the truth, and to the depth of our religious practice; it is important for us to love one another and to walk together in the light of the truth, as Saint John says in his Third Letter addressed to Gaius.

This was an opportunity that left its mark on me. Personally, I was very impressed by the depth of the Muslim practices in my country. In every locality, at the hour for prayer, the Muslims stop and pray. It is the greatest sign that they love a God who is part of their lives. The Islam in Guinea is spiritual, devoted to rather moving practices. I am not afraid to say that the Islam in my country is a fraternal, peaceful religion. The possibility of conversion exists, and the newly baptized are not obliged to hide, as in other countries. Overall, this religious approach is the one found throughout West Africa.

How would you describe the nature of Cor unum, the dicastery to which you devoted several years of your life, in its fight against all sorts of poverty? Furthermore, why do you speak so often about the close relation between God and the poor?

The Gospel is not a slogan. The same goes for our activity to relieve people's suffering; it is not a matter of talking or holding forth, but of working humbly and having a deep respect for the poor. For example, I remember being disgusted when I heard the advertising slogan of a Catholic charitable organization, which was almost insulting to the poor: "Let us fight for zero poverty".... Not one saint—and God alone knows the tremendous number of saints of charity that the Church has brought forth in two thousand years—ever dared to speak that way about poverty and poor people.

Jesus himself had no pretention of this sort. This slogan respects neither the Gospel nor Christ. Ever since the Old Testament, God has been with the poor; and Sacred Scripture unceasingly acclaims "the poor of Yahweh". A poor person feels dependent on God; this bond is the foundation of his spirituality. The world has not favored him, but all his hope, his sole light, is in God. The exhortation of Psalm 107 is particularly significant: "Let them thank the LORD for his merciful love, for his wonderful works to the sons of men! For he satisfies him who is thirsty, and the hungry he fills with good things. Some sat in darkness and in gloom, prisoners in affliction and in irons.... But [God] raises up the needy out of affliction, and makes their families like flocks."

Poverty is a biblical value confirmed by Christ, who emphatically exclaims: "Blessed are the poor in spirit, for theirs is the kingdom of heaven" (Mt 5:3). Saint Paul also says that "our Lord Jesus Christ,... though he was rich, yet for your sake he became poor, so that by his poverty you might become rich" (2 Cor 8:9).

Yes, poverty is a Christian value. The poor person is someone who knows that, by himself, he cannot live. He needs God and other people in order to be, flourish, and grow. On the contrary, rich people expect nothing of anyone. They can provide for their needs without calling either on their neighbors or on God. In this sense, wealth can lead to great sadness and true human loneliness or to terrible spiritual poverty. If in order to eat and care for himself, a man must turn to someone else, this necessarily results in a great enlargement of his heart. This is why the poor are closest to God and live in great solidarity with one another; they draw from this divine source the ability to be attentive to others.

The Church must not fight against poverty but, rather, wage a battle against destitution, especially material and spiritual destitution. It is critical to make a commitment so that all men might have the minimum they require in order to live. From the earliest centuries in her history, the Church has sought to transform hearts so as to push back the frontiers of destitution. *Gaudium et spes* invites us to fight against different kinds of destitution, not against poverty: "The spirit of poverty and charity is the glory and witness of the Church of Christ" (88).

There is a fundamental distinction between destitution and poverty. Francis, in his yearly Lenten message in 2014, distinguishes between moral destitution, spiritual destitution, and material destitution. The pope says that spiritual destitution is still the most serious because man is cut off from his natural source, which is God. Thus he writes that "we experience ... *spiritual destitution* ... when we turn away from God and reject his love. If we think we don't need God who reaches out to us through Christ, because we believe we can make do on our own, we are headed for a fall. God alone can truly save and free us." In contrast, material destitution leads in fact to a subhuman sort of life that is the source of great suffering. It seems that there are no prospects left.

But we do not have the right to confuse destitution and poverty, because in doing so we would seriously be going against the Gospel. Recall what Christ told us: "The poor you always have with you, but you do not always have me" (Jn 12:8). Those who want to eradicate poverty make the Son of God a liar. They are mistaken and lying.

The pope wanted to espouse what Saint Francis called "Lady Poverty". The *Poverello* of Assisi recommended to his friars that they wear poor habits, live by their own work to support the community, and never claim a salary as something due. He asked them to acquire no material goods but rather to be in every place "pilgrims and strangers in this world, serving the Lord in humility". Saint Francis of Assisi wanted to be poor because Christ chose poverty. If he calls poverty a royal virtue, it is because it shone brilliantly in the life of Jesus, the King of kings and Lord of lords, and in the life of his mother, Mary of Nazareth. Let us not forget the magnificent, heartfelt cry of our pope when he declared to journalists from all over the world on March 16, 2013, at the dawn of his pontificate: "Oh, how I wish for a Church that is poor and for the poor!"

Similarly, I often think about the vow of poverty taken by religious; does our world still know that the men and women who pronounce it do so in order to be as close as possible to Christ? The Son wanted to be poor so as to show us the best path by which we can return to God. The "zero poverty" program liquidates and physically eliminates the vows of religious and priests.... I know that not all priests necessarily take a vow of absolute poverty. But I firmly believe, in contemplating Christ, that the priesthood is linked to poverty. The priest is a man of God, a man of prayer and humility, a contemplative who seeks to help his brethren to penetrate the mystery of the love of God. To be a priest is to behave as Jesus did, to have nothing, to desire nothing, and to belong to God alone: "Mihi vivere Christus est et mori lucrum" (For to me to live is Christ, and to die is gain) (Phil 1:21).

As president of the Pontifical Council *Cor unum*, I devoted my days to fighting against destitution, particularly on the most distressing fronts in the world. This was a demanding struggle to bring first aid to those who no longer had anything: no food or clothing or medications. In my prayer, I often think of the destitution of loneliness and of those who have no human consideration.

Mankind has never been so rich, yet it reaches astounding heights of moral and spiritual destitution because of the poverty of our interpersonal relationships and the globalization of indifference. In the fight against destitution, there is one fundamental dimension, which consists of restoring to man his vocation as a child of God and his joy in belonging to the family of God. If we do not include the religious aspect, we fall into a kind of philanthropy or secular humanitarian activity that forgets the Gospel. There you have the distinction between Christian charity and the activity of civil organizations; the difference is Christ!

The Son of God loves the poor; others intend to eradicate them. What a lying, unrealistic, almost tyrannical utopia! I always marvel when *Gaudium et spes* declares: "The spirit of poverty and charity is the glory and witness of the Church of Christ" (GS 88).

We must be precise in our choice of words. The language of the UN and of its agencies, who want to suppress poverty, which they confuse with destitution, is not that of the Church of Christ. The Son of God did not come to speak to the poor in ideological slogans! The Church must banish these slogans from her language. For they have stupefied and destroyed peoples who were trying to remain free in conscience.

Are you not afraid of being misunderstood in employing this sort of distinction?

It is a lack of charity to shut one's eyes. It is a lack of charity to remain silent in the face of confusing words and slogans!

We must not be afraid to assert that the Church's battle to relieve human needs is inseparable from the Gospel. It will only make our struggle more intense. If you read the Latin text of *Gaudium et spes* carefully, you will immediately notice this distinction. Well, then, are they going to think me naïve? Certainly I can make a mistake. It is not always easy to distinguish a poor person from a crook who is disguising his wealth beneath his rags.... Nevertheless, if I really listen to the teachings of Jesus, I would rather be robbed than lack charity.

I remember an incident that I experienced at the beginning of my episcopal ministry in Conakry. A woman originally from Ivory Coast came to see me at my residence to tell me that she had been the victim of a robbery. I was in a hurry because I had to prepare a conference and I was getting ready to travel to Abidjan. She was weeping because her mission was to buy some loincloths to bring them back to her country. A large part of the sum of money belonged to friends of hers, women who had asked her to make similar purchases for them. If she brought back nothing, she feared that she would be suspected of having diverted the money to her personal use. I asked the diocesan purchasing agent to give her a sum that would set her mind at ease. The next day at the airport I again met that woman who was taking the plane, just as I was. She had assured me that she had nothing left; obviously she had fooled me. But if I had not responded to her tears, I would not have responded to the appeal of Christ, who asks us to help those in distress. I was certain that I had acted according to the words of Saint Paul: "Love ... believes all things, hopes all things, endures all things" (1 Cor 13:7). It was up to that woman to deal with her conscience. Indeed, discernment of the intentions of others must not prevent us from living a life of charity. In heaven, we will be judged on love, as Saint John of the Cross used to say. Let us never forget the words from the Gospel of Matthew: "Truly, I say to you, as you did it to one of the least of these my brethren, you did it to me" (Mt 25:40).

In Latin America, liberation theology intended precisely to help the poorest of the poor in societies with great inequalities. What do you think about that movement?

I heard about liberation theology when I was still in Africa. As I began my reading, I was interested by this way of putting the poor at the center of attention. In my country, and in many other African regions, we were experiencing economic difficulties similar to those in Latin American countries. In Africa, however, our search was more cultural, inasmuch as we wanted to understand the best way to connect our traditional heritage to Christianity. Still, liberation theology was not without a certain charm. Personally, when I understood the Marxist origins of some proponents of that theology, I immediately distanced myself from it. I saw too well in my country the consequences of the Communist ideology. The theory of class struggle was central to the politics of Sékou Touré. This bleak view of social realities was at the origin of many of the social ills in Guinea. In claiming to help those who are destitute, without promoting their freedom and responsibility, they were only aggravating the distress of the population. I did not see how the word "struggle" itself could become the center of Christian doctrine.

The Church's battle is focused on the conversion of hearts. This is possible only if there is human soil ready to be sown by God's grace. Finally, in Africa, liberation theology had limited repercussions. I would even say that the deviations in that theology did not suit the African soul.

Today what are the stakes in the new evangelization?

In his apostolic exhortation *Evangelii nuntiandi*, dedicated to evangelization in the modern world, Paul VI had already tried to address this major topic. Then John Paul II again gave the necessary impetus to the Church with his very extensive teaching on the subject. When the peoples in Eastern Europe had just regained their freedom, he decided to give to the world the encyclical *Redemptoris missio* in order to set a demanding horizon, in particular an urgent call to conversion.

Indeed, when we observe today the many deficiencies of faith, the eclipse of the sense of God and of man, the lack of real familiarity with the teaching of Jesus Christ, the detachment of some countries from their Christian roots, and what John Paul II called a "silent apostasy", it is urgent to think about a new evangelization. This movement presupposes that we go beyond mere theoretical knowledge of the Word of God; we must rediscover personal contact with Jesus.

It is important to give individuals the opportunity for the experience of close encounters with Christ. Without such a heart-to-heart conversation, we are fooling ourselves if we think that people will follow the Son of God in the long term.

The importance of this personal experience reminds me of a saying of the Desert Fathers that left a deep impression on me during my biblical studies in Jerusalem. Translated from Coptic, it expresses the importance of the indispensable interior life in being a Christian: "One monk met another and asked him: 'Why do so many abandon the monastic life? Why?' The other monk replied: 'Monastic life is like a dog chasing a rabbit. It runs after the rabbit, barking; many other dogs, hearing the bark, join it, and they all run together after the rabbit. But after a while, all the dogs that run without seeing the rabbit wonder: Where are we going? Why are we running? They become tired, get lost, and stop running, one after the other. Only the dogs that see the rabbit continue to pursue it to the end, until they catch it.'" The moral of the story is: Only those whose eyes are fixed on the person of Christ on the Cross persevere to the end....

Many circumstances and deep motives, or the people around us, may have led us to follow Jesus. Then comes the moment of maturity, when only our personal experience of Christ guides us. This personal encounter is decisive for the rest of our life. Saint Paul experienced this moment on the road to Damascus, just as Saint Augustine did under a fig tree in Cassiciacum. And so the former could say: "To me to live is Christ" (Phil 1:21). He added: "It is no longer I who live, but Christ who lives in me; and the life I now live in the flesh I live by faith in the Son of God, who loved me and gave himself for me" (Gal 2:20).

The Gospel is not a theoretical path; it must not become a sort of school reserved for the elite. The Church is a plainly evident path to the Risen Lord.

Without this union with Christ, it will not be possible to bridge the gap between his Word and the people, especially in Western countries. New laws take as their point of departure anthropological foundations that are opposed to the teaching of Jesus; they are the clear indication of the burning questions that now separate men from Christ.

I think that the immense economic, military, technological, and media influence of a godless West could be a disaster for the world. If the West does not convert to Christ, it could end up making the whole world pagan; the philosophy of unbelief feverishly seeks followers in new parts of the globe. In this sense, we are facing an atheism that is proselytizing more and more. The pagan culture is determined to extend the domain of its struggle against God. In order to bring about their rebirth, the former countries of the old Christian tradition need to reenergize by embarking on a new evangelization.

When I think of the Holy Ghost missionaries of my childhood, I have no doubt that they were men who had given everything. For them, intellectual knowledge of Christ was not enough in itself. They had totally abandoned themselves into God's hands and considered themselves merely clumsy, inadequate instruments of his Son. They were certain that evangelization remains essentially the work of God.

The Father acts and wants to involve us in such a way that our activities, our concerns, and our missionary labors are theandric, so to speak, done by God with our commitment and the involvement of our whole being.

In reality, when we commit ourselves to the new evangelization, it is always a form of cooperation with God. Saint Paul says the same thing: "God is at work in you, both to will and to work for his good pleasure" (Phil 2:13). Evangelization lies in our will and our ability to be together with God, while generously offering him our humble collaboration. It is founded on prayer and on the real presence of God in us: "The Lord himself has spread [the] gospel throughout the world", and "all who belong to the Lord are to drink it in, each according to his capacity", Saint Augustine says in his *Commentary on the Gospel of John*.

Benedict XVI established a close connection between love and faith in all missionary work. At the start of the Ordinary General Assembly of the Synod of Bishops on the new evangelization, commenting on the hymn for Terce, he made a connection between *confessio* (profession of faith) and *caritas*. The *confessio* involves our being, our heart, our lips, and our intellect. But the *confessio* is not something purely abstract and intellectual. And so he said: "St. Bernard of Clairvaux told us that God, in his revelation, in the history of salvation, gave our senses the possibility to see, to touch, to taste revelation. God ... has entered the world of the senses, and our senses must be filled with this taste, with this beauty of God's Word, which is true.... [Thus] we must be penetrated by the *'confessio'*, which has to *'personare'*; the melody of God must [set the tone for] our being in its entirety." And so *confessio* and *caritas* are the two pillars of the new evangelization.

In the current situation, there is a burning question on our lips. How can we help people to rediscover the faith? With the utmost vigor, Saint John solemnly proclaims: "What we have seen with our eyes, what we have looked upon and touched with our hands, what we have contemplated, we proclaim also to you" (cf. 1 Jn 1:1). We cannot say who Christ is by means of intellectual concepts; what is needed is an experience that is both spiritual and "physical" at the same time. Of course, the catechism for children and theology for seminarians are phases of basic apprenticeship. Therefore, to prepare for the new evangelization, John Paul II decided to issue a Catechism of the Catholic Church, entrusting the project to Joseph Ratzinger as editor-in-chief. The entire doctrine of the Church is found in this document. And we have an urgent obligation, says Saint Athanasius, to study "the ancient tradition, teaching, and faith of the Catholic Church, which was revealed by the Lord, proclaimed by the apostles, and guarded by the Fathers. For upon this faith the Church is built, and if anyone were to lapse from it, he would no longer be a Christian either in fact or in name." But the faith is strengthened by way of the heart, through a personal encounter with and experience of Jesus. Every day we must once again choose Christ as our guide, our light, and our hope. Baptism demands some sort of daily actualization. I am not afraid to recall that spiritual combat is first of all a war against the evil that is within us.

In this struggle, I think that bishops have a primordial role; I am completely in agreement with Pope Francis when he asks the successors of the apostles to be permanently on the front lines of evangelization. The Holy Father rightly thinks that Rome should not replace the bishops in certain matters. They always have a threefold responsibility in the implementation of the new evangelization: to sanctify, govern, and teach. For example, there was a time when the means of communication were very slow; Rome was very far away, and the bishops had to go ahead fearlessly, while taking their risks. Let us not forget that at a time when a brush with martyrdom was an everyday experience for Christians, Saint Paul told Timothy to exhort in season and out of season.... Think also of Saint Augustine, who taught every day!

My God, how right Francis is to denounce "airport bishops"! Incidentally, missionary congregations ought to reflect on the dangers to which they expose their young members by making them fly like butterflies from one country to another. These young religious could settle down to superficiality and tourism, having no roots, incapable of establishing real ties with any Christian community. They accumulate experiences, but they could not be the pastors of any flock.

You seem to be very critical, perhaps even a bit harsh, with regard to the development of the old Christian Europe.

I know very well that not all the aspirations permeating the Western world are bad. I would never dare to contradict John Paul II, who sought reasons for hope and encouraging signs in our world. Following Benedict XVI, I am convinced that one of the most important tasks of the Church is to make the West rediscover the radiant face of Jesus. Europe must not forget that its entire culture is imbued with Christianity and the fragrance of the Gospel. If the Old Continent cuts itself off from its roots definitively, I fear that it will cause a major crisis for all mankind, and I see some beginnings of it here and there. Who can fail to deplore the legalization of abortion and euthanasia, the new laws about marriage and the family?

I do not forget that together with my family I came to know about Christ thanks to some French missionaries. My parents and I believed thanks to Europe. My grandmother was baptized by a French priest as she was leaving this world. I might never have left my village if the Holy Ghost Fathers had not spoken about Christ to some poor villagers. How can we Africans comprehend the fact that Europeans no longer believe what they gave us so joyfully, in the worst possible conditions? Allow me to repeat: without the missionaries who came from France, I might never have known God. How can we forget this sublime heritage that the Westerners seem to leave to gather dust?

I am not the only one critical of the West. Aleksandr Solzhenitsyn had harsh words for those who perverted the meaning of liberty and set up a lie as a rule of life. In 1980, in his book *L'erreur de l'Occident*,[7] he wrote: "The Western world has arrived at a decisive moment. Over

---

[7] Alexandre Soljenitsyne, *L'Erreur de l'Occident* (Paris: Grasset, 1980).

the next few years, it will gamble the existence of the civilization that created it. I think that it is not aware of it. Time has eroded your notion of liberty. You have kept the word and devised a different notion. You have forgotten the meaning of liberty. When Europe acquired it, around the eighteenth century, it was a sacred notion. Liberty led to virtue and heroism. You have forgotten that. This liberty, which for us is still a flame that lights up our night, has become for you a stunted, sometimes disappointing reality, because it is full of imitation jewelry, wealth, and emptiness. For this ghost of the former liberty, you are no longer capable of making sacrifices but only compromises.... Deep down, you think that liberty is won once and for all, and this is why you can afford the luxury of disdaining it. You are engaged in a formidable battle, and you behave as though it were a ping pong match." This man who experienced repression in the gulags of the former USSR can use such language. He knows firsthand what true liberty is.

Today in Europe, there are forces in the world of finance and in the media that are trying to prevent Catholics from exercising their liberty. In France, the "Manif pour tous" [a demonstration supporting traditional marriage] offers an example of the necessary initiatives. It was a manifestation of the spirit of Christianity.

The Church is always reforming herself: Ecclesia semper reformanda, *according to the adage. But what should we understand by reform? Is reform necessarily a sort of progress or is it instead a hope?*

Reform is an ongoing necessity. We are the one, holy, catholic, and apostolic Church. Saint Paul called all baptized persons "the saints". If we really read the Gospel, we find that one saying recurs constantly: "Convert and believe the Good News!" It is also the first thing that Jesus calls for in the Gospel of Mark. Reform, therefore, is this interior work that everyone must accomplish, at both the personal level and the ecclesial level, in order to correspond better to what Christ expects of us. It is not just a matter of reorganizing structures, because organizations may be perfect, but if the persons who run them are bad, the work will be vain and illusory. We all must march to the same drum as Christ. The Church is reformed when the baptized march more resolutely toward holiness, allowing themselves to be recreated in the likeness of God by the power of the Holy Spirit. Only the contagion of sanctity can transform the Church from within. From the earliest Christian times, there has always been a call to reform, understood as a greater closeness to God. Reform is a way of corresponding more perfectly to the absolute demands of the Christian vocation. Christ gives us just what we need for this reform, through his Word and prayer, which are the core of all regeneration; the Gospel brings God's life and grace to our souls. The sacraments are the means of constant healing, reform, and renewal.

Nostalgia and the search for God have never been so insistent, because our world is going through an unprecedented moral crisis. At the same time, the forces that want to reject God are so powerful that the Church has difficulty responding to this search. The great challenge lies in this unquenchable thirst for the beyond.

I often think of the Greeks who came to Jerusalem and said to Philip: "We want to see Jesus." Indeed, the world has not changed; our contemporaries still expect Christians to show them Christ. And so the baptized ought to live out their faith joyfully. The times of great troubles for the Church are precisely the eras in which Christians live in a way contrary to Gospel principles. I think that I am not too far from the truth in saying that both the clergy and the laity today are in urgent need of conversion. I know that many are not living the Gospel message. This is why the most ambitious reform is the one that leads the Church to be more fiercely determined in her march toward sanctity and her proclamation of the Good News. The world's pleas, as feeble as they may be, to go beyond false materialistic and ideological values are opportunities that the Church cannot afford to miss. Through these opportunities, men are turning their attention toward God. In this busy world, in which there is no time for family or for oneself, much less for God, true reform consists of rediscovering the meaning of prayer, the meaning of silence, the meaning of eternity.

Prayer is the greatest need of the contemporary world; it remains the tool with which to reform the world. In an age that no longer prays, time is, so to speak, abolished, and life turns into a rat race. This is why prayer gives man the measure of himself and of the invisible world. I wish that we would not forget the path that Benedict XVI decided to take for the Church on the day of his resignation from the See of Peter. He chose a way dedicated exclusively to prayer, contemplation, and listening to God. This is the most important route, because it grasps the meaning of God's glory. Finally, Francis' plan to reform the Roman Curia consists of putting it face to face with God....

How would you describe precisely what Francis intends for the government of the Church?

The institutional framework of all interior reform is important. If structures become obstacles to evangelization and the Church's mission, one must not pretend to look elsewhere; I think that this goes to the heart of the governmental reform courageously desired by Francis. It had become apparent that some aspects of the life of the Roman Curia would have to be the object of real reflection.

We addressed these issues a lot during the discussions that preceded the beginning of the conclave, in March 2013. Personally, I think that it must be stressed that the members of the Curia are not high-ranking officials; they are laymen, priests, bishops, and cardinals who must not forget their vocation. Today, the pope's difficult job is to clean up the structures. But above all the Holy Father wants to restore a greater interior dynamism to those who work alongside him. This is why he wanted the Curia to make a long spiritual retreat in Lent of 2014, outside of Rome and far from everyday activities.

At another level, I think that the reform he envisages has to do with our relationship to power, money, and wealth. In this regard, there is a big job ahead that extends beyond the Roman Curia alone; the whole Church, alas, is concerned about the problem of careerism, that frantic search for power, privileges, honors, social status, and political and financial power. Only a true conversion will make it possible to get beyond these failings, which are nothing new.

True power in the Church is essentially humble and joyful service in imitation of Christ, who "came not to be served but to serve, and to give his life as a ransom for many" (Mt 20:28). If we ignore Christ's poverty, forgetting that he reminded us that we cannot serve two masters, God and the golden calf, no reform will be possible. Once again, the only solution is found in prayer that pastors might place themselves once more facing Christ and their vocation; in this sense we must not let apathy and weariness obscure the promises of our priestly ordination or of our religious profession.

Since the origins of the Church, prayer is often combined with fasting; our body must be completely involved in the search for God in the silence of prayer. It would be false to put God first in our lives if our bodies were not really involved. If we are not capable of denying this body not only foods but also certain pleasures and basic biological needs, out of love for God, we will lack an interior disposition. This is why, from the beginning of Christian tradition, chastity, virginity, consecrated celibacy, and fasting became indispensable expressions of the primacy of God and of faith in him.

Concerning this connection to the body and to sexuality, I am not forgetting that some members of the clergy, worldwide, have been accused of genuine crimes. The Holy See has been the subject of publicity campaigns of unprecedented violence, as though old enemies who are still ready to kill were seeking to take advantage of a great weakness. But I am perfectly aware of the abominable acts that have been committed by some priests.

The abandonment of sexuality is one of the promises made by a priest, except in the Eastern Church, where the ordination of married men is possible, even though the most ancient tradition seemed to retain abstinence as a rule. We understand then that reform involves the whole man, including his corporeal nature. The Holy Ghost Fathers I knew had a real mastery of their body, the result of a solid formation and a real contact with God that filled their heart.

When I think back to my seminary years, I remember a large number of rules that helped us to control our instincts. For example, it was positively forbidden to take even the smallest snack outside of meals. In the superiors' view, someone who could not obey that strict dietary rule did not have a vocation; indeed, he was not capable of controlling one of his natural needs. This discipline of the body was essential in the discernment of future priests. I have not forgotten, either, that it was absolutely forbidden to go to the dormitory outside of the hours prescribed by the rule. Our entire days were considered in terms of a discipline of the mind and body. This asceticism was understood as a path of sanctification and an imitation of Jesus.

All the seminarians desired to make progress in sanctity. They had to have a spiritual director who could help them at any moment to confront a crisis situation. In life, we are like the creepers in the forest. In Africa, a creeper is a flexible stem that is incapable of lifting itself up. Therefore it creeps along the ground until it meets a hardy tree. Then it latches on to this support and climbs to the top. For it, too, would like to see the sun. It is the same with us. If we do not find a solid tree whose roots are nourished by God, so as to ascend toward heaven, there is no chance of our being able to see the light. Recall also the proverb in the

Mossi language: "The desert creeper, finding no tree around which to wind, winds around God."

In the desert, and at certain times in our life, we can count on God alone.

Of course, I am not unaware of the fact that a wolf can always get into the sheepfold. In my formation I had the chance to learn from professors and priests who transformed us by their example and led us daily to Christ.

One of the reasons for the moral crisis no doubt had its origins in the hedonistic sexual revolution of the 1970s. When confronted with that "liberation" of the body, which was directed toward its impulses and rejected all restraints, and given the eroticization of entire sectors of society, the Church made no effort to form her ministers more thoroughly. The start of the reform must concentrate on Catholic schools and seminaries.

I know that what I say may sound controversial; I do not mean to offend anybody, much less pass judgment on anyone at all, but how can we deny that the reform desired by Francis is urgent?

V

CORNERSTONES AND FALSE VALUES

For love is strong as death, jealousy is cruel as the grave. Its flashes are flashes of fire, a most vehement flame. Many waters cannot quench love, neither can floods drown it.

—Song of Solomon 8:6–7

NICOLAS DIAT: *How should we view the authentic connection between Christianity and morality? Benedict XVI thought that the two should not be confused, at the risk of distorting the nature of each. Do you agree with this analysis?*

ROBERT CARDINAL SARAH: Yes, in *Deus caritas est*, Benedict XVI writes that at the origin of being Christian there is not an ethical decision, a philosophical or moral idea, but an encounter with an event, a Person. This man who comes to us, Christ, gives life a new prospect and, thereby, its decisive orientation.

Benedict XVI thus repeated an idea of the theologian Romano Guardini, for whom Christianity is not the result of an intellectual experience but an event that comes from outside to meet me. Christianity is Someone bursting into my life. This movement also implies the historicity of Christianity, which is based on facts and not on an insight into the depths of my own interior world.

Taking as examples the mysteries of the Incarnation and the Trinity, Romano Guardini correctly writes that we will not discover the three Divine Persons by appealing to our intellect.

Saint John Chrysostom says in his *Homilies on Saint Matthew*: "We see that Jesus came from us and our human nature and that he was born of a Virgin Mother. But we do not understand how this prodigy could have happened. Let us not weary ourselves in trying to discover it but, rather, humbly accept what God has revealed to us, without curiously investigating what God keeps hidden from us."

For many cultures, Christianity is a scandal and foolishness: "Jews demand signs and Greeks seek wisdom, but we preach Christ crucified, a stumbling block to Jews and folly to Gentiles" (1 Cor 1:22–23). This statement by the apostle Paul shows the extent to which our religion is essentially bound up with a person who comes to us to appeal to our hearts and to give us a new orientation that will upset our whole world view.

Although Christianity cannot be reduced to morality, it nevertheless has moral consequences; love and faith give to the life of a man a new orientation, depth, and breadth. Man leaves the darkness of his past life. His life is enlightened by the light that is Christ. He lives by Christ's life. From now on he can walk only in the company of Jesus, who is light, truth, and life. After his encounter with Jesus, a real Christian changes his conduct.

In the same way, a society imbued with a Christian spirit advances with a new ambition that is entirely unlike the precepts of a pagan society. From this perspective, I am very fond of the *Letter to Diognetus*: "The Christians ... are in the flesh, but they do not live according to the flesh. They pass their days on earth, but they are citizens of heaven. They obey the prescribed laws, and at the same time surpass the laws by their lives", because they faithfully follow Jesus Christ, who is the way, the truth, and the life.

Yes, Christianity is summed up in a person who comes to reveal and offer his love: "God so loved the world that he gave his only-begotten Son, that whoever believes in him should not perish but have eternal life" (Jn 3:16). This is certainly not about "moralism" but about "morality". The first moral precept is love of God and of neighbor, is it not? The fulfillment of the Law, Saint Paul says, is love (Rom 13:10).

Love is the very being of God: "You see the Trinity when you see charity", Saint Augustine wrote. If we discover love, our conduct in relation to good and evil will be different. In certain eras of the Church, there was a sort of an antiseptic fixation on moral questions. That trend could not produce good fruits because it obscured the true character of revelation, the radical irruption of God.

The Church has sometimes been brushed aside because of a narrow moralism that some clerics promoted. How many of the faithful had the sense that they were not understood, that they were sometimes even rejected? When Christ comes into a life, he unsettles it and transforms it from top to bottom. He gives it a new orientation and new ethical points of reference; baptism is a break [with the past] in the form of a covenant, and not a moral pact! Authentic moral conduct is the reflection of the One whom I have received in my heart, and he is defined by his love, perfection, sanctity, and goodness.

Pope Francis rightly refuses to give a pervasive place to moral questions, without minimizing them, however. He considers that the most important encounter is with Christ and his Gospel; the Holy Father acts like Benedict XVI, who tried to distinguish morality from the essence of Christianity. During his visit to Saint Catherine's Monastery at Mount Sinai, in February 2000, John Paul II himself explained that the path marked out by the divine Law is not a moral police ordinance, but the mind of God. God's Law, promulgated by Moses, contains the major principles, the absolutely necessary conditions for the spiritual survival of men. All the prohibitions that it contains are a safeguard to prevent man from falling over the brink of evil into the abyss of sin and death.

A life enlightened by love of God does not need to take shelter behind moralizing barriers that are often the expression of unspoken fears. Morality is fundamentally a consequence of the Christian faith.

How can the Church get through the mountains of misunderstanding that have risen up since the encyclical Humanae vitae *by Paul VI, published in 1968? Is it still possible to overcome the opposition between Christian morality and the dominant values of Western societies?*

It is important to situate this antagonism in the context of secularization and de-Christianization; whole sectors of modern society have turned away from the Church's moral teaching; this phenomenon has gone hand in hand with ignorance and rejection of her doctrine or of her cultural heritage. There is a complex set of factors that we have to take into account, an indifference toward God that goes beyond the simple problem of moral rules. I think that priests and bishops must display the riches of pedagogy (while being cautious not to take refuge in dogmatic presentations that are too learned) so as to make it clear that questions of sexual morality are not the sum total of the Church's message; today, the model offered by Francis ought to be a powerful help to them.

Yet the Church must remain vigilant with regard to the overturning of values, which leads to confusion between good and evil; in our relativistic societies, good becomes what pleases the individual and is convenient to him. Hence the Church's moral teaching is misunderstood or despised and rejected as the emanation from a false good. The media often do their part deliberately to discredit the Church's position, to distort it, or to silence it. The prevailing narrative constantly seeks to present the idea of an outmoded, medieval Church—what ignorance of the Middle Ages!—that refuses to adapt to the development of the world, is hostile to scientific discoveries and anxious about old ideals. Given this mudslinging, we must be firm and clear, not naïve, yet beyond reproach; we must pray and stay in union with God. The attacks will pass if they are unfair.

How can we not thank Paul VI for the courage he had in issuing the encyclical *Humanae vitae*? This document was prophetic in developing a morality that could defend human life. Despite many pressures within the Church herself, the pope saw what John Paul II called "the culture of death" forming on the horizon. I have not forgotten the violent critiques aimed at him because he refused to abdicate the elementary principles of life. In his turn, John Paul II lavishly produced a very rich teaching on the human body and sexuality. Despite the respect that he enjoyed, especially after his decisive interventions to free the peoples of Eastern Europe from the yoke of Communist dictatorship, how many bitter critiques have not been made against his view of morality? He had understood, nevertheless, that the Church must not lower her arms. By his steadfastness, he obeyed Jesus, who once said to Peter: "And when you have turned again, strengthen your brethren" (Lk 22:32).

I think that history will prove the Church right, for the defense of human life is the defense of mankind. Today, so many organizations and groups advocate women's liberation so that they can be in control of their own bodies and destinies.... In fact, women's bodies are exploited, utilized in many circumstances, often for publicity and commercial purposes, so that they become mere merchandise and a sex-object. In a hyper-eroticized society, which tries to convince people that man is fulfilled only through unbridled sexuality, it seems to me that women's dignity has had major setbacks. The West is the continent that most shamefully humiliates and despises women by publicly stripping them naked and utilizing them for hedonistic commercial purposes.

But we must rejoice over the fact that many women now have access to higher education. Similarly, the right to vote was granted to them in Europe, although too late. It is important also that women should be able to have a job that is compatible with motherhood.

Nevertheless, the West is losing its way because of its illusions, thinking that moral liberalism makes it possible for civilization to advance. How can anyone pretend that free access to pornography through the new means of communication, which is spreading a despicable view of sexuality—something sacred in itself, however—throughout society and even among very young people, is an example of progress in the world? How are we to understand the fact that the major UN agencies that claim to champion human rights do not fight vigorously against the powerful European and American sex industry? All of these dark clouds are signs of a world that lives far from Christ. Without the Son of God, man is lost and humanity has no more future.

Today the Church must fight against prevailing trends, with courage and hope, and not be afraid to raise her voice to denounce the hypocrites, the manipulators, and the false prophets. For two thousand years the Church has faced many contrary winds, but at the end of the most difficult journeys the victory was always won.

Do you think therefore that the world has let itself be hypnotized by the Western world?

At the risk of shocking some people, I think that Western colonialism continues today, in Africa and Asia, more vigorously and perversely through the imposition of a false morality and deceitful values. I do not deny the fact that European civilization was able to offer great benefits, particularly with its missionaries, who were often great saints. It spread the word of the Gospels everywhere, along with beautiful cultural expressions that had been shaped by Christianity.

Benedict XVI correctly emphasized [in a 2006 essay entitled "Europe and Its Discontents"] that an important element of "European identity" is "monogamous marriage ... both as a fundamental structure for the relation between men and women and as the nucleus for the formation of the state community", and that the institution of marriage was "forged in the biblical faith". Conversely, there are repeated attempts to implant a new culture that denies the Christian heritage.

Concerning my continent of origin, I wish to denounce vehemently an attempt to impose false values while using political and financial arguments. In some African countries, ministries dedicated to gender theory have been created in exchange for economic aid! A few African governments, fortunately in the minority, have already given in to pressures in favor of universal access to sexual and reproductive rights. It is very painful for us to note that reproductive health has become a worldwide political "norm", containing the most perverse things that the West has to offer to the rest of the world, which is seeking comprehensive development. How can Western heads of state exert such pressure on their counterparts in countries that are often fragile? Gender ideology has become the perverse condition for cooperation and development.

In the West, homosexual persons demand that their life together be recognized legally, so as to be comparable to marriage; echoing their demands, some organizations are exerting massive pressure on African governments, too, to recognize this model in the name of respect for human rights. In this specific case, to my way of thinking, we are departing from the moral history of mankind. In other cases, I have noticed the existence of international programs that impose abortion and the sterilization of women.

These policies are all the more hideous because most African populations are defenseless, at the mercy of fanatical Western ideologues. The poor are asking for a little aid, and some people are cruel enough to poison their minds. Africa and Asia absolutely must protect their cultures and their own values. International agencies in fact have no right to practice this new Malthusian, brutal colonialism. Out of ignorance or complicity, African and Asian governments would be guilty of allowing their people to be euthanized. Mankind would lose much if these continents were to fall into the huge, formless magma of globalization, which is directed toward an inhumane ideal that is in fact hideous, barbaric oligarchy.

The Holy See must play its part. We cannot accept the propaganda and the pressure groups of the LGBT lobbies—lesbian, gay, bisexual, and transgendered. The process is all the more unsettling for being rapid and recent. Why this frenzied desire to impose gender theory? An anthropological vision that was unknown a few years ago, the product of the strange thought of a few sociologists and writers like Michel Foucault, should suddenly become the world's new El Dorado? It is impossible to remain complacent in the presence of such an immoral and demonic deception.

Pope Francis is right to critique the action of the devil, who works to undermine the foundations of Christian civilization. Behind this Promethean vision of Africa or Asia there is the mark of the devil.

The chief enemies of homosexual persons are the LGBT lobbies. It is a serious error to reduce an individual to his behavior, especially sexual behavior. Nature always ends up having its revenge.

In your opinion, therefore, the battle of John Paul II against this "culture of death" is still quite relevant?

In the early 1990s, the pope, seeing the peoples of Eastern Europe sinking little by little into the oppression of materialism and moral relativism, which is even more insidious than Soviet ideology, initiated a great struggle. John Paul II had understood that the new attacks on human life were becoming a veritable social system, rampant slavery. I think that the Malthusian ideology is still just as powerful; his idea endures, and his plan of action is to promote anti-birth policies in many poor countries. Likewise, international statistics on abortions are horrifying. Worldwide, in 2014, around one pregnancy out of four was voluntarily interrupted. That means a little more than forty million abortions in just one year. What makes this figure even more ghastly is that the "right to abortion", that is, legal permission to kill an innocent baby, fortunately remains very limited in three-quarters of the countries in the world.

During the Extraordinary Synod on the Family, in October 2014, Archbishop Paul Bùi Văn Đoc of Thành-Phô Hô Chí Minh, explained to us that the most tragic case in the world was Vietnam. Indeed, this country performs 1,600,000 abortions per year, 300,000 of them on young women between the ages of fifteen and nineteen. This is a real catastrophe for the country.

In France, 220,000 elective abortions are performed each year, which is one abortion for every three births.

A war has been declared against human life, with gigantic financial resources. How is it conceivable that so many defenseless children should be eliminated in their mothers' wombs under the pretext of a woman's right to control her body freely? Women's dignity is a noble, important cause to fight for, but it is not achieved by murdering unborn children.

John Paul II had understood that well-meaning intentions concealed a veritable battle plan against life. In Africa, when I see the astronomical sums that are promised by the Bill and Melinda Gates Foundation, which aims to increase exponentially access to contraception for unmarried girls and women, thus opening up the way for abortion, I can only protest against such a lethal project.

What are the hidden motivations of these large-scale campaigns that will end in tens of thousands of deaths? Could it be a well-designed plan to eliminate the poor in Africa and elsewhere? God and history will tell us some day.

Euthanasia has become a new ideological battlefield of Western postmodernity today. When a person seems to have finished his race on this earth, some organizations, under the pretext of relieving his sufferings, consider that it is better to put him to death. In Belgium this "right", which is not a right, has just been extended to minor children! While ostensibly helping a child who is suffering, it is possible to put him to death in cold blood. Proponents of euthanasia prefer to ignore the fact that palliative means today are perfectly suited to those who have no more hope of a cure; cold-hearted, brutal death has become the only answer. Euthanasia is the most acute indication of a Godless, subhuman society that has lost hope. I am astonished at how those who propagate this culture strike a conscientious pose and put on airs as though they were the heroes of a new humanity. In a strange sort of inversion of roles, pro-life people become monsters to be slain, barbarians from another age who reject progress. With the help of the media, the wolves persuade the unwary that they are well-meaning lambs siding with the weak! But this just makes the plan of those who promote abortion, euthanasia, and all the attacks on human dignity that much more dangerous.

If we do not overcome the culture of death, mankind is headed for its perdition. Now, at the beginning of the third millennium, the destruction of human life is no longer a barbaric act but a sign of progress in civilization; the law takes a right to individual liberty as the pretext for giving man the option to kill his neighbor. The world could become a real hell. This is no longer a sort of decadence but, rather, a dictatorship of horror, a programmed genocide of which the Western powers are guilty. This relentless campaign against life is a new, definitive stage in the relentless campaign against God's plan. Nevertheless, in all my travels, I notice a reawakening of consciences. The young Christians of

North America are gradually taking the lead to drive back the culture of death. God has not fallen asleep. He truly is with those who defend life!

Do you think that John Paul II was a prophet?

All the saints are prophets. They faithfully transmit to us the vision, the will, the love, and the hope of God for mankind. Today this extraordinary pope is numbered among the saints of the Church. But I think that we have not fully understood the extent to which he was a visionary. The way in which John Paul II made the sacredness and inviolability of human life the priority of his pontificate opens up an immense field, even beyond his presence among us. All he did was to recall God's holy law: "You shall not kill"; at the same time, the simple grandeur of his words and his power to convince others were liberating for those who watched the darkness advance.

His exclamation "Be not afraid" is the most beautiful continuation that Paul VI could have imagined; he had suffered so much from the critiques that poured out like a torrent of hatred after his encyclical *Humanae vitae*. John Paul II had no use for the syrupy objections of the proponents of anti-Christian humanism. He intended to sow seeds that would help give birth to a new culture. This pope had an even more acute insight into these problems inasmuch as he himself had experienced firsthand attacks on the most fundamental rights. Through the Nazi and Communist dictatorships, he had a personal knowledge of real combat for human liberty. That is why he could not allow the proponents of the culture of death to hide behind the screens of a false promotion of human rights in order to promote their destructive plans. In 1995, in *Evangelium vitae*, he wrote: "In this way, and with tragic consequences, a long historical process is reaching a turning-point. The process which once led to discovering the idea of 'human rights'— rights inherent in every person and prior to any Constitution and State legislation—is today marked by a surprising contradiction. Precisely in an age when the inviolable rights of the person are solemnly proclaimed and the value of life is publicly affirmed, the very right to life is being denied or trampled upon, especially at the more significant moments of existence: the moment of birth and the moment of death" (EV 18).

John Paul II wanted to denounce the schizophrenia of today's world that paints over abominable situations with good intentions. He knew that the era would witness the proliferation of false prophets, strategists of evil, and heralds of a future without hope, but Karol Wojtyła did not seek to be a hero, because he was simply a messenger of God. In France, the many large-scale demonstrations that have sprung up to protest against the institution of a false marriage between persons of the same sex are another response to the appeal made by John Paul II in Bourget on June 1, 1980, during his first journey to France: "Today in the historical capital of your nation, I would like to repeat these words that constitute your title of pride: France, eldest daughter of the Church.... There is just one problem, that of our fidelity to the Covenant with the Eternal Wisdom, which is the source of a true culture, in other words, of human growth, and the problem of fidelity to our baptismal promises in the name of the Father, the Son, and the Holy Spirit. Allow me then to ask you: France, eldest daughter of the Church, are you faithful to your baptismal promises? Allow me to ask you: France, eldest daughter of the Church and teacher of the people, are you faithful, for the good of all mankind, to your alliance with the Eternal Wisdom? Forgive me for this question. I asked it as the priest does at the moment of baptism. I asked it out of solicitude for the Church, of which I am the first rock and the first servant, and for the love of man, whose final grandeur is in God, Father, Son, and Holy Ghost." The pope from Poland reawakened the revolutionary spirit of the saints who have marked off the eras throughout French history.

In many speeches, and in this book, you explicitly denounce gender theory. Why this repeated insistence?

African philosophy declares: "Man is nothing without woman, woman is nothing without man, and the two are nothing without a third element, which is the child." Fundamentally, the African view of man is trinitarian. In each of us there is something of the divine; the one Triune God dwells within us and imbues our whole being.

According to gender theory, there is no ontological difference between man and woman. It claims that masculine and feminine identities are not inscribed in nature but are only the result of a social construct, a role played by individuals through social tasks and functions. For these theorists, gender is performative, and the differences between man and woman are nothing but oppressive norms, cultural

stereotypes, and social constructs that have to be undone so as to arrive
at parity between man and woman. The idea of a constructed identity
actually denies in an unrealistic way the importance of the sexed body.
A man will never become a woman, and she will never become a man,
no matter what mutilations one or the other agrees to undergo. To say
that human sexuality no longer depends on the identity of a man or
a woman but rather on sexual orientations, such as homosexuality, is
nightmarish totalitarianism.

I see no possible future for such deception. I am more worried about
the way in which States and international organizations are trying to
impose by any means, often rapidly, the so-called deconstructive philosophy of *gender*. If sexuality is only a social, cultural construct, we end
up calling into question the way in which mankind has reproduced itself
since its origins. Indeed, it is almost difficult to take such an outrageous
view seriously. If some scholars go along with this fantastic, dangerous
talk, that is their business; but I will never agree to let these theories be
imposed directly or insidiously on defenseless populations. How do you
expect a little child or a young adolescent from the remote African countryside to be able to defend himself against such deceitful speculations?

It is one thing truly to respect homosexual persons, who have a right
to authentic respect, and quite another thing to promote homosexuality
as a role model.

This way of understanding human relations is actually an attack on
homosexual persons, who are victims of ideologues who do not care
about their lot. Certainly, we must make sure that homosexuals do not
become the target of often shameful and insidious attacks. Nevertheless,
I think that it is an aberration to try to set up that sexuality as a progressive ideology. I observe an attempt by some influential structures
to make homosexuality the cornerstone of a new global ethic. Every
extremist ideological project bears within it its own failure; in the short
term, I fear that homosexual persons will be the first victims of such
political excesses.

*African culture assigns great importance to the family. How can this model be of
interest to the Church and the rest of the world?*

In the first place, the African family is built around a common life. For
many people, money has a secondary place. My family was poor, but we

were still happy and close-knit. In Guinea, the family has remained the primordial cell of society, the place where we learn to be attentive to others and to serve them unostentatiously. I think that Europe and the West must rediscover the meaning of the family by looking at the traditions that Africa never abandoned. On my continent, the family is the melting pot of the values that irrigate the whole culture, the place where customs, wisdom, and moral principles are handed down, the cradle of unconditional love. Without the family, neither society nor the Church exists any more. In a family, the parents transmit the faith. The family lays the foundations on which we construct the building of our life. The family is the little Church where we begin to encounter God, to love him, and to form personal ties with him.

My father taught me great love for the Virgin Mary. I can still see him kneel down on the sand of Ourous to pray the Angelus every day at noon and in the evening. I never forgot those moments when he closed his eyes to give thanks to Mary. I imitated him and recited my prayers to the Mother of Jesus at his side.

Parents are man's first educators. In a family, man can learn to live and to manifest the presence of God. If Christ is the bond that holds a family together, then it will have an indestructible solidity. In Africa, an important place is reserved for the elderly; the respect due to old people is one of the cornerstones of African society. I think that Europeans do not realize how shocked the peoples of Africa are by how little attention is paid to the elderly in Western countries. This tendency to hide old age and marginalize it is the sign of a worrisome selfishness, heartlessness, or, more accurately, hard-heartedness. To be sure, old people have all the comfort and the physical care they need. But they lack the warmth, closeness, and human affection of their relatives and friends, who are too busy with the professional obligations, their recreation, and their vacations.

Indeed, the family is a place where man learns to be of service to society. In Africa, the family has never closed in on itself; it takes its place within a larger social fabric. The tribe and the village are generally the natural extension of the family; the tribe conveys the culture, protects and transmits some very ancient traditions. An African proverb says, "It takes a whole village to educate a child." Everyone receives and, in the same action, participates in the survival of the group; I speak about survival, because nothing is easy. Certainly I am not unaware of the fact that this sense of belonging can be seriously perverted, particularly when some tribes resort to the logic of pride, hatred, and disdain for others.

Nevertheless, nothing replaces the family, where we can understand the depth of giving and of love. I learned from my parents how to give. We were accustomed to receiving visitors, which impressed on me the importance of welcoming and generosity. For my parents, and all the inhabitants of my village, receiving others as guests implied that we were seeking to make them happy. Familial harmony can be the reflection of the harmony of heaven. That is the real treasure of Africa!

Other regions of the world would be in serious danger if they came to lose this "source of giving". Back in November 1981, in his apostolic exhortation *Familiaris consortio*, John Paul II felt the urgent need to write that "the situation in which the family finds itself presents positive and negative aspects: the first are a sign of the salvation of Christ operating in the world; the second, a sign of the refusal that man gives to the love of God. On the one hand, in fact, there is a more lively awareness of personal freedom and greater attention to the quality of interpersonal relationships in marriage, to promoting the dignity of women, to responsible procreation, to the education of children. There is also an awareness of the need for the development of interfamily relationships, for reciprocal spiritual and material assistance, the rediscovery of the ecclesial mission proper to the family and its responsibility for the building of a more just society. On the other hand, however, signs are not lacking of a disturbing degradation of some fundamental values: a mistaken theoretical and practical concept of the independence of the spouses in relation to each other; serious misconceptions regarding the relationship of authority between parents and children; the concrete difficulties that the family itself experiences in the transmission of values; the growing number of divorces; the scourge of abortion; the ever more frequent recourse to sterilization; the appearance of a truly contraceptive mentality" (FC 6).

I know that the African family still has magnificent prospects ahead of it. I wish I could be sure that such opportunities existed for European, American, Asian, and Oceanic families, too. The battle to preserve the roots of mankind is perhaps the greatest challenge that our world has faced since its origins.

VI

ISSUES IN THE POSTMODERN WORLD

You understand absolutely nothing about modern civilization unless you first admit that it is a universal conspiracy against all interior life.

—Georges Bernanos, *La France contre les robots*

NICOLAS DIAT: *Some thinkers maintain that the Church must now confront the conjunction of two challenges: the atheism of Enlightenment philosophy and the moral liberalism resulting from the social revolution in the 1960s. What is your judgment on what the philosopher Alberto Methol Ferré, a friend of Pope Francis, called libertine atheism?*

ROBERT CARDINAL SARAH: Today the West lives as if God did not exist. How could countries with ancient Christian and spiritual traditions cut themselves off from their roots to such an extent? The consequences appear to be so tragic that it is essential to understand the origin of this phenomenon.

The West decided to distance itself from the Christian faith under the influence of the Enlightenment philosophers and the resulting political currents. Although Christian communities exist that are still vital and missionary, most Western populations now regard Jesus as a sort of idea but not as an event, much less as a person whom the apostles and many witnesses of the Gospel met and loved and to whom they consecrated their whole life.

This estrangement from God is not caused by reasoning but by a wish to be detached from him. The atheistic orientation of a life is almost always a decision by the will. Man no longer wishes to reflect on his relationship to God because he himself intends to become God. His model is Prometheus, the mythological character of the race of Titans

167

who stole sacred fire so as to give it to men; the individual has embarked on a strategy of appropriating God instead of adoring him. Before the so-called "Enlightenment" movement, if a man ever tried to take God's place, to be his equal, or to eliminate him, these were isolated individual phenomena.

Atheism has its principal origin in the heightened individualism of European man. The individual-king, who aspires more and more to a sort of absolute autonomy or independence, tends to forget God. On the moral level, this search for absolute liberty implies the gradual, indiscriminate rejection of ethical rules and principles. The individualist universe comes to be centered solely on the person, who no longer tolerates any constraint. Hence God is considered someone who creates obstacles to confine our will by imposing laws; God becomes the enemy of autonomy and liberty. Wishing to be totally free, man refuses to accept what he considers to be constraints and even goes so far as to reject any form of dependence on God. He rejects the authority of God, who nevertheless created us free so that, by the reasonable exercise of our freedom, we might go beyond our wild impulses and tame all our instincts by taking full responsibility for our life and growth.

Atheism is thus a decision to ignore reason, which would bring us back to our Creator, the true light that should enlighten us, guide us, and show us the paths of life. In keeping with this logic, some philosophers speak about God no longer as a Father but as a great architect of the universe.

The rejection of God is situated in a movement of scientific and technological conquest that characterized Europe in the early eighteenth century. Man intends to dominate nature and to assert his independence. Technology gives him the impression that he is master of the world. He therefore becomes the sole ruler in a realm without God. Science, however, should not separate man from God. On the contrary, it should bring man closer to divine love.

Of course, the great mystery of evil can drive some persons to doubt and atheism. Indeed, if God is our Father, how can he allow so many innocent persons to suffer? There is no need to insist on the unfathomable quantity of evils with which mankind is afflicted. In Africa we have, unfortunately, paid a heavy tribute to wars, famines, and epidemics. At *Cor unum*, I witnessed many sufferings that we try to alleviate with means that are ridiculous in comparison with the extent of the needs.

I will never be able to forget the work that we accomplished in Haiti. How could God allow people who were already so poor, deprived of everything, to suffer one misfortune after another, like the gigantic earthquake in 2010, followed by floods and epidemics? How could I ever erase from my memory the refugee camps in Jordan and the faces of so many women who had lost their husbands, their houses, their belongings? They had to take care of their children, who because of the hardships were emotionally unstable and increasingly needy.

The question of evil, which goes down through the ages, remains the same: How can God allow such horrible trials and sufferings to be imposed on innocent victims? In this regard I like to cite Albert Camus. As a philosopher, he looked for reasonable certitudes by which to live. He saw faith as a "leap into the irrational" that turns the mind away from reality, in which man denies his faculty of reason, his "lucid awareness". But what solidified the thinker's atheistic position even more was the existence of evil, which he, like the Enlightenment philosophers, could not associate with the divine omnipotence and wisdom. He was unable to accept "the paradox of a God who was almighty and maleficent, or beneficent and sterile", as he describes it in *L'Homme révolté*.[1] How can you believe in God when innocent children are suffering?

However, we do not know to what extent we cause most of the evils on this earth. How many wars and slaughters could have been avoided? Very often Western countries, who boast of being architects and promoters of peace, are the chief producers or the main traffickers of weapons of mass destruction. With cynical hypocrisy, they sell them to the poor nations and exchange them for their mineral or petroleum resources. The world today is rife with hatred, violence, and barbarism, and many innocent people pay dearly because of those who hold power.

Look at the chaos and disaster in Iraq, Syria, Libya, Palestine, Israel, Egypt, Afghanistan, the Democratic Republic of Congo, Mali.... Angola went through thirty long years of a similar situation. But in vast regions of the world, suffering has not made people lose their faith. On the contrary, God is a light that permits people who no longer have anything to continue to hope. I recall also the peaceful faces and the serene voices of the Filipinos who confided to me in 2013: "Typhoon Haiyan leveled

---

[1] Albert Camus, *L'Homme révolté* (Paris: Gallimard, 1951).

everything, destroyed everything in its path, except our faith, which remains firmly planted like a rock in the middle of a turbulent sea!"

The brutal statements of Nietzsche in *The Gay Science* sum up the problem of atheism that I have just described. He sets a scene in which a madman goes through the city in broad daylight, with a lantern in his hand, shouting: "I seek God! ... Where is God gone? ... I mean to tell you! *We have killed him,*—you and I! We are all his murderers! But how have we done it? How were we able to drink up the sea? Who gave us the sponge to wipe away the whole horizon? What did we do when we loosened this earth from its sun? Whither does it now move?... Do we not stray, as through infinite nothingness? Does not empty space breathe upon us? Has it not become colder? Does not night come on continually, darker and darker? Shall we not have to light lanterns in the morning? Do we not hear the noise of the grave-diggers who are burying God? Do we not smell the divine putrefaction?—for even Gods putrefy! God is dead! God remains dead! And we have killed him!" And Friedrich Nietzsche finishes his account by writing: "It is further stated that the madman made his way into different churches on the same day, and there intoned his *Requiem aeternam deo.* When led out and called to account, he always gave the reply: 'What are these churches now, if they are not the tombs and monuments of God?' "[2]

Since we claim to have celebrated God's funeral, how can we be surprised that a godless world has become a hell on earth? Morality, love, freedom, technology, and science are nothing without God's presence. Man can devise the most magnificent works, but they will be mere sand castles and shifting illusions unless they are related to God. Nietzsche was twenty years old when he wrote his poem to the unknown God: "I want to know you, Unknown One, you who have reached deep within my soul...."

In your reflection you seem to infer that atheistic philosophy is by nature militant and combative....

Today, in the rich and powerful countries, the eclipse of God leads man toward practical materialism, disorderly or abusive consumption, and the creation of false moral norms. Material well-being and

---

[2] *The Gay Science*, trans. Thomas Common (Digireads.com Publishing, 2009), 79–80.

immediate satisfaction become the only reason for living. At the end of this process, it is no longer even about fighting God; Christ and the Father are ignored. The reason for this is obvious: God no longer interests anyone. He is dead, and his departure leaves us indifferent. We have passed from atheistic materialism to fluid "New Age" thinking. Those in control of this world no longer think that they have to fight; they have reached another stage that consists essentially of creating the new man. Some researchers even speak about "transhumanism", a technological process that would go "beyond" man the human being. What a proud illusion!

For the Church and for Christians, the danger therefore becomes still more menacing. Western man seems to have made up his mind; he has liberated himself from God; he lives without God. The new rule is to forget heaven so that man might be fully free and autonomous. But the death of God results in the burial of good, beauty, love, and truth; if the source no longer flows, if even that water is transformed by the mud of indifference, man collapses. Good becomes evil, beauty is ugly, love becomes the satisfaction of several primal sexual instincts, and truths are all relative. We should not be surprised, therefore, Benedict XVI said in 2008 in a Letter to the Diocese of Rome, that today we have doubts "about the value of the human person, about the very meaning of truth and good, and ultimately about the goodness of life".

Modern atheism, the heir to an aggressive movement against God and Christianity, now seeks to ignore God so as to make the world ignorant of him. The laws of the Father, the message of the Gospel are hidden beneath mountains of clever tricks cynically designed to stupefy man. With consummate hypocrisy, the same ones who try to turn man away from his Creator arrogantly say: God does not care about our sufferings; he is absent; this earth is a valley of tears where each one can count only on himself. . . .

Whether it is militant or still in the larval state, atheism always leads to the same consequences. Man is treated as an object, cut off from his spiritual roots and blinded by the artificial lights of material goods or achievements. Finally, all atheism seeks to change the very nature of man. The persecutions are no longer the ones in the concentration camps of the formerly Communist countries, those horrible prisons where my predecessor in Conakry, Archbishop Tchidimbo, had been isolated, tortured, and humiliated, not even having the right to celebrate

Mass during the first five years of his detention. Now the persecution has acquired greater subtlety.

In the postmodern world, God has become a superfluous hypothesis, more and more detached from the different spheres of life. I think that people who want to keep the presence of God in their lives must be aware of the subtleties that can easily lead them toward practical atheism and the loss of the salt of faith; they, too, could become like the pagans of yore, those men "having no hope and without God in the world" described by Saint Paul for the Christians of Ephesus (Eph 2:12). Today we cannot be unaware of the way in which God is systematically cast back into the darkness; anaesthetized, men board a ship that leads them ever farther away from heaven.

The best example of the disappearance of the head-on battles of the past is still the Russian Orthodox Church. After so much violence, so much destruction, it is now at the center of the debates. Reversing the movement of insidious atheism that has carried off practically all of Western Europe, Orthodoxy has allowed the Russian nation to avoid the traps, so that now it is a country that makes significant room for God and faith.

Confronted with all these difficulties, it is necessary to return to the foundations of Christian hope and to declare that life on this earth is only part of our existence, which will be prolonged and completed in eternity. In season and out of season, the Church must recall that life cannot be summed up in terms of the satisfaction of material pleasures, without moral rules. At the end of a journey without God there is only the unhappiness of a child deprived of his parents. Yes, hope abides in God alone!

In an age when relativity is the rule, how can the Church still make comprehensible the dogmas that are one of her most important foundations?

Subjectivism is one of the most significant traits of our time. Feelings and personal desires are the only norm. Often modern man regards traditional values as archaeological artifacts.

Since the social revolution in the sixties and seventies, it has been common practice to pit individual liberty against authority. Within this context, even among the faithful, it may seem that personal experience becomes more important than the rules established by the Church. If the individual is the central point of reference, everyone can interpret the Church's message in his own way, adapting it to his own ideas. I regret that many Christians allow themselves to be influenced by this pervasive individualism; they may sometimes have difficulty feeling at home within the Catholic Church, in her traditional forms, with her dogmas and teachings, her laws, exhortations, and Magisterium. Of course, the disparity is even more significant with respect to moral questions.

Consequently, it is not inaccurate to say that there is a sort of rejection of the dogmas of the Church or a growing distance between people, the faithful, and the dogmas. On the question of marriage, there is a gulf between some people and the Church. The question, therefore, becomes quite simple: Must the world change its attitude, or must the Church change her fidelity to God? Can the distance between these two realities be maintained over time, at the risk of seeing the misunderstandings deepen? For if the faithful still love the Church and the pope but do not put doctrine into practice and change nothing in their lives, even after coming to Rome to hear the successor of Peter, what sort of future can we envisage?

Many of the faithful rejoice to hear talk about divine mercy, and they hope that the radical demands of the Gospel can be relaxed even for the benefit of those who by their lives have chosen to break away from the crucified love of Jesus. They do not appreciate the price paid by him on the Cross, which delivered every one of us from the yoke of sin and death. They think that because of the Lord's infinite goodness everything is possible, while at the same time deciding to change nothing in their lives. Many expect, as something normal, that God should pour out his mercy on them while they remain in sin....

But sin destroys me: How can the energies of divine life be grafted onto nothingness? Despite the repeated appeals of Saint Paul, they cannot imagine why light and darkness cannot coexist: "What shall we say then? Are we to continue in sin that grace may abound? By no means! How can we who died to sin still live in it? Do you not know that all of us who have been baptized into Christ Jesus were baptized into his death?... What then? Are we to sin because we are not under law but under grace? By no means!" (Rom 6:1–3, 15).

This confusion calls for rapid responses. The Church can no longer go on as though the reality did not exist; she can no longer be content with ephemeral enthusiasm that lasts for the duration of major meetings or liturgical gatherings, as beautiful and rich as they may be. We cannot long do without practical reflection on subjectivism as the root of most contemporary errors. What good is it to know that the pope's Twitter account is followed by thousands if people do not change their lives concretely? What good is it to compile amazing statistics about the crowds that throng to see the popes if we are not sure that their conversions are real and deep and if we do not know whether Jesus and his Gospel are the reference point and guide of our faithful? That being said, the World Youth Days have also made possible some beautiful and generous responses to God's call.

Given the wave of subjectivism that seems to be sweeping everyone away, men of the Church must beware of denying reality by becoming inebriated with deceptive appearances and glory. Certainly, some events can prompt interior changes and genuine conversions. For example, I am sure that the funeral of John Paul II and the ceremonies for his canonization, at the same time as that of John XXIII, gave great impetus to many Catholics; that immense crowd gathered around the Lord's altar managed to deepen the message of Karol Wojtyła and the universal call to holiness voiced by the Second Vatican Council, which the two popes embodied in their everyday lives. In order to start a concrete, radical change in people's lives, the teaching of Jesus and of the Church must reach human hearts. Two millennia ago, the apostles followed Christ. They left everything, and their lives were never again the same. The path taken by the apostles is still a model today.

The Church has to rediscover a vision. If her teaching is not understood, she must not be afraid to go back to the drawing board a hundred times. This is not about relaxing the requirements of the Gospel or changing the doctrine of Jesus and the apostles to adapt to fleeting fashions but, rather, about challenging ourselves radically with regard to how we ourselves live the Gospel of Jesus and present dogma.

The lack of comprehension seems to reach the level where even the philosophical heritage of Christianity is denied. For example, few thinkers recall the Church's fundamental contribution to the establishment of humanism. In addition, are we not witnessing now the emergence of a humanism that no longer knows Christ?

Yes, indeed, the Christian religion put man at the center of all its concerns, unlike the pagan beliefs that preceded it. The hope for salvation proclaimed by Christ is addressed to all mankind. But only Christ Jesus, the God-man, fully manifests man to himself and reveals to him the sublimity of his vocation. And if it is true that Christ fully reveals man, then it is also fair to say that if we reject Christ, or if we obscure his face, the consequences appear a hundredfold in our confusion about what man is.

Sin blurs man's face. Now Christ came not only to save mankind but also to repair what sin had broken, to snatch man away from everything that disfigures him, so as to restore to human destiny all its breadth and fulfillment.

Following Saint Irenaeus and Saint Athanasius of Alexandria, Saint Thomas Aquinas states that the only Son of God assumed our nature in order to divinize men. Athanasius says "in order to make us God". *A contrario*, Enlightenment philosophy wanted to de-Christianize humanism. But the moment God is no longer creator, man is debased. In Genesis it says that God has a plan for man, to which the latter must be faithful. If man tries to liberate himself from God, he loses his trinitarian structure and becomes dehumanized. Humanism that tries to ignore Christ empties out its own substance and becomes merely materialism.

By preserving a few meager spiritual roots, materialism can sometimes create an illusion. But it no longer has anything in common with humanism that is shaped by Christianity, which is absolutely centered on the face of man, the unique reflection of God. Without a true humanism founded on Christ, man no longer understands himself. He cannot even love truly, or if he does love, he will do so with a lot of selfishness and difficulty.

In order for man to be fully actualized, he is, so to speak, ontologically connected to God by Jesus Christ. There is a vital relation with God. It is impossible from now on to separate man from Jesus, the God-man; this prompted Paul VI to say at the conclusion of the Second Vatican Council that the path to God goes by way of man. The discovery of God goes by way of the discovery of man. The service of God goes by way of the service of man.

What do you mean by "the trinitarian structure" of man?

How do we describe the Trinity? One God in three Persons. The Son is from the Father, and the Spirit is with the Father and the Son; he is the *Vinculum caritatis* between the Father and the Son, the bond of love between the Father and the Son. The Trinity is a communion of knowledge and love. Strictly speaking, man is a relational being. He is driven toward God and toward other men. If man loses this orientation, he has nothing left but to look at himself perpetually, and this egotism can take different forms.

Apart from his trinitarian nature, in which he fully actualizes his vocation to be united to God, man becomes closed in on himself. Another person becomes a problem and is no longer an extension of himself. The abandonment of the Trinity is taken to its ultimate consequences when man seeks to divinize his own nature, in a passionate, desperate quest for himself, far from Jesus Christ.

Saint Irenaeus, in his treatise *Against Heresies (Contra haereses)*, develops a Christian anthropology close to Saint Paul's. We find in it, as though reflected in a mirror, the divine plan to remake man in his own image. For Irenaeus of Lyons, man is modeled by the Holy Spirit in the divine likeness: "At present we receive a share in the Spirit who perfects us and prepares us for incorruptibility and little by little accustoms us to receive God." Christ is the Archetype of the new man. And so Irenaeus can write: "Life in man is the glory of God; the life of man is the vision of God. If the revelation of God through creation gives life to all who live upon the earth, much more does the manifestation of the Father through the Word give life to those who see God."

In separating himself from the Triune God, man forgets the true order of things, for God became man so that man might become God. Indeed, the elimination of God causes great violence. Without the Father, man finds himself dependent exclusively on little personal deals, which lead to great loneliness. Without Christ, man becomes a wolf to his fellowman, and he no longer can love as Jesus does. Without the Spirit, man's intellect increasingly contemplates itself and finally goes into decline; with the Spirit, reason functions in hope and joy.

Benedict XVI called unceasingly for a productive dialogue between fides *and* ratio, *faith and reason. Today most philosophical reflection seems to be cut off from all transcendence. What do you think of this development?*

The encounter between Greek philosophy and Christianity was a unique moment in the history of mankind. This powerful dialogue was willed by God.

How can we define philosophy? I think that it is not solely about love of wisdom but, above all, an incessant search by the human intellect for the truth and for a contemplative knowledge of the deeper causes of things. This search went aground on many reefs, and it was consolidated with Socrates and reached a very high level with Plato and Aristotle.

Through its encounter with the Christian faith, with Saint Augustine, Saint Thomas Aquinas, and others, the human intellect shaped by non-Christian thinkers no longer loves natural wisdom alone but loves eternal wisdom, wisdom incarnate, Christ, who declared, "I am the Truth." Thus Greek philosophy receives Christian baptism and is purified so as to become within the Church the servant of theology.

There is no disputing the fact that Saint Thomas Aquinas was the man who gave his life to prepare the way for this providential encounter. He is the one who witnesses and blesses the exchange of consent at the marriage of Greek wisdom and eternal wisdom. . . .

At the end of a long, fine, honest, and patient search, the Greek philosophers, such as Aristotle, understood the essence of nature, of matter, of life, and of the spirit. Despite the perfection of the thought that he was able to elaborate, with an ordered vision of the universe and of man, Aristotle, who played one of the greatest roles in the history of philosophical reflection, recognized his limits. In his *Nicomachean Ethics*, Aristotle writes: "O my friends, no one is a true friend!" This bitter admission could be translated into other terms: "There is no communion!" This is the painful recognition of the fact that man's thirst is never quenched by the human intellect alone. Philosophy, by itself, is incapable of leading man to his total fulfillment, to his encounter with eternal truth, even though "since the creation of the world [God's] invisible nature . . . has been clearly perceived in the things that have been made" (Rom 1:20).

The very idea of a creation "from nothing" never crosses Aristotle's mind. Thus Greek wisdom brings us very close to the truth. Nevertheless, in its highest expression, it is still far from the concept of a God who would lower himself to deal with man. Philosophical thought still does not understand the foundations of the human person. This ignorance explains its inability to perceive the radical equality of all men and to guess at the ineffable grace of divine adoption, which is supernatural. We all become brethren, not by nature, but by God's grace. Greek wisdom cannot explain evil or suffering or redemption or hope. Nevertheless, this thirst for divine friendship is still a marvelous attempt and a preparation for revelation, for the Logos.

Even though several passages by Aristotle seemed to depart explicitly from Christian doctrine, and despite all the gaps in Greek wisdom, Saint Thomas Aquinas later tried to understand Aristotle, to receive his thought in order to improve it for the purpose of instruction, because the philosopher's approach seemed to him to espouse the correct method of seeking the truth. Furthermore, Saint Thomas considered this method a useful instrument with which to study the doctrine of the faith. He did not intend, like other theologians of his era, to reject pagan wisdom because of its shortcomings or its partially erroneous philosophical expressions; instead, he made use of them after purifying them of their pagan overtones....

Earlier, Saint Basil, in his fight against the Greek culture of his time, found himself confronted with a similar task. In his book *On the Way to Jesus Christ*, Joseph Ratzinger refers to a text by Saint Basil in which he adapts a verse from the Book of the Prophet Amos to the problem of pagan culture. "Then Amos answered Amaziah, 'I am no prophet, nor a prophet's son; but I am a herdsman, and a dresser of sycamore trees" (Amos 7:14). The Septuagint Greek translation of this prophetic book renders the last expression more concretely as follows: "I was a herdsman who cuts sycamore fruits." This translation is based on the fact that the fruits of the sycamore tree must be cut before they are harvested, so that they mature after a few days. In his commentary on Isaiah 9:10, Basil presupposes familiarity with this practice when he writes: "The sycamore is a tree that bears very plentiful fruit. But it is tasteless, unless one carefully slits it and allows its sap to run out, whereby it becomes flavourful. That is why, we believe, the sycamore is a symbol of the pagan world: it offers a surplus, yet at the same time it is insipid. This comes from living according to pagan customs. When one manages to slit them by means of the Logos, it [the pagan world] is transformed, becomes tasty and useful." Applying this reasoning to the contemporary scene, Joseph Ratzinger commented: "The Logos itself must slit our cultures and their fruit, so that what is unusable is purified and becomes not only usable but good.... Only the Logos himself can guide our cultures to their true purity and maturity, but the Logos makes us his servants, the 'dresser of sycamore trees'."[3]

---

[3] Joseph Ratzinger, *On the Way to Jesus Christ* (San Francisco: Ignatius Press, 2005), 46–47.

This passage symbolizes in a way the role of the Gospel in the forum of culture and philosophical thought. The Gospel is not only focused on the individual; it also irradiates culture by assisting the growth and development of the person, his way of thinking, his productiveness for God and the world. The Gospel is a "slit" or a "cut", a purification that brings about maturation and healing. Obviously this "cut" is not a momentary matter but a patient encounter between the Logos and the culture.

Today, after such productive encounters as that of ancient Greece and the Gospel, philosophy's thirst has not been quenched. Philosophy, even without revelation, can achieve transcendence and arrive at God as the Creator and final cause. But the rejection of God once again confines philosophy to questions about matter alone. Jesus Christ, the perfect man, comes to magnify all research into human nature. Why should a thinker want at any cost to commit himself to a sort of regression and to reject a discovery of man? Contemporary philosophy is interested in him in a very superficial way. This new wisdom ultimately touches only on phenomena external to man. Often it is more about sociology than about philosophy! The time has come to restore certain human sciences to their place, has it not?

Let us set aside the cultural question to address politics in the broad sense of the term. Would you say likewise that democracy is an invention of Christianity?

Indisputably. There is a Christian concept of the equality of man. Christ grants equal dignity to everyone; there is no barrier to his salvation. Only Christ guarantees respect for and protection of the fundamental rights of every human person. He alone imposes on every man and every woman the duty to carry out their responsibilities with regard to individual conscience and society, in order to promote justice, liberty, and the common good. Christ places at the heart of societies the primacy of fraternal love and service to others. These are a few elements that must be taken into account in the constitution of a true democracy.

This form of government is not exactly majority rule, but it approximates it. Does a majority still deserve the name when it crushes racial, religious, and political minorities with the help of oppressive laws? In *Deus caritas est*, Benedict XVI recalled that "the just ordering of society and the State is a central responsibility of politics. As Augustine once said, a State which is not governed according to justice would be just a bunch of thieves: '*Remota itaque iustitia quid sunt regna nisi magna latrocinia?*' "

(DCE 28). Such situations and realities are not uncommon today. It is good for every power to be checked and balanced by other powers. And so democracy, which is an ideal and a practice, is acknowledged as the least bad political system. But if democracy excludes religion, explicitly or not, it is no longer a good for the people; hence the constitutional State no longer is, either.

The Christian message is revolutionary: all men are brothers and have one and the same Father. We are equal in dignity, for we are all created in the image of God. Nevertheless, true democracy cannot be the arbitrary rule of the majority. For is the majority necessarily just? Obviously the answer is no. Sometimes the minorities are the ones who hold the truth....

I am convinced that a democracy that contributes to the integral development of mankind cannot continue without God. When a head of State knows that God is above him, his conscience more easily appeals to him to be a humble servant. Without a Christian reference, in ignorance of God, a democracy becomes a sort of oligarchy, an elitist, inegalitarian regime. As always, the eclipse of what is divine means the debasement of what is human.

On Monday, April 18, 2005, during the Missa pro eligendo Romano Pontifice, *a few hours before his election to the throne of Peter, Cardinal Ratzinger had decided to denounce the dictatorship of relativism. You seem to think that the insights of this speech are still quite relevant today.*

Yes, and I would like first to cite a long passage from this homily. Joseph Cardinal Ratzinger then declared: "How many winds of doctrine have we known in recent decades, how many ideological currents, how many ways of thinking. The small boat of the thought of many Christians has often been tossed about by these waves—flung from one extreme to another: from Marxism to liberalism, even to libertinism; from collectivism to radical individualism; from atheism to a vague religious mysticism; from agnosticism to syncretism and so forth. Every day new sects spring up, and what Saint Paul says about human deception and the trickery that strives to entice people into error (cf. Eph 4:14) comes true. Today, having a clear faith based on the Creed of the Church is often labeled as fundamentalism. Whereas relativism, that is, letting oneself be 'tossed here and there, carried about by every wind of doctrine', seems the only attitude that can cope with modern times. We are building a dictatorship of relativism that does not recognize anything as definitive and whose ultimate goal consists solely of one's own ego and desires. We, however, have a different goal: the Son of God, the true man. He is the measure of true humanism. An 'adult' faith is not a faith that follows the trends of fashion and the latest novelty; a mature adult faith is deeply rooted in friendship with Christ. It is this friendship that opens us up to all that is good and gives us a criterion by which to distinguish the true from the false, and deceit from truth. We must develop this adult faith; we must guide the flock of Christ to this faith. And it is this faith—only faith—that creates unity and is fulfilled in love. On this theme, Saint Paul offers us as a fundamental formula for Christian existence some beautiful words, in contrast to the continual vicissitudes of those who, like children, are tossed about by the waves: make truth in love. Truth and love coincide in Christ. To the extent that we draw close to Christ, in our own lives too, truth and love are blended. Love without truth would be blind; truth without love would be like 'a clanging cymbal' (1 Cor 13:1)."

Today relativism appears to be the philosophical basis for Western democracies that refuse to consider that Christian truth might be superior to any other. They altogether take for granted their denial of Christ's words: "I am the way, and the truth, and the life; no one comes to the Father, but by me" (Jn 14:6).

In a relativistic system, all ways are possible, like fragmentary components of the march of progress. The common good, from this perspective, is the product of a continual dialogue of everyone, a meeting of different private opinions, a fraternal Tower of Babel in which everybody has a particle of the truth. Modern relativism goes so far as to claim that it is the embodiment of liberty. In this sense, liberty becomes the aggressive obligation to believe that there is no higher truth; in this new Eden, if man rejects the truth revealed by Christ, he becomes free. Life together in society assumes the form of an impassable horizon within which each individual can control his own moral, philosophical, and religious views. Consequently, relativism drives man to create his own religion, populated by multiple more or less pathetic deities, which are born and die in response to impulses, in a world that is somewhat reminiscent of the ancient pagan religions.

In this totalitarian yoke, the Church loses her absolute character; her dogmas, her teaching, and her sacraments are practically prohibited or else diminished in their rigor and their demands. The Bride of the Son of God is marginalized, in a disdain that engenders hatred of Christianity, because it is a permanent obstacle. The Church becomes one among others, and the final objective of philosophical relativism still is her death by gradual dilution; relativists, along with the prince of this world, impatiently await that great dusk. They work for the coming of the kingdom of darkness.

John Paul II and Joseph Ratzinger, as prefect of the Congregation for the Doctrine of the Faith, had grasped the importance of the lethal danger of relativistic theories. The declaration *Dominus Iesus* is largely a response to relativism. In the introduction, which has lost none of its insightful relevance, Joseph Ratzinger correctly wrote: "The Church's constant missionary proclamation is endangered today by relativistic theories which seek to justify religious pluralism, not only *de facto* but also *de iure* (or in principle). As a consequence, it is held that certain truths have been superseded; for example, the definitive and complete character of the revelation of Jesus Christ, the nature of Christian faith as compared with that of belief in other religions, the inspired nature of the books of Sacred Scripture, the personal unity between the Eternal Word and Jesus of Nazareth, the unity of the economy of the Incarnate Word and the Holy Spirit, the unicity and salvific universality of the mystery of Jesus Christ, the universal salvific mediation of the Church, the inseparability—while recognizing the distinction— of the kingdom of God, the kingdom of Christ, and the Church, and the subsistence of the one Church of Christ in the Catholic Church. The roots of these problems are to be found in certain presuppositions of both a philosophical and theological nature, which hinder the understanding and acceptance of the revealed truth. Some of these can be mentioned: the conviction of the elusiveness and inexpressibility of divine truth, even by Christian revelation; relativistic attitudes toward truth itself, according to which what is true for some would not be true for others; the radical opposition posited between the logical mentality of the West and the symbolic mentality of the East; the subjectivism which, by regarding reason as the only source of knowledge, becomes incapable of raising its 'gaze to the heights, not daring to rise to the truth of being'; the difficulty in understanding and accepting the presence of definitive and eschatological events in history; the metaphysical emptying of the historical incarnation of the Eternal Logos, reduced to a mere appearing of God in history; the eclecticism of those who, in theological research, uncritically absorb ideas from a variety of philosophical and theological contexts without regard for consistency, systematic connection, or compatibility with Christian truth; finally, the tendency to read and to interpret Sacred Scripture outside the Tradition and Magisterium of the Church. On the basis of such presuppositions, which may evince different nuances, certain theological proposals are developed—at times presented as assertions, and at times as hypotheses—in which Christian revelation and the mystery of Jesus Christ and the Church lose their character of absolute truth and salvific universality, or at least shadows of doubt and uncertainty are cast upon them" (DI 4).

Relativism is a widespread evil, and it is not easy to combat it. The task becomes more complex inasmuch as it arbitrarily serves as a sort of charter for a way of communal life. Relativism attempts to complete the process of the social disappearance of God. It guides mankind with an attractive logic that proves to be a perverse totalitarian system. The Church continues today the battle of Benedict XVI against the liquidation of God. And this is a battle on behalf of mankind.

If we follow the reasoning of Benedict XVI, liberty is in danger of being no longer a choice but an obligation, echoing somewhat the words of the French Revolutionary Saint-Just: "No liberty for the enemies of liberty."

God created man free; the latter has freedom because he comes from God, who is the very source of all liberty. Saint John writes elsewhere: "So if the Son makes you free, you will be free indeed" (Jn 8:36). A person living in a state of captivity still possesses one treasure that the cruelest dictator cannot take away from him, for God has given every being interior freedom.

But liberty does not consist of emancipation from all limits or norms. Such liberty is a myth. For liberty must always be guided by the truth; it is intrinsically connected to our creaturely nature. The liberty of one individual must, furthermore, take into account that of his neighbor. Today, I think that the liberty of some is being imposed on others. Recently, the great French demonstrations against the distortion of marriage were able to prove that. This false liberty is the extension of a godless egalitarianism.

Man has the right to express himself according to his conscience without being obliged to undergo external pressures. Thus, interior freedom absolutely must be something that is constantly being won and built up. Liberty without truth is deceitful; the absence of a moral connection between liberty and truth can only produce a form of anarchy. Liberty continues to be real when it truly accomplishes the supreme good of human existence, which is to live in the truth of God.

Today all our freedoms are threatened. Economic, political, and media pressures never cease to diminish the connection between liberty and truth. But I think, too, that we must not give up when faced with this daily combat to win our true liberty. For man, shackled and thrown into a prison, whether physical or symbolic, is a free being. In captivity, he has a prodigious power to decide for himself, to choose and to orient his life toward the good. He also has the dizzying ability to love his torturers; this is the ineffable and eternal message of the Gospel. But liberty requires interior discipline, choices and acts of self-denial that lead our life toward whatever disposes us to be at the service of others. This struggle is collective; it is unthinkable to wage a battle alone. Mankind needs the Church and personal and communal prayer in order to be brought to the truth.

The evangelist John expresses this problem perfectly when he writes: "Jesus then said to the Jews who had believed in him, 'If you continue in my word, you are truly my disciples, and you will know the truth, and the truth will make you free.' They answered him, 'We are descendants of Abraham, and have never been in bondage to any one. How is it that you say, "You will be made free"?' Jesus answered them, 'Truly, truly, I say to you, every one who commits sin is a slave to sin. The slave does not continue in the house for ever; the son continues for ever. So if the Son makes you free, you will be free indeed. I know that you are descendants of Abraham; yet you seek to kill me, because my word finds no place in you. I speak of what I have seen with my Father, and you do what you have heard from your father.' They answered him, 'Abraham is our father.' Jesus said to them, 'If you were Abraham's children, you would do what Abraham did, but now you seek to kill me, a man who has told you the truth which I heard from God; this is not what Abraham did. You do the works of your father.' They said to him, 'We were not born of fornication; we have one Father, even God.' Jesus said to them, 'If God were your Father, you would love me, for I proceeded and came forth from God; I came not of my own accord, but he sent me' "(Jn 8:31–42).

For his part, Saint Augustine forcefully testifies that what shackles man's liberty is sin. Liberty is given to us when we have chosen God freely.

Yes, God created man free, endowed with free will. He can choose between good and evil. However, man will be fully himself only by choosing good and by submitting in a filial way to God. But the Father was excluded from this "freedom of the children of God", as Saint Paul says, by original sin.

I often think of this realistic reflection by Saint Augustine in his treatise on lying: "So great blindness, moreover, has occupied men's minds, that to them it is too little if we pronounce some lies not to be sins; but they must needs pronounce it to be sin in some things if we refuse to lie."[4]

All human life is a struggle against the shackles of evil, against the slavery of sin, in order to regain true freedom.

Clearly Benedict XVI dedicated his pontificate and a large part of his theological work to the dialogue between faith and reason. What is your view today of the importance of that decision?

In fact, Benedict XVI never tired of returning to this major theme, because it seemed to him essential that we be able to understand the sources of our belief. He thought that the true work of a theologian consists of entering into the Word of God so as to seek to grasp it rationally, to the extent possible, and to share it with the utmost clarity with the people of his time. And so the theologian must develop answers to the great questions of mankind. Baptized persons have the duty to believe not only with their heart but also with their intellect. Benedict XVI says that religion should not become self-enclosed, nor should it cut itself off from the help of reason. Likewise, it seemed to him very important not to fall into the trap of those who seek to dissociate reason and faith, following in the wake of Enlightenment philosophy; some people think that reason can only regress when it comes into contact

---

[4] Augustine, *On Lying*, 43, in *Nicene and Post-Nicene Fathers*, vol. 3, first series, ed. Philip Schaff (Peabody, Mass.: Hendrickson, 1995), 477.

with faith. On the contrary, faith and reason are like two lights that require each other.

Every believer holds in his heart a treasure, and he has the option of deepening his faith also through the intermediary of reason. This marvelous complementarity is a gift of God. Scientific rigor should not discourage Christians at all. For scientific research is always an advance in our understanding of revelation and of the world. The barriers that some have tried to set up between faith and reason are groundless because they are artificial: there can be no contradiction in God.

Both John Paul II and Benedict XVI treated this question in works that are exceptional in the history of the Church. How can we forget John Paul II's encyclical *Fides et ratio*, published in September 1998? I never tire of quoting the first lines of this document: "Faith and reason are like two wings on which the human spirit rises to the contemplation of truth."

Our world, which no longer wants to hear talk about God, even supposing that it no longer needs him, can find great riches in the dialogue between faith and reason. Men will then be able to understand that the finest human intellect is nothing without the light from heaven, of which the Father gives us a spark through faith.

Along these lines, it is still important to meditate on this passage from *Fides et ratio*: "In my Encyclical Letter *Veritatis Splendor*, I drew attention to 'certain fundamental truths of Catholic doctrine which, in the present circumstances, risk being distorted or denied' (4). In the present Letter, I wish to pursue that reflection by concentrating on the theme of *truth* itself and on its *foundation* in relation to *faith*. For it is undeniable that this time of rapid and complex change can leave especially the younger generation, to whom the future belongs and on whom it depends, with a sense that they have no valid points of reference. The need for a foundation for personal and communal life becomes all the more pressing at a time when we are faced with the patent inadequacy of perspectives in which the ephemeral is affirmed as a value and the possibility of discovering the real meaning of life is cast into doubt. This is why many people stumble through life to the very edge of the abyss without knowing where they are going. At times, this happens because those whose vocation it is to give cultural expression to their thinking no longer look to truth, preferring quick success to the toil of patient enquiry into what makes life worth living. With its enduring appeal to the search for truth, philosophy has the great responsibility of forming thought and culture;

and now it must strive resolutely to recover its original vocation. This is why I have felt both the need and the duty to address this theme so that, on the threshold of the third millennium of the Christian era, humanity may come to a clearer sense of the great resources with which it has been endowed and may commit itself with renewed courage to implement the plan of salvation of which its history is part" (FR 6).

Can scientific research and the Church therefore go in the same direction?

Certainly, since truth is one. In a few cases, some men of the Church may have been imprudent and disrespectful toward scientists. In his address to the participants in the plenary session of the Pontifical Academy of Sciences on October 31, 1992, John Paul II clearly acknowledged the errors committed in the case of Galileo. His remarks were even more well-founded because he did not hesitate to emphasize how far Galileo had gone outside his field by confusing, like most of his adversaries, "the scientific approach to natural phenomena and a reflection on nature, of the philosophical order, for which that approach generally calls". John Paul II explained as follows: "That is why he rejected the suggestion made to him to present the Copernican system as a hypothesis, inasmuch as it had not been confirmed by irrefutable proof. This was, however, a requirement of the experimental method of which he was the inspired founder. Secondly, the geocentric representation of the world was commonly admitted in the culture of the time as fully agreeing with the teaching of the Bible, certain expressions of which, taken literally, seemed to affirm geocentrism. The problem posed by theologians of that age was, therefore, that of the compatibility between heliocentrism and Scripture. Thus the new science, with its methods and the freedom of research that they presupposed, obliged theologians to examine their own criteria of scriptural interpretation. Most of them did not know how to do so. Paradoxically, Galileo, a sincere believer, showed himself to be more perceptive in this regard than the theologians who opposed him. 'If Scripture cannot err,' he wrote to Benedetto Castelli, 'some of its interpreters and commentators can and do so in many ways.' We also know of his letter to Christine de Lorraine (1615), which is like a short treatise on biblical hermeneutics.... The majority of theologians did not recognize the formal distinction between Sacred Scripture and its interpretation, and this led them unduly to transpose into the realm of the doctrine of the faith a question that in fact pertained to scientific investigation." Benedict XVI, too, discussed Galileo in a major address to the Roman Curia on December 22, 2005.

Actually, it is not fair to generalize on the basis of a few particular examples. The Church's fiercest opponents have managed to create a myth, as though she did everything in her power to fight against science! Some powerful media groups are now largely responsible for establishing the image of a backward, obscurantist Church. This is a witch hunt, which is all the more serious because when the Church fights against some research projects—such as human stem cell research, to give a current example—she makes her arguments on the basis of a particularly well-supported ethical system and while taking into account the most recent discoveries.

Indeed, the Church has often been involved in a large number of scientific research projects, either institutionally or else through many researchers, whether Christian or not; her attitude is always motivated by the good of man and the improvement of his living conditions, especially in the field of medicine.

The Church does not want to absolutize scientific findings as though they were new dogmas. There are scientific research projects that pose serious moral dangers for the very future of man and his dignity or for respect for life. The popes, assisted particularly in recent decades by the Pontifical Academy of Sciences and by many Catholics throughout the world, work so that governments might set ethical limits to some research programs. The Church must say how far we can go, and science has the obligation to respect the good of the human person; it cannot ruin man's very being in the name of a boundless march of progress.

Does the Church believe in progress or in hope?

She encourages both. . . . She is in favor of progress if it promotes the real good of mankind; as for hope, it is born of faith: it is, as the poet Péguy said, "faith that loves".

Indeed, progress is not the same thing as the hope of heaven. The former seems to be attracted to essentially material concerns. Man aspires to have a better life, to rule over nature, to discover more sophisticated technologies, more rapid communications, a more efficient economy. . . .

The mistake is to become locked into a materialistic vision and to make progress an absolute. Too often in Western societies, and in many large cities of the world, any spiritual progress that leads to hope is almost forbidden.

Christ alone enables man to realize his full potential. Jesus introduces those who believe in him into the trinitarian communion. True progress allows a human being to come to terms with his origins by rediscovering God; this is the way to the Father. True progress lifts our sights, our efforts, and our hope toward the things of eternity!

Man is not happy when he accumulates material goods; he flourishes if he conforms his whole life to Christ's teaching. Wealth can lead to solitude and sadness, whereas Christ always gives joy. Progress without God is a false happiness.

Pope Francis thinks that "spiritual destitution" is the greatest tragedy of modern man. In his Lenten message in 2014, he wrote: "No less a concern is *moral destitution*, which consists in slavery to vice and sin. How much pain is caused in families because one of their members—often a young person—is in thrall to alcohol, drugs, gambling, or pornography! How many people no longer see meaning in life or prospects for the future, how many have lost hope! And how many are plunged into this destitution by unjust social conditions, by unemployment, which takes away their dignity as breadwinners, and by lack of equal access to education and health care. In such cases, moral destitution can be considered impending suicide. This type of destitution, which also causes financial ruin, is invariably linked to the *spiritual destitution* which we experience when we turn away from God and reject his love. If we think we don't need God who reaches out to us through Christ, because we believe we can make do on our own, we are headed for a fall. God alone can truly save and free us. The Gospel is the real antidote to spiritual destitution: wherever we go, we are called as Christians to proclaim the liberating news that forgiveness for sins committed is possible, that God is greater than our sinfulness, that he freely loves us at all times and that we were made for communion and eternal life. The Lord asks us to be joyous heralds of this message of mercy and hope! It is thrilling to experience the joy of spreading this good news, sharing the treasure entrusted to us, consoling broken hearts and offering hope to our brothers and sisters experiencing darkness. It means following and imitating Jesus, who sought out the poor and sinners as a shepherd lovingly seeks his lost

sheep. In union with Jesus, we can courageously open up new paths of
evangelization and human promotion."

*You often denounce the modern drama of fanatical egalitarianism, whether ideo-
logical or societal. What do you mean by that?*

Soviet Communism showed how possible it was to lead mankind into
misery while promising absolute equality. In my country we experienced true hell under Sékou Touré, who claimed to fulfill Marx's promises with the class struggle. The myth of equality resulted in a bloody
dictatorship. God willed that human beings should be complementary
so as to aid and support one another mutually. Equality is not God's
creation.

Today gender theory seems to be toying with this same illusory battle
for equality. The dream, the illusion, and the artificial paradises very
quickly turn into a nightmare. Man and woman form a unity in love; the
denial of their differences is a destructive utopia, a deadly impulse born
in a world cut off from God.

Egalitarianism is an ideology that thrives when religion is forgotten.
All ideologies end up disappearing, like Communism. Thus the fall of
ideologies is inevitable inasmuch as they are nothing but mere products
of man without God. But at what cost!

In April 2014, Pope Francis denounced the harmful consequences
of the egalitarian ideology of gender for the development of children.
Speaking to a delegation from the International Catholic Child Bureau,
he plainly affirmed, in his characteristically direct language: "the right
of children to grow up in a family with a father and a mother capable of
creating a suitable environment for the child's development and emotional maturity". He added that "children and young people ... are not
lab specimens! The horrors of the manipulation of education that we
experienced in the great genocidal dictatorships of the twentieth century have not disappeared; they have retained a current relevance under
various guises and proposals and, with the pretense of modernity, push
children and young people to walk on the dictatorial path of 'only one
form of thought'. A little over a week ago a great teacher said to me: 'At
times with these projects—referring to actual educational projects—one
doesn't know whether the child is going to school or to a re-education
camp.' Working for human rights presupposes the vital aim of fostering

anthropological formation, of proper knowledge of the reality of the human person, and knowing how to respond to the problems and challenges posed by contemporary culture and the mentality propagated by the mass media. Obviously this does not mean we should take refuge in hidden protected areas that today are unable to foster life, that belong to a past culture.... No, not this, this is not good.... We should face the challenges the new culture launches with the positive values of the human person. For you, this means offering your managers and operators continuing formation on the anthropology of the child, because that is where rights and duties have their foundation. It is against this background that educational projects must be planned and developed, mature and adapt to the signs of the times, always respecting the human identity and freedom of conscience."

And so, when a female advocate of women's rights, within the very precincts of the United Nations Organization, in October 2014, called on members of Planned Parenthood International to denounce the distribution of outdated contraceptives, which are dangerous to the health, to poor, defenseless African women, she was fully joining the battle of Pope Francis.

In abandoning God, man loses his reason and becomes blind. The ideological search for equality is an unreal path that fuels the worst tragedies.

Do you think therefore that modern man loses himself in deceptive pastimes so as not to face the real problems?

A Godless society, which considers any spiritual questions a dead letter, masks the emptiness of its materialism by killing time so as better to forget eternity. The farther material things extend their influence, the more man takes pleasure in sophisticated, narcissistic, and perverse amusements; the more man forgets God, the more he observes himself. In looking at himself, he sees the deformations and the ugliness that his debauchery has encrusted on his face. Then, to delude himself that he still shines with the original splendor of a creature of God, he puts on his make-up. But the hidden evil is like the glowing coal beneath the ashes.

Without God, man builds his hell on earth. Amusements and pleasures can become a true scourge for the soul when it sinks into pornography, drugs, violence, and all sorts of perversions.

There is great sadness in claiming to want to indulge in limitless pleasures, whereas the most beautiful joy is to remain simply with God, allowing him to clothe us in light and purity.

In his *Pensées* Blaise Pascal writes about diversions: "When I have set myself now and then to consider the various distractions of men, the toils and dangers to which they expose themselves in the Court or the camp, whence arise so many quarrels and passions, such daring and often such evil exploits, etc., I have discovered that all the misfortunes of men arise from one thing only, that they are unable to stay quietly in their own chamber. A man who has enough to live on, if he knew how to dwell with pleasure in his own home, would not leave it for sea-faring or to besiege a city. An office in the army would not be bought so dearly but that it seems insupportable not to stir from the town, and people only seek conversation and amusing games because they cannot remain with pleasure in their own homes.... [Diversion is something so necessary to men of the world that they are miserable without it.] We seek repose by resistance to obstacles, and so soon as these are surmounted, repose becomes intolerable. For we think either on the miseries we feel or on those we fear. And even when we seem sheltered on all sides, weariness, of its own accord, will spring from the depths of the heart wherein are its natural roots, and fill the soul with its poison. The counsel given to Pyrrhus to take the rest that he was seeking through so many labours, was full of difficulties."[5] "To bid a man live quietly is to bid him live happily. It is to advise him to be in a state perfectly happy, in which he can think at leisure without finding therein a cause of distress. As men who naturally understand their own condition avoid nothing so much as rest, so there is nothing they leave undone in seeking turmoil. So we are wrong in blaming them. Their error does not lie in seeking excitement, if they seek it only as a diversion; the evil is that they seek it as if the possession of the objects of their quest would make them really happy. In this respect it is right to call their quest a vain one. Hence in all this both the censurers and the censured do not understand man's true nature. [Vanity is the pleasure of making a show to others.]"[6]

---

[5] *The Thoughts of Blaise Pascal*, trans. Charles Kegan Paul (Whitefish, Mont.: Kessinger, 2010), 56, 59.

[6] Blaise Pascal, *Thoughts*, trans. W. F. Trotter, Harvard Classics 48 (New York: Collier & Son, 1910), 54.

According to the philosopher, since men could not remedy death, misery, and ignorance, they decided that it would make them happy not to think about them at all. This definition of diversion is indeed connected with several of Pascal's concepts: misery, because one seeks diversions in order to forget it; vanity, because there is no worse proof of vanity than this remedy to human ills; the supreme good, because ignorance of man's true good is what drives him to pursue illusory goods.

Diversion has a twofold origin. It is reminiscent of Montaigne's diversion, which consists of the ability to turn one's thoughts away from the evils that one is suffering so as to endure them better, but it is also inspired by the Augustinian idea that man is capable of excluding his final end and God from his thoughts. Saint Augustine is right: the search for different pleasures is connected to the abandonment of God.

The man who ignores God and turns his own instincts into godlike standards for all things is headed for destruction. Today we are confronted with one of the last stages of the civilization of diversion. The alternative is simple: if mankind reforms itself, it will live, but if its headlong flight persists, civilization will become a hell.

Could you say that a society that rejects God always ends by seeking replacements in various superstitions and magical rites? From your personal experience, are you not acquainted with a traditional society that is still largely built on pagan foundations without Christian hope?

For a long time I have thought that superstition is born of fear and that true serenity comes from God. If we do not know our Father, or if no one has taught us about him, there is a more or less significant situation of anxiety. In order to ease the fear, rituals, beings, or objects are invested with sacred powers. Paganism can occur in traditional societies or in modern countries, but its manifestations remain identical. To curb depression, the ritual becomes a tranquilizer.

In Africa, paganism was often based on animal sacrifices offered to invisible forces or on the veneration of sacred trees and mountains, which were supposed to contain the presence of deities and spirits. Hence cults seek to mitigate the violence of negative forces. But superstition leaves people in anxiety, ignorance, and doubt. In Guinea, I was able to realize that the fear resulting from animism was being transmitted from generation to generation; it had become cultural. And even some Christians, although saved from death and fear by Jesus, had difficulty in freeing themselves from paganism.

The result is an irrational *continuum* in which society constantly indulges in libations and sacrifices of all sorts in order to appease the spirits. If man becomes open to the knowledge of God, superstition tends to disappear. I am aware that many Christians may remain bound by old fears. Animism, which looks at the world as being ruled by spirits, is still powerful. Some Christians, weakened by a superficial faith, may be tempted to offer pagan sacrifices to the spirits in order to draw down their favors.

The second type of superstition is connected with the abandonment of God. When man turns away from his fundamental roots, it is necessary for him to commend himself to other forces. Paradoxically, modern materialistic societies are based on magical beliefs. Men make false gods for themselves. The search for power without God generates a greater susceptibility to the thirst for liberating illusions. In this context, it is clear that the first words of John Paul II after his election, repeating Jesus' invitation: "Be not afraid!", seek to bring man closer to God so as to restore to him his true liberty.

In many of your reflections, you denounce the increase of symbolic or physical violence against Christians....

This is a reality that runs through the whole history of Christianity, starting with Christ himself, from his birth until the day of his crucifixion. The apostles were the victims of serious violence. The Son of God had announced to his disciples that they would never be at peace on this earth. The only way to win this great combat is union with God. Christians will never succeed in overcoming the challenges of the world by appealing to political tools, human rights, or respect for religious liberty. The only true rock for the baptized is prayer and the encounter with Jesus Christ. Men whose strength is in prayer are unsinkable. Jesus began his public ministry with forty days of prayer in the desert, and he finished his life with a cry that is a final prayer: "Father, forgive them; for they know not what they do" (Lk 23:34).

The violence against Christians is not just physical; it is also political, ideological, and cultural: "Do not fear those who kill the body but cannot kill the soul; rather fear him who can destroy both soul and body in hell" (Mt 10:28). Many Christians, in Nigeria, in Pakistan, in the Middle East, and elsewhere, courageously undergo this physical martyrdom daily, in order to be faithful to Christ, without ever giving up their freedom of soul.

The persecution is more refined when it does not destroy physically but demolishes the teaching of Jesus and of the Church and, therefore, the foundations of faith by leading souls astray. By this violence, some people try to neutralize and depersonalize the Christians, so as to dissolve them in a fluid society without religion and without God. There is no greater disdain than indifference. This insidious war springs from a diabolical hatred of Jesus Christ and of his true witnesses. I can still hear the powerful echo of the voice of John Paul II in Lyon [October 4, 1986], warning us about the danger of an environment that may imprison us in forgetfulness, turn us away from the faith, and leave us defenseless against the fumes of rampant idolatry: "Of course, today you are not thrown to the beasts; no one tries to put you to death because of Christ. But is it not necessary to acknowledge that another sort of trial surreptitiously affects Christians? Currents of thought, life-styles, and sometimes even laws opposed to the true meaning of man and of God undermine the Christian faith in the lives of individuals, families, and society. Christians are not mistreated, they even enjoy all sorts of freedoms, but is there not a real risk that their faith will be, so to speak, imprisoned by an environment that tends to relegate it to the domain of an individual's private life? Nowadays there is a massive indifference among many people with regard to the Gospel and the moral behavior that it demands; is this not a way of sacrificing little by little to the idols of selfishness, luxury, consumption, and pleasure, which are sought without limits and at any price? This form of pressure or seduction could kill the soul without attacking the body. The spirit of evil that opposed our martyrs is still at work. With other means, it continues to seek to turn people away from the faith."

In the West, this violence is increasingly insidious, especially since it is careful to hide its true face. In the Gospel of John, Christ's words are plain: "If the world hates you, know that it has hated me before it hated you. If you were of the world, the world would love its own; but because you are not of the world, but I chose you out of the world, therefore the world hates you. Remember the word that I said to you, 'A servant is not greater than his master.' If they persecuted me, they will persecute you; if they kept my word, they will keep yours also. But all this they will do to you on my account, because they do not know him who sent me. If I had not come and spoken to them, they would not have sin; but now they have no excuse for their sin. He who hates me hates my Father also. If I had not done among them the works which no one else did, they would not have sin; but now they have seen and hated both me and my Father. It is to fulfill the word that is written in their law, 'They hated me without a cause'" (Jn 15:18–25).

Now the refinements of evil are becoming ever more insidious. A man who falls asleep for a moment must take care not to fall into a trap that is so pleasant that it is all the more formidable.

As we conclude this reflection, how should we understand the development of modern secularization?

Sometimes I get the feeling that the Western part of the world definitely intends to lock everything up in this world, in an aggressive rejection of transcendental relations. The separation between earth and heaven becomes so radical that religion becomes a foreign object, a lost island inhabited by individuals from another era. This oligarchic attitude of the promoters of atheism not only is based on oversimplifications but also is dangerous.

The fact remains that man lives in two dimensions, the heavenly and the earthly. He is created for this life and for the next. Here below it is important to harmonize the two by responding to corporal and spiritual needs without neglecting either. A society that forgets God hungers, without realizing it, for the spiritual foods that man cannot do without. This is why the secularization process that reduces the religious dimension to the smallest possible extent results in a division of man by depriving him of one of his lungs. Man is both on earth and in heaven; but man's only roots are in heaven! Without its ramifications, what is human loses its strength. In April 2014, during a homily at his morning Mass in Saint Martha's, Pope Francis commented on the dialogue between Moses and God on Mount Sinai as a way of addressing the question of prayer: "This prayer is a real struggle with God," Francis explained, "a struggle on the part of the leader of a people to save his people, who are the people of God. Moses speaks freely in front of the Lord and in doing so teaches us how to pray without fear, freely, even with insistence."

Prayer must be a "negotiation with God" to which we bring "our arguments", Francis advised. For him, "Prayer changes our heart. It helps us better understand our God." Therefore, it is important to speak normally with him, as with a friend, "Even rebuking the Lord a little: 'You promised me this, but you did not do it ...'", speaking face to face. When Moses comes down from the mountain, he returns changed by his experience, for he thought that the Lord was going to punish and destroy his people for idolizing the golden calf. The pope added that during his prayer, Moses "tries to convince God, but in doing so, he rediscovers the memory of his people and God's mercy." He understands that "Our God is merciful. He knows how to forgive." Moses goes back down full of energy, telling himself that he knows the Lord better. In prayer, therefore, Moses finds the strength to lead his people toward the Promised Land.

Prayer is reinvigorating because it is a struggle with God, just as Jacob wrestled all night until the dawn. If we hold firm, we will have the same experience: "When the man saw that he did not prevail against Jacob, he touched the hollow of his thigh; and Jacob's thigh was put out of joint as he wrestled with him." Then he gives Jacob a new name and blesses him (Gen 32:23–32). Saint Paul, too, considers prayer to be a struggle: "Epaphras, who is one of yourselves, a servant of Christ Jesus, greets you, *semper certans pro vobis in orationibus* [always fighting for you in his prayers] that you may stand mature and fully assured in all the will of God" (Col 4:12). The apostle is sure that spiritual work has no impact if it is not supported by intercessory prayer. To the Romans, but also to us, Saint Paul writes: "I appeal to you, brethren, by our Lord Jesus Christ and by the love of the Spirit, to strive together with me in your prayers to God on my behalf, that I may be delivered from the unbelievers in Judea, and that my service for Jerusalem may be acceptable to the saints" (Rom 15:30–31).

VII

TO BE IN THE TRUTH

Prayer was the glue that enabled my freedom.

—James Foley, American journalist assassinated
in Syria on August 19, 2014

NICOLAS DIAT: *How would you define the word "faith"?*

ROBERT CARDINAL SARAH: Faith is like the response of an engaged couple. By their "yes", which will involve their whole lives, two beings dedicate their love. This loving sentiment is based on a mutual faith that gives credit to the other and counts on his fidelity in the future. Thus the two become one flesh. In their love, each one humbles himself before the other, flourishes and grows in the other. "Love has grown in me", Saint Thérèse of Lisieux used to say timidly and vigorously. In faith and love, God grows in me and lifts me up to him. But faith is also a gift from God, because man always responds freely to the call of heaven. This is not about some theoretical response, but about a personal experience of God, as he is.

In responding to God, we base our life on him, and the Father places his hope in us. God always wants to conform man to his image and likeness. It is important to understand that faith is a covenant of love that causes us to become one and the same being with the beloved person.

In his book *The Sign of Jonas,*[1] Thomas Merton wondered whether it was possible to declare that "by Love, the soul receives the very 'form' of God." In the language of Saint Bernard, this form, which we could associate with a divine likeness, is the identity for which we are created.

---

[1] Thomas Merton, *The Sign of Jonas* (New York: Harcourt, Brace, 1956), 276.

And so we can say: "Caritas haec visio, haec similitudo est" (Charity is this vision, this sameness). Through love we have a direct resemblance to God, and through mystical love, we "see" him here below, in the sense that we already have the experience of God as he is in himself.

Faith is the most beautiful experience of God. One extraordinary example of this is given by Abraham. After hearing a call, he set out with confidence. We are the children of Abraham, our father in faith, and we belong to the lines of the spiritual descendants of the people of the Exodus, traveling through the desert. In the same way, Christians are also the children of Jesus' disciples, those who followed him. Thus, faith can be defined as a spiritual walk that is led and guided solely by God's voice. To put it differently, I would say that faith is adherence to a word that is known to come from a place farther on and higher than me. The whole Bible ceaselessly unfolds this providential gift.

Faith is also an act that gradually and definitively transforms us.

Since Abraham had to agree to sacrifice his son Isaac, the son of the promise, faith is an act that makes us radically different. After the trial of the sacrifice of his son, neither Abraham nor Isaac was the same; Isaac was no longer the same son for Abraham. He had been given and commended to God; he became the sign of another filiation. Similarly, Abraham no longer lived merely as the man who had received a gift from God: the gift of his son Isaac. Now he was the one who had agreed to be dispossessed of this gift and to recover it as a spiritual heritage.

In fact, faith is always a Paschal journey in search of the Father's will, in line with Abraham's fidelity and obedience even to the altar on which he was to sacrifice his son, Isaac. Saint Paul defines faith as obedience to the Father (Rom 1:5; 16:25). Yet we must understand that our obedience can lead to the mountain of sacrifice. Thus, the journey of faith is the journey of man's consent to God's will. The Father's commandments are always a charter for life that requires our loving consent. Faith consists of willing what God wills, loving what God loves, even if that leads us to the Cross.

We place our faith in Jesus Christ. We rely on him, because he is "the pioneer and perfecter of our faith" (Heb 12:2). Through him, we say "Amen" to God for his glory (2 Cor 1:20). The word *amen*, in Hebrew, refers to something firm and worthy of confidence. This word, therefore, expresses the response of man's fidelity to God's fidelity in Jesus Christ. We can rely on God as though on a rock, with the conviction and assurance that, even though it is situated on the edge of an abyss, it will not crumble. In a relationship of faith, God is my stronghold, my fortress, and my rock.

Faith does not presuppose any guarantees. The believer walks in the dark, like a pilgrim seeking the light. What he knows he knows only in the half-light of evening, walking with the help of a *cognitio vespertina* and not yet of a *cognitio matutina*, a knowledge of clear vision, according to the beautiful terminology of Saint Augustine and Saint Thomas.

If I may refer to a very suggestive medieval etymology, I cannot forget that the verb to believe, *credere*, supposedly meant also *cor-dare*, "to give one's heart" and to place it unconditionally into the hands of an Other.

The man who believes agrees, like Abraham, to become the prisoner of the invisible God; he agrees to let the Father possess him in obedient listening, docility of heart, and the lights of his intellect. His walk toward God is consent and abandonment, without expecting to benefit from reassuring guarantees. Saint Paul gave us this magnificent program: "I press on to make [the resurrection from the dead] my own, because Christ Jesus has made me his own" (Phil 3:12).

In April 2014, Pope Francis recalled in a homily that he gave at Saint Martha's that "Christianity is not a philosophical doctrine, it is not a program of life that enables one to be well formed and to make peace. These are its consequences. The Cross is the mystery of the love of God who humbles himself. There is no Christianity without the Cross. There is no way for us to abandon sin unaided. Christ humbles himself to save us. And so just as in the desert sin was lifted up, here God made man was lifted up for us. And all of our sins were there. One cannot understand Christianity without understanding this profound humiliation of the Son of God, who humbled himself and made himself a servant unto death on the Cross. To serve." The Holy Father added: "The heart of God's salvation is his Son, who took upon himself our sins, our pride, our self-reliance, our vanity, our desire to be like God. A Christian who is not able to glory in Christ Crucified has not understood what it means to be Christian. Our wounds, those that sin leaves in us, are healed only through the Lord's wounds, through the wounds of God made man who humbled himself, who emptied himself."

I like this reflection by the pope very much, because it shows that faith is a commitment of our entire being. Faith taken to its ultimate degree is an absolute act of dispossession in God. On this earth, I think that the Carthusian monks, the sons of Saint Bruno, who place all their hope in God, are one of the finest examples of lives given entirely to God. In their hermitages, nothing matters anymore except divine hope.

How exactly can this hope be summoned up?

Hope is nothing other than Christian optimism. It allows man to remain firm in the faith, fully assured by God's promises. In hope, God is the guarantor of my future and of my serene stability. Christians must always be optimistic and joyful; but this is an attitude that results from faith in the power of a God who never loses a battle so that man might experience peace and glory with him. Faith is the foundation of hope, a new dimension of man that leads him toward divinity. And so, in his Letter to the Romans, Saint Paul writes: "Therefore, since we are justified by faith, we have peace with God through our Lord Jesus Christ. Through him we have obtained access to this grace in which we stand, and we rejoice in our hope of sharing the glory of God. More than that, we rejoice in our sufferings, knowing that suffering produces endurance, and endurance produces character, and character produces hope, and hope does not disappoint us, because God's love has been poured into our hearts through the Holy Spirit who has been given to us" (Rom 5:1–5).

Since our faith and our hope rest in God, we have nothing to fear. The Christian can say with assurance: "And now, Lord, for what do I wait? My hope is in you.... I am silent, I do not open my mouth; for it is you who have done it" (Ps 39:7, 9).

In 2007, in his encyclical *Spe salvi*, Benedict XVI wrote brilliantly about hope: " 'Hope', in fact, is a key word in Biblical faith—so much so that in several passages the words 'faith' and 'hope' seem interchangeable. Thus the Letter to the Hebrews closely links the 'fullness of faith' (10:22) to 'the confession of our hope without wavering' (10:23). Likewise, when the First Letter of Peter exhorts Christians to be always ready to give an answer concerning the *logos*—the meaning and the reason—of their hope (cf. 3:15), 'hope' is equivalent to 'faith'. We see how decisively the self-understanding of the early Christians was shaped by their having received the gift of a trustworthy hope, when we compare the Christian life with life prior to faith, or with the situation of the followers of other religions. Paul reminds the Ephesians that before their encounter with Christ they were 'without hope and without God in the world' (Eph 2:12). Of course he knew they had had gods, he knew they had had a religion, but their gods had proved questionable, and no hope emerged from their contradictory myths. Notwithstanding their gods, they were 'without God' and consequently found themselves in a dark world, facing a dark future. *In nihil ab nihilo quam cito recidimus* (How quickly we fall back from nothing to nothing): so says an epitaph of that period. In this phrase we see in no uncertain terms the point Paul was making. In the same vein he says to the Thessalonians: you must not 'grieve as others do who have no hope' (1 Thess 4:13). Here too we see as a distinguishing mark of Christians the fact that they have a future: it is not that they know the details of what awaits them, but they know in general terms that their life will not end in emptiness. Only when the future is certain as a positive reality does it become possible to live the present as well. So now we can say: Christianity was not only 'good news'—the communication of a hitherto unknown content. In our language we would say: the Christian message was not only 'informative' but 'performative'. That means: the Gospel is not merely a communication of things that can be known—it is one that makes things happen and is life-changing. The dark door of time, of the future, has been thrown open. The one who has hope lives differently; the one who hopes has been granted the gift of a new life" (SS 2).

Why, then, is Christian joy no longer understood?

For Saint Paul, joy is the distinctive mark of the Christian. Recall how he liked to exhort the Christians by telling them: "Rejoice in the Lord always; again I will say, Rejoice. Let all men know your forbearance.... Have no anxiety about anything, but in everything by prayer and supplication with thanksgiving let your requests be made known to God" (Phil 4:4–6). Without prayer there is no true joy. Similarly, Paul exclaimed: "Christ is proclaimed; and in that I rejoice. Yes, and I shall rejoice. For I know that through your prayers and the help of the Spirit of Jesus Christ this will turn out for my deliverance" (Phil 1:18–19). Prayer is the source of our joy and serenity because it unites us to God, who is our strength. A sad man is not a disciple of Christ. Someone who relies on his own strength is always saddened when it declines. In contrast, a believer cannot be in sorrow because his joy comes from God alone. But spiritual joy depends on the Cross. By beginning to forget ourselves for the Love of God, we find him, at least obscurely. And since God is our joy, this joy is proportionate to our self-denial and union with him.

Jesus himself invites us to live a life full of generosity, a life of giving but also of joy. Pope Francis speaks a lot about the simple happiness of the Gospel. In his apostolic exhortation *Evangelii gaudium*, "The Joy of the Gospel", he writes: "With Christ joy is constantly born anew" (EG 1). The Holy Father correctly points out that it is necessary to pray daily so as not to lose this sweet fullness. The many demands of the world can torment Christian joy. One can even say that worldly happiness cannot understand Christian joy. We must be happy to follow Christ in all circumstances. The battle always proves to be rough, for there is no lack of sufferings. A smile does not come naturally when we face suffering and disappointment. If God truly possesses us, if Christ abides in us, joy always returns.

Indeed, joy cannot be forced; it springs spontaneously from an interior source that is God. His love constantly leads to true happiness. Thus, the peoples of the rich nations that have abandoned God are always sad, whereas the poor nations of believers radiate a true joy; they have nothing, but God is a constant light for them because he dwells in their hearts. I was able to observe this again during my last trip to the Philippines, with the pope, in January 2015.

Similarly, many observers tend to emphasize that Francis has placed his pontificate under the key word of mercy. What do you think?

According to the etymology, mercy, *misericordia*, is casting one's heart upon someone else's misery, loving the other in the midst of his misery. But before flooding us with its benevolence, mercy demands truth, justice, and repentance. In God, mercy will become "forgiveness". Thus we are at the center of the Gospel message.

Forgiveness is the most striking face of God's love for mankind. Thus Saint Peter asked Jesus: " 'Lord, how often shall my brother sin against me, and I forgive him? As many as seven times?' Jesus said to him, 'I do not say to you seven times, but seventy times seven' " (Mt 18:21–22). In other words, tirelessly.

Indeed, we must love as God loves. God knows man's failures and great weaknesses, but he casts his Heart upon our misery. God rejoices to forgive us. Forgiveness is beginning again to love with more gratuitousness and generosity when love has been badly hurt.

Without God's grace, unless we fix our eyes on the crucifix, from which we hear the voice of Jesus praying for his executioners, and unless we open our flawed hearts to graft them onto the pierced Heart of the One who comes to consume our sins with the fire of his overflowing love, it will be difficult for us to forgive, because this act requires us to give in abundance. It is necessary to be overflowing with love, it is necessary to have a superabundant love in order to attain the truth of forgiveness. The best imitation of Jesus is forgiveness. In the Gospel, the prodigal son, the adulterous woman, Mary Magdalen, are marvelous examples of forgiveness given to us by Christ to imitate.

God is forgiveness, love, and mercy; the radical newness of Christianity is found here and nowhere else. Men must forgive as God himself forgives, tirelessly. We were made by God, and it is enough for us to remember our divine origins in order to comply easily with his will, which asks us to be perfect as our heavenly Father is perfect in his mercy. Forgiveness always allows man to be recreated, for this is an opportunity that has come from heaven. . . .

Who is this God of forgiveness?

The Book of Jonah declares that this God is "a gracious God and merciful, slow to anger, and abounding in mercy, [who repents] of evil" (Jon 4:2).

As for Jeremiah, he reveals to us a God trembling with tenderness for Ephraim: "Is Ephraim my dear Son? Is he my darling child? For as often as I speak against him, I do remember him still. Therefore my heart yearns for him; I will surely have mercy on him, says the LORD" (Jer 31:20).

The prophet Isaiah puts it this way: God has carved us on the palms of his hands. The Father surpasses and overwhelms the tenderness of all the mothers in the world: "Can a woman forget her sucking child, that she should have no compassion on the son of her womb? Even these may forget, yet I will not forget you. Behold, I have graven you on the palms of my hands; your walls are continually before me" (Is 49:15–16).

Finally, Jesus reveals a God whose love is unfathomable. When his prodigal children return home, he gives them a lengthy embrace and restores to them their dignity as children of heaven.

God is good and beautiful, and his creatures are all in his image; Genesis, with its account of the beginning of the world, is magnificently imbued with God's beauty. This beauty shines for man. God does nothing for himself; all creation is designed for his offspring.

God's beauty, which is reflected in creation but can be destroyed by man, can always be reborn thanks to forgiveness. If man rejects forgiveness, he detaches himself from God and falls into a subhuman life dominated by ugliness, lying, and evil. If he accepts forgiveness, good is reborn.

How are we to understand the quest for universality that runs through the entire history of Christianity?

Man always seeks to be in a group larger than himself, so as to strengthen and develop his life. Now, from her origins, the Church has wished to include everyone in this great community of the baptized which was willed by God. She wants to gather them into a common dignity, the same destiny. In this, the Bride of Christ magnificently echoes a quest that is inherent in man himself. This is always about a desire for enrichment by turning to the other. The Holy Spirit unites and gives rise to distinct charisms: there is diversity in this unity. The other is always a treasure offered to me by God in order to enrich my humanity and to help me to grow in my own vocation. I in turn, however poor I may be, owe it to myself to promote the riches and unique qualities of the other. I, too, am a gift—as modest as it may be—for the other. We form one human family, each one contributing his own richness, in a marvelous mosaic of cultures and traditions. There are treasures of mankind that are not empty words.

Moreover, the universal must not destroy the particular identity. Over the centuries, the Church has taken care to give a dominant place to local expressions. The finest example of this has been the specific liturgical rites, such as the Ambrosian Rite, the Lyonese Rite, or the Mozarabic Rite.

The Church is one and different at each place on earth.

Today, for many Christians, it is sometimes difficult to have confidence in the future. . . .

In Christian life doubts sometimes arise, but confidence always returns. The best synonym for the word "confidence" is the word "faith"! Indeed, confidence is the best sign that man is turned toward God. His Word cannot deceive me or lead me astray. A Christian's confidence consists of abandoning himself totally to the eternal fidelity of Christ. Today some French literature is haunted by the problem of transparency; it seems that everything has to be transparent in order for there to be sincerity. But true transparency is Christ. Confidence is born of this light of truth that is never spent. Circumstances can become difficult, winds may buffet our life, and storms may destroy our human landmarks, but Jesus remains with us always: "Blessed is the man who trusts in the LORD, whose trust is the LORD. He is like a tree planted by water, that sends out its roots by the stream, and does not fear when heat comes, for its leaves remain green" (Jer 17:7–8).

In her meditations, Saint Teresa of Avila wrote some magnificent lines on true confidence in the Son of God: "Let nothing trouble you, let nothing scare you, all is fleeting, God alone is unchanging. Patience everything obtains. Who possesses God nothing wants. God alone suffices."[2]

The nuns, by their pure, demanding way of life, show an everlasting hope in the Word of God. They possess abundantly the simple, beautiful, exemplary confidence of little children. They have confidence because God alone truly suffices for them. They know that God will not deceive them. The key to such great self-denial in everyday life is confidence, prayer, and absolute love for God. Love is a fire; this blaze inflames them with a desire that is not immediately directed toward action but, rather, toward God alone.

The entire life of nuns is dedicated to prayer. But how can prayer be defined precisely?

If man does not have a well, he cannot draw water. Similarly, without prayer, man becomes arid, because he no longer has depth or an interior life or a fountain to irrigate his soul. Prayer opens onto a limitless oasis. It does not consist fundamentally of speaking with God. Of course, it is normal that two friends should want to talk so as to get to know each other. From this perspective, Moses is a good example: he spoke with God in a sublime face-to-face conversation; the Old Testament tells us that when he emerged from these intimate dialogues, his face shone. We cannot really meet God without his light shining upon us. Through prayer we allow God to engrave on our face the splendor of his Face.

---

[2] "Efficacy of Patience", in St. Teresa of Avila, *The Collected Works*, trans. Kieran Kavanaugh, O.C.D., and Otilio Rodriguez, O.C.D., vol. 3 (Washington, D.C., ICS Publications, Institute of Carmelite Studies, 1985), 386.

In fact, prayer ultimately consists of being silent so as to listen to God, who speaks to us, and so as to hear the Holy Spirit, who speaks in us. I think it is important to say that we do not know how to pray alone and cannot do so: the Holy Spirit is the one who prays in us and for us. Saint Paul tells us: "It is the Spirit himself bearing witness with our spirit that we are children of God." He continues: "Likewise the Spirit helps us in our weakness; for we do not know how to pray as we ought, but the Spirit himself intercedes for us with sighs too deep for words" (Rom 8:16, 26).

Of course, there is no doubt that men must speak to God, but true prayer leaves God free to come to us according to his will. We must know how to wait for him in silence. It is necessary to go on in silence, in resignation, and in confidence. To pray is to be able to be quiet for a long time; we are so often deaf, distracted by our words.... Unfortunately, we cannot take it for granted that we know how to listen to the Holy Spirit who prays in us. The more we persevere in silence, the greater chance we will have of hearing God's whisper. Recall that for a long time the prophet Elijah remained hidden in a cave before hearing the soft whispering of heaven. Yes, I will say it again, prayer consists in the first place of remaining silent for a long time. We must often nestle close to the Virgin of silence to ask her to obtain for us the grace of loving silence and of interior virginity, in other words, a purity of heart and a willingness to listen that banishes any presence except God's. The Holy Spirit is in us, but we are often filled with orchestras that drown out his voice....

Prayer is a long time of desert and aridity when we want to go back to the easy joys of the world instead of waiting for God. When many thoughts distract us from God, it is important not to forget that the Holy Spirit is still present. The greatest saints themselves had doubts about their own prayer life, so severe was their dryness sometimes; Saint Thérèse of Lisieux even wondered whether she believed in the words that she recited in her daily prayers.

I think that prayer calls somehow for an absence of words, because the only language that God really hears is the silence of love. The contemplation of the saints is nourished exclusively by a face-to-face encounter with God in abandonment. There is no spiritual fruitfulness except in a virginal silence that is not mixed with too many words and interior noise. It is necessary to be able to strip oneself bare before God, without make-up. Prayer needs the honesty of a spotless soul. Virginity is the very essence of the absolute in which God keeps us.

God enveloped Moses' poverty with his ineffable light. He unbur-
dened his heart of all difficulties. Moses was stripped bare so as to hear
truly the hope offered by God. True prayer leads to a sort of disappearance of our personal clutter.

When John Paul II prayed, he was submerged in God and seized by
an invisible presence, like a rock that seemed totally foreign to what was
going on around him. Karol Wojtyła was always on his knees before
God, still, motionless, and as though dead in his silence before the majesty of his Father. In thinking of that saintly successor of Peter, I often
recall this remark by John of the Cross in the *Ascent of Mount Carmel*:
"All objects living in the soul—whether they be many or few, large or
small—must die in order that the soul enter divine union."[3]

God never communicates himself fully except to a heart that resembles the pure light of a summer morning full of beautiful promises.

I am not unaware of the fact that the body constantly draws us out of
prayer. Man consists of imagination, too, which is skillful at taking us on
long voyages far from God....

And so, for a long time I have thought that prayer can take shape only
in the night. In darkness, we are illumined only by God. Like Jacob, and
after the example of monks, it is important to learn to pray in the middle
of the night, while all creation is seeking sleep. Prayer at night plunges us
back into the darkness of the death of Jesus Christ, which we commemorate during the ceremonies of the Paschal Vigil. Then, according to
Thomas Merton in *The Sign of Jonas*, "darkness is like a font from which
we shall ascend washed and illumined, to see one another now no longer
separate but one in the Risen Christ."[4]

Through prayer, man is recreated in the immensity of God; it is a
small anticipation of eternity. Through prayer we resemble Christ, who
loved to be recollected all night: "In these days he went out to the hills
to pray; and all night he continued in prayer to God" (Lk 6:12).

To turn to another level, how would you define contemplation?

In his *Nicomachean Ethics*, Aristotle speaks about it admirably. For him,
contemplative activity is in itself the most exalted action of man on this

---

[3] *Ascent of Mount Carmel*, in *The Collected Works of St. John of the Cross*, trans. Kieran Kavanaugh, O.C.D., and Otilio Rodriguez, O.C.D. (Washington, D.C.: ICS Publications, Institute of Carmelite Studies, 1979), 99.

[4] Merton, *Sign of Jonas*, 297.

earth. Thus contemplation is the exact opposite of practical activity; by definition, it is the most important moment in human life. He explains that the wisdom of a contemplative person includes marvelous pleasures, both by its purity and by its firmness. The wise man, even when left completely alone, can still devote himself to contemplation. The greater the wisdom, the more important is the place in life occupied by contemplation. Aristotle explains that the wise man has the duty to lead other persons to contemplative activity. He anticipates the Desert Fathers and all the contemplatives who decided to devote their lives to God, who is Wisdom and the source of all wisdom. Of course, the divine realities of which Aristotle speaks are quite far from our God and Christ. The philosopher merely calls his contemporaries to lift up their minds and hearts.

Indeed, there is in man a sort of nostalgia for God's company. We have within us a profound desire and a will to be face to face with divinity. On the Christian level, contemplation is actually an intimate conversation with God in silence and solitude. It is impossible in the agitation of the world, but even more so in the distractions of interior noise. The tumults that are most difficult to contain are still our own interior storms.

With Christ, contemplation resembles the joy of two lovers who look silently at each other. I often think of the little peasant who used to come each day to the church in Ars. He remained for a long time absolutely immobile in front of the tabernacle. One day, the saintly Curé asked him, "What are you doing there, dear friend?" He replied, "I look at him, and he looks at me." The little peasant said nothing, because he had no need to speak in order to tell Christ that he loved him; in return, he had no need of any sign from the Son of God, because he knew that he was truly loved. In love, words are not necessary. The more dense the life of silence, the more alone the soul is with God. And the more virginal the soul, the more it withdraws from the agitated world.

Nevertheless, we must not think that it is possible to contemplate God only in the silence of a monastery, a church, or in the solitude of the desert. John Paul II exhorted Christians to be "contemplatives in action". In the commentary on the Gospel of John by Saint Thomas Aquinas, there is a particularly illuminating passage. Jesus turns to Andrew and John, who have asked him: "Rabbi (which means Teacher), where are you staying?" And he answers: "Come and see." Saint Thomas thus gives a mystical sense to words that actually mean that only an encounter and personal experience can enable us to know Christ. This experiential knowledge of God in us is the heart of contemplation. Christ's sacred humanity is always the way by which to arrive at God: to allow him to speak in the silence, before the Blessed Sacrament, looking at a crucifix, in the presence of a sick person who is another Christ, Christ himself. Each soul, of course, has its path. John Paul II used to say that although sometimes he felt that the time was ripe for him to ask God for things, on other occasions that was not the case.

For Saint Thomas, practically speaking, there is no contradiction between contemplation and activity. Thus a monk can brave a spiritual storm in his cell or in the monastery church and find God again after working in the fields.... Sacrifice, obedience, mortification are capable of bringing him back to the Father. Intense intellectual or manual work purifies the mind of preoccupations that make conscious union with God impossible. "Ora et labora" sums up the two paths to contemplation offered not only to monks but to all disciples of Christ.

Contemplation leads us toward the divine in an irreversible movement. The man who contemplates and encounters his Creator will never be the same again; he may fall a hundred times, sin a hundred times, deny God a hundred times, but a part of his soul has already arrived in heaven definitively.

It would be regrettable if prayer turned into long, vague chatter that led us away from authentic contemplation. Garrulous prayer does not allow the soul to hear God. This is a danger of modern life, in which silence sometimes becomes disturbing. We ceaselessly need to hear the noise of the world: today logorrhea is a sort of imperative, and silence is considered a failure....

Contemplation is a precious moment in the encounter between man and God. The battle continues, but that is the price of the superb victory.

This may be a challenge, but could you sum up in a few words the search for God of which you speak so often?

Psalm 42 says: "As a deer longs for flowing streams, so longs my soul for you, O God. My soul thirsts for God, for the living God. When shall I come and behold the face of God?" I think that these verses express the desire that is permanently in the depths of our soul; man absolutely needs God, as a newborn needs his mother.

The Father made us for himself, but our heart is anxious, divided by a dull restlessness. In fact, it is simply waiting to rest in God; he alone can satisfy us. This is why, consciously or not, we are constantly in search of the Father.

We must not be afraid of seeking him always, because God is hidden by so many events in our life, so many temptations, so many false lights that blind us; we can easily lose him.

Nevertheless, the desire for God remains engraved on the heart of man. Yes, man was created by God, for God, and God never stops drawing him. Only in God will man find the truth and happiness that he feverishly seeks. Saint Augustine spoke magnificently about this passionate attraction of man toward the city of God and, in contrast, about all the perishable charms of the earthly city.

Man wishes for what is exceptional, which is God, but he has never really encountered him. In our time of religious indifference, the search is even more vital. For temporal things are in league with eternity. Although the aridity of the era seems frightening, we must not forget that the divine source is still more present than ever. Man may search without knowing why, or he may even reject the path toward God; but his quest exists in the depths of his soul. How can we reveal this interior thirst, so as to help mankind to go beyond the veil of sensible appearances?

I think that man will never be indifferent toward God. He can try to forget him, by following fashions or by an ideological mind-set. But this timid withdrawal is merely circumstantial. In this sense, atheism does not exist. Paradoxically, the very fact of not believing is already the declaration of a repressed faith.

The Church speaks about supernatural happiness. What does this expression mean?

For theologians, beatitude consists of seeing and possessing God. On earth we do not see God; we know that he exists, but we do not see him. According to Saint Thomas, the vision of God in heaven will be immediate.

On earth, we would like to love with all our heart, but we do not succeed. Why? Because we do not see God. In heaven, our souls will be silent, perfectly docile, and transparent to the light. The soul will be immobile. Man's perpetual restlessness on earth leads him to pursue fleeting appearances. In heaven we will possess being.

The promise of a transformation and a resurrection does not cease to astonish even after more than two thousand years. It is certainly difficult to prepare on this earth for the true happiness of heaven. The only sure method is to remain united with God, who is present in our hearts. The vision of eternity is not given to us during our present life, but we have faith, which is a way of possessing in the darkness.

In this world, certainty about God's perfection has to be enough for us. Saint Augustine is said to have expressed this sentiment in a famous, paradoxical formula: "My God, if you were to offer to change places, so that I would become God and You Augustine, I would say: No! I prefer that you be God and that I be Augustine or whatever, what does it matter? You are my happiness, and not me."

Christians know that at the end of time Christ will come again in glory. According to the Bible, he will be escorted by all the angels, and all peoples will assemble before him. He will separate men as a shepherd separates the sheep from the goats. He will place some on his right, to live with him in eternity, and the rest, who have chosen their position, will remain separated from his light. The earthly city is not our true homeland; it is a transitory moment. We are born to take a great journey toward the city of God and to become "fellow citizens with the saints and members of the household of God" (Eph 2:19).

Despite this sublime destination, we are called to be God's artisans here below, so that some drops of eternity might descend even in this world. The vision of heaven cannot make us forget that we have to combat the powers of evil that search relentlessly to corrupt mankind, God's creation. The kingdom of God must begin *hic et nunc* (here and now).

On earth we have the treasure of prayer, which is the language of heaven.

In this language, all the words translate only one thought, one truth that soon invades the soul and thoroughly imbues it so as to direct and ennoble it; Christ himself proclaims this truth: I am infinite love; all that is mine I give to you so that we may be one as the Father and the Son are one (see Jn 17:22–23).

The Latin proverb says: "Soli Deo." Does this mean that God alone must always attract man?

Man must not be turned toward himself. Precisely the opposite orientation assures him of balance and life. Man must snatch himself away from himself. As long as he is locked into his ego, his own interior prison remains a veritable hell.

"God alone" is the open road by which we can escape from ourselves. Only the thought of God can give us at the same time freedom and purity and the balance between the two. Not by taking other men as our model, even the best of them, will we know what we should do, but rather by turning to God; he is the one who will show us what sacrifices are demanded of us, and he alone will give us the strength to make them, too.

When we are in darkness and no longer manage to see God, not even the idea of him, we must have a bit of courage while patiently remaining turned toward him. In those somber hours, we advance more rapidly toward the goal. The "tunnels" of faith are shortcuts to God; to become distracted then is to lose great graces. Many saints have experienced this....

If we are faithful in always directing our soul toward the divine light, we will become luminous in turn, as flowers take on a resemblance to the sun.

The normal orientation will produce order, balance, tranquility, and peace. Then, we will be on the way to sainthood, which consists of being more interested in God than in oneself and in living by his eternal beauty.

This is the spiritual testament of Mother Teresa of Calcutta, who was able to write at the end of her life: "Make every effort to walk in the presence of God, to see God in everyone you meet.... In the streets in particular, radiate the joy of belonging to God, of living with Him and being His."[5]

---

[5] Mother Teresa of Calcutta, *Love a Fruit Always in Season*, ed. Dorothy S. Hunt (San Francisco: Ignatius Press, 1987), 58.

VIII

THE MYSTERY OF INIQUITY
AND GREAT DOUBTS

Except for one's own sins, so many, many projects for the dehumanization of man are Satan's works, simply because he hates man.

—Pope Francis, Homily on Monday, September 29, 2014

NICOLAS DIAT: *What is your reaction to the scandal of pedophile priests?*

ROBERT CARDINAL SARAH: If children have been entrusted to a priest who is supposed to lead them to God, and these fragile little creatures are the object of sexual abuse, this is evil and criminal behavior and a very serious matter. Pedophilia is one of the most abominable moral deviations.

The bishops who have deliberately hidden these scandals are a small minority. Nevertheless, there is no disputing the fact that their mismanagement did great harm to the Church. However, let us not forget that many of the predatory priests or religious had devised subtle strategies to make sure that their criminal acts would remain secret. Often, unfortunately, many victims did not report these incidents because they took place in situations of terrible psychological suffering. I am quite aware of the fact that respect for the office of the priest may also have played a role in establishing a culture of silence.

During the pontificate of John Paul II, Joseph Ratzinger was very courageous in his determination not to turn a blind eye to such crimes. It is important to remember these uncompromising words of Christ: "Whoever receives one such child in my name receives me; but whoever causes one of these little ones who believe in me to sin, it would be better for him to have a great millstone fastened round his neck and to be drowned in the depth of the sea" (Mt 18:5–6). It is essential to recall that Jesus is pitiless and that he does not forgive the scandal given to children, just as he does not tolerate our lukewarm faith either: "I know your works: you are neither cold nor hot. Would that you were cold or hot! So, because you are lukewarm, and neither cold nor hot, I will spew you out of my mouth" (Rev 3:15–16).

The bishops who transferred pedophile priests from parish to parish to conceal their attacks behaved despicably. How could anyone imagine that those crimes would stop as if by magic?

This practice was used particularly in Ireland. In that country, cases of sexual abuse reached exceptional levels. The letter of Benedict XVI to Irish Catholics, published in March 2010, did not try to disguise the extent of the tragedies experienced because of betrayal by members of the clergy.

When I was archbishop of Conakry, I never had a problem with pedophilia in my diocese, and there is no disputing the fact that this scandal has not affected Africa much. On the other hand, on another level, I had to confront priests who were involved in clandestine affairs with women; the faithful were always very shocked by these excesses of their pastors. Besides, the situation of priests who lead a double life with wives and children, thus profaning the image of the high priest Jesus Christ and the grace of the priesthood, is no less serious. "Do not be deceived," Saint Paul says, "God is not mocked, for whatever a man sows, that he will also reap. For he who sows to his own flesh will from the flesh reap corruption; but he who sows to the Spirit will from the Spirit reap eternal life" (Gal 6:7–8).

Indeed, I think that many bishops were not prepared to confront such weighty problems. Furthermore, we often are unaware of the complexity of the medical treatment of pedophiles. Those in charge of certain dioceses should have consulted qualified medical personnel, which in itself presented a set of considerable difficulties.

Today, I think that the Church has addressed with great courage and true effectiveness the problem of sexual predators. It is important to understand that John Paul II truly did not know about this problem. His illness prevented him from becoming aware of the extent of the betrayal of certain men. With great lucidity, Joseph Ratzinger opened up a new path. Benedict XVI and, then, Francis adopted radical methods to kill the roots of this horror.

In many countries, the civil institutions that are supposed to address such problems could take as their inspiration the transparency of the

Church. I am not afraid to say that we acted in such a way that the procedures implemented by the Church are now a model.

What is the best way to understand the shocking statement made by Francis during the press conference on his trip to the Holy Land, comparing the acts of pedophile priests to black Masses?

The pope gave mature reflection to the full scope of such a comparison. Francis decided to make that statement because he thinks that pedophilia is a satanic act. I strongly support the Holy Father's accusation. How can a priest who has been able to attack an innocent child with such extraordinary violence then celebrate Holy Mass?

After committing such a serious sexual crime, a priest can no longer carry the consecrated Host in his hands. If he decides to continue celebrating Mass, his disrespect for the Son of God has become so great that, consciously or not, he has made a pact with the devil. A pedophile priest who says Mass commits a sacrilege.

A pedophile act ontologically affects the very being of a priest; consequently, the priestly bond that attaches him to Christ is gone. The breach is so extreme that he can no longer enter into communion with Jesus.

How can a priest reach the point of such perversion and forget the sacred, serious, and momentous words pronounced at his priestly ordination: "Receive the oblation of the holy people, to be offered to God. Understand what you do, imitate what you celebrate, and conform your life to the mystery of the Lord's cross."

Francis decided to denounce black Masses so as to flush out the devil and bring his misdeeds into the light of day. An act of pedophilia is the corruption of innocence, the denial of God's creation; the battle against divine purity is essentially the devil's delight. The body of a child is virginal, and Satan cannot tolerate that virginity.

Francis deserves our thanks and gratitude for his courage. For the devil will seek his revenge.

How does one speak without useless polemics, with complete objectivity, about the betrayal of some men of the Church?

In the seminaries, a small minority of men were able to hide the problems that put them deeply at odds with the priestly vocation. I cannot understand how they could have accepted ordination, only to find themselves afterward in a situation where they regularly profaned the sacraments.

In his pastoral letter to the Catholics of Ireland, Benedict XVI had very stern words about the priests and religious who have abused children. He wrote: "You betrayed the trust that was placed in you by innocent young people and their parents, and you must answer for it before Almighty God and before properly constituted tribunals. You have forfeited the esteem of the people of Ireland and brought shame and dishonor upon your confreres. Those of you who are priests violated the sanctity of the sacrament of Holy Orders in which Christ makes himself present in us and in our actions. Together with the immense harm done to victims, great damage has been done to the Church and to the public perception of the priesthood and religious life. I urge you to examine your conscience, take responsibility for the sins you have committed, and humbly express your sorrow. Sincere repentance opens the door to God's forgiveness and the grace of true amendment. By offering prayers and penances for those you have wronged, you should seek to atone personally for your actions. Christ's redeeming sacrifice has the power to forgive even the gravest of sins, and to bring forth good from even the most terrible evil. At the same time, God's justice summons us to give an account of our actions and to conceal nothing. Openly acknowledge your guilt, submit yourselves to the demands of justice, but do not despair of God's mercy." (7)

A man of the Church who commits such sins is lying to himself and betraying God. Christ gave him all the means to carry out his priesthood, but he preferred to make a pact with the forces of darkness. And so the grace that was given him on the day of his ordination is seriously thwarted. A seminarian is never forced to become a priest. Well, then, what possible reason could a man who experiences such lethal impulses have for choosing the path of priesthood? Some specialists in these matters think that a pedophile always gravitates toward a setting where he knows he will be able to meet children. This explanation shows the extent to which the Church must strengthen her controls so as to detect this type of individual, which is certainly a small minority.

The pedophile is guilty of a threefold betrayal, of himself, of the Church, and of the baptized people, but he is also responsible for radically challenging the teaching of Christ. The worst criminal always has the possibility of divine forgiveness, but the pedophile priest puts himself into a situation of head-on combat with the Son of God.

What lesson should we learn from the terrible story of Father Marcial Maciel, the founder of the Legionaries of Christ?

A moment ago I mentioned the problem of bishops who do not know the horrors committed by certain priests. Allow me to tell you a little personal anecdote. When I was archbishop of Conakry, I read a book by Father Maciel on the formation of seminarians and clergy. I found his analysis magnificent.... In point of fact, I was entirely unaware of his real life and his unworthy conduct. Furthermore, how could I ever have imagined that this work had not been written by him and, worse yet, that whole passages were lifted from other treatises on spirituality?

Before I came to Rome, my knowledge about that congregation was limited. Moreover, I never met Father Maciel. Later, when I worked at the Congregation for the Propagation of the Faith, I was struck by the luxuriousness of the Legion's houses of formation and spiritual centers; from that perspective, I often wondered about their ability to travel to poor mission countries.

Nevertheless, I was impressed by the significant number of priestly vocations that they generated. During a theology conference at the Pontifical Athenaeum *Regina Apostolorum*, which is run by the Legion of Christ, I had admired the good comportment of all those seminarians, who had come primarily from Latin America. They were a symbol of the new evangelization desired by John Paul II. My admiration for those young members of the Legion of Christ has never diminished. For God often lets the weeds and the good grain live together until the harvest. And we can admire their generous gift of their life and their commitment to following Christ.

Of course, there is always one burning question. How could a man as corrupt as Father Maciel fool the Roman authorities and the popes themselves for so many years? I think that the founder of the Legion of Christ betrayed the graces that heaven had given him. Little by little the devil took hold of his soul and inspired in him all the despicable acts that we know about now. I do not think it possible to suppose that that man was ever, even for a single day, in a relationship with Jesus Christ. It seems obvious that he constantly rejected the help that the Son of God could have given him.

According to the revelations that investigations of his life have brought to light, Marcial Maciel had already committed abominable acts at a very young age. His duplicity is all the more impressive since he succeeded in placing the government of the Legion at the service of all his corruption. The mystery remains, because he founded a flourishing religious family. Father Maciel instituted a work for the good of the Church while never renouncing his own sin.

Indeed, this man built up a work of God while at the same time carrying in his own person the seeds of its destruction. There certainly was a battle between good and evil; God gave much, while secret, maleficent actions never ceased to spread their diabolical poisons. While God was building a magnificent work, the devil did his utmost, in ever more hideous ways to ruin the work down to its foundations.

It must not be forgotten that the Legionaries of Christ have made an enormous contribution to the Church over the course of the last fifty years. The esteem that John Paul II had for the Legion was first of all an appreciation of its authentic missionary work.

After so many difficulties and attacks by the Evil One, I am certain that the better side will triumph. We must remember with gratitude the way in which Joseph Ratzinger was able to address with courage and lucidity such a complex problem that others pretended not to see. In many respects, Benedict XVI saved the Legion of Christ from major chaos.

What is evil, actually?

God is love and freedom. He leaves everyone free to love him or not; his love constrains no one. Evil is therefore the opposite of God, whatever is contrary to him. Saint John writes that evil is fundamentally a struggle against God. Our Father is the supreme good, and evil is in every respect what God is not.

What are the roots of evil? I think that it comes from the ability of each created being to make a free decision for good or for evil. According to revelation, evil comes from the Evil One, from Satan, who rebelled against God and tempted our "first parents" to turn away from God's will. Evil is fundamentally a rebellion against God, against good, and against love.

Paradoxically, while no one wants evil, we do not hesitate to cooperate with it. Saint Paul, who was seeking to reject evil, exclaimed (Rom

7:14–20, 24): "We know that the law is spiritual; but I am carnal, sold under sin. I do not understand my own actions. For I do not do what I want, but I do the very thing I hate. Now if I do what I do not want, I agree that the law is good. So then it is no longer I that do it, but sin which dwells within me. For I know that nothing good dwells within me, that is, in my flesh. I can will what is right, but I cannot do it. For I do not do the good I want, but the evil I do not want is what I do. Now if I do what I do not want, it is no longer I that do it, but sin which dwells within me.... Wretched man that I am! Who will deliver me from this body of death?" In the Letter to the Romans, the apostle thus describes in particularly realistic terms the struggle within every man. We are not unaware that something is forbidden; yet we sin. Indeed, the prohibition itself does not prevent sin, quite the contrary. Everything happens as though the law itself aroused the desire to transgress it.

Finally, evil can be defined by its relation to good. Without God, sin has no full meaning, because then it is impossible to appreciate in a truly certain way the nature of good or of evil. This is the tragedy of contemporary man. If man becomes a god, he plunges into a pitch-black night in which values have no meaning, since good and evil no longer exist. Mankind could thus be lost in a sort of chaos, because without a boundary between good and evil, the foundations of justice are dangerously erased.

In the divine plan, evil remains a great mystery for us. After our death, we will be able to understand many things that are difficult to accept here below.

Since the beginning of his pontificate, Francis has frequently spoken about the existence of the devil. Isn't that a rather difficult subject to understand?

Revelation teaches us with certainty about the existence of evil spirits who oppose God by refusing to serve him and who incite men to rebel against God. The devil is the one who divides, who sets men against one another.

There is no better way to understand the existence of the devil than through his works. Like all spirits, he is not visible. Moreover, Satan loves nothing so much as the darkness in which he lies; the more hidden the devil, the more effective he is.

The prince of this world can be recognized also by all the temptations into which we fall. Through the Scriptures we know that he tempted Christ. Saint Luke writes as follows: "Jesus, full of the Holy Spirit, returned from the Jordan, and was led by the Spirit for forty days in the wilderness, tempted by the devil. And he ate nothing in those days; and when they were ended, he was hungry. The devil said to him, 'If you are the Son of God, command this stone to become bread.' And Jesus answered him, 'It is written, "Man shall not live by bread alone."' And the devil took him up, and showed him all the kingdoms of the world in a moment of time, and said to him, 'To you I will give all this authority and their glory; for it has been delivered to me, and I give it to whom I will. If you, then, will worship me, it shall all be yours.' And Jesus answered him, 'It is written, "You shall worship the Lord your God, and him only shall you serve."' And he took him to Jerusalem, and set him on the pinnacle of the temple, and said to him, 'If you are the Son of God, throw yourself down from here; for it is written, "He will give his angels charge of you, to guard you," and "On their hands they will bear you up, lest you strike your foot against a stone."' And Jesus answered him, 'It is said, "You shall not tempt the Lord your God."' And when the devil had ended every temptation, he departed from him until an opportune time" (Lk 4:1–13).

I would like to quote also words by Paul VI, spoke on June 29, 1972, during a Mass at Saint Peter's Basilica. The pope did not hide his pain and anguish: "Given the situation in the Church today, we have the impression that through some cracks in the wall the smoke of Satan has entered the temple of God: it is doubt, uncertainty, questioning, dissatisfaction, confrontation. There is no confidence in the Church. Instead people put their trust in the first secular prophet who comes along to talk to us about a newspaper editorial or a social movement, and they run after him to ask him whether he has the formula for true life, ignoring the fact that we already have it, that we are the owners of that formula. Doubt has entered our consciences, and it entered through windows that should have been open to the light. Science exists to give us truths that do not separate from God, but make us seek him all the more and celebrate him with greater intensity; instead, science gives us criticism and doubt. Scholars are those who more thoughtfully and more painstakingly exert their minds. But they end up teaching us: 'I do not know, we do not know, we cannot know.' The school becomes the gymnasium of confusion and sometimes of absurd contradictions. Progress is celebrated, only so that it can then be demolished with the strangest, most radical revolutions, so as to negate everything that has been achieved and to become primitives again after having so exalted the advances of the modern world. In the Church, too, this state of uncertainty prevails; it was thought that after the Council a day of sunshine would dawn for the history of the Church. What dawned instead was a day of clouds and storms, of darkness, of searching and uncertainties. We preach ecumenism, but we constantly separate ourselves from others. We seek to dig abysses instead of filling them in. How could that have happened? There has been an intervention of an adverse power. Its name is the devil, this mysterious being to whom Saint Peter also alludes in his Letter. How many times Christ speaks to us in the Gospel about this enemy of men! We believe in the action of Satan, who is active today in the world precisely to disturb, to suffocate the fruits of the Ecumenical Council, and to prevent the Church from breaking into the hymn of joy at having renewed in fullness her awareness of herself. This is why we wish, today more than ever, to be able to perform the duty entrusted by God to Peter, to strengthen our brothers in the faith. We wish to communicate to you this charism of certitude that the Lord gives to the one who represents him on this earth, however unworthily. Faith gives us certitude, assurance, when it is based on the Word of God and is accepted and acknowledged as being in conformity with our reason and our human soul."

Saint John Vianney rightly said that "the Holy Spirit dispels the mists that the devil puts ahead of us to make us lose the way to heaven."

And so it is important for dioceses to have well-trained priest exorcists, imbued with sanctity and protected by Mary's virginal mantle. The manifestations of the devil are very significant and widespread today. Under his influence, yesterday's sins have become virtues. The devil is finally celebrating because he is making substantial gains. We must not have any doubt, however, because the definitive victory will be for God alone. Saint Matthew records these magnificent words that Christ spoke to Peter: "And I tell you, you are Peter, and on this rock I will build my Church, and the gates of Hades shall not prevail against it" (Mt 16:18).

God promised us victory over the forces of evil. Our hope must remain strong.

"In every man, at every hour, there are two solicitations, one toward God, the other toward Satan. The call toward God or spirituality is a desire to ascend in rank; the one toward Satan or animal instincts is a joy to descend." Does this

reflection by Charles Baudelaire in Les Fleurs du mal *(The flowers of evil) seem enlightening to you?*

That great poet agrees with the remarks of Saint Paul about the difficulty of doing good. Remember that the apostle said: "I delight in the law of God, in my inmost self, but I see in my members another law at war with the law of my mind and making me captive to the law of sin which dwells in my members" (Rom 7:22–23). In man there is a nostalgia for God, a connatural attachment and an aspiration to go toward the Father. However, man still has two sides; he is divided between his search for the good and the power of darkness. Every day the devil seeks to trap us in the nets of temptation. Man looks toward heaven, but the heaviness of the devil attracts him incessantly. From this perspective, prayer, supplemented by penance, is an act of resistance, a sign of not submitting to the prince of this world. I think that the Christian philosopher Simone Weil was right when she said in her book *Gravity and Grace*: "Creation: good broken up into pieces and scattered throughout evil. Evil is limitless, but it is not infinite. Only the infinite limits the limitless." This reflection states the truth of our earthly condition. In the same way, she fittingly concluded with this promise about the outcome of our combat: "To say that the world is not worth anything, that this life is of no value, and to give evil as the proof is absurd, for if these things are worthless what does evil take from us?"[1]

In the history of mankind, God promised us that evil would not have the last word. Through the tribulations of this great struggle, we need to know that we are not alone. Without the help of grace, we are lost children; man is a vine that seeks to climb toward the sun, but it needs a firm tree. For mankind, the Church is that tree; and for the Church, this tree around which to wind, in order to make her children climb to heaven, is Christ.

In the final analysis, does hell exist, or is this just an old-fashioned fable to frighten people?

Hell denotes a definitive separation between God and man. But God never sends someone to hell; damnation is the result of a free choice.

[1] Simone Weil, *Gravity and Grace*, trans. Emma Crawford and Mario von der Ruhr (1952; London and New York: Routledge Classics, 2002), 69, 84.

Thus, hell exists through an unshakeable will to cut oneself off from God.

However, although no one seeks suffering, the decision not to acknowledge God results in unavoidable consequences. Separation from the Father is a serious act, because man cuts himself off from God, whose son he is. Hell is the opposite of flourishing in God. This suffering is compared to a burning fire because there is nothing more terrible than to kill one's parents, to make them disappear definitively from one's heart and from one's sight.

Today hell is a problem that has been completely erased from approved thought; Satan has even become a sort of purely fictional character. Hence the devil rejoices, because his acts are forgotten and hidden.

Nevertheless, the visions of hell granted to the great saints of the Church are terrifying. I would like to cite the words of Saint Mark, which are particularly clear: "If your hand causes you to sin, cut it off; it is better for you to enter life maimed than with two hands to go to hell, to the unquenchable fire. And if your foot causes you to sin, cut it off; it is better for you to enter life lame than with two feet to be thrown into hell. And if your eye causes you to sin, pluck it out; it is better for you to enter the kingdom of God with one eye than with two eyes to be thrown into hell, where the worm does not die, and the fire is not quenched. For every one will be salted with fire" (Mk 9:43–49).

Hell is a reality, not an idea. The depictions of the Last Judgment over the entrances to cathedrals are explicit. Certainly, in the West, we have insolently dismissed the question of hell. But in Africa, we believe in the harmfulness of the forces of evil. It would never occur to anyone to deny their existence, their misdeeds, and their methods.

Even today, the devil's shrewdest trick is to make people believe that he does not exist. However, Pope Francis has not been afraid to talk about Satan from his first Mass after his election to the See of Peter, when he declared: "When we do not profess Jesus Christ, the saying of Léon Bloy comes to mind: 'Anyone who does not pray to the Lord prays to the devil.' When we do not profess Jesus Christ, we profess the worldliness of the devil, a demonic worldliness."

In the Gospel, Christ says explicitly that it is possible to drive out the devil only by prayer and fasting. The Church cannot remain silent about such a powerful teaching.

How is purgatory defined?

I am not unaware of the fact that this notion is very difficult to understand. Some saints have said a lot about this question, for example, Catherine of Siena, who wrote: "If miserable men had any idea of what purgatory and hell are, they would prefer to die ten times than to endure such tortures for a single day." Likewise, Saint Augustine did not hesitate to address this subject in his sermons: "The apostle says: 'He will be saved as though through fire. . . .' We think little of this fire because of the words 'he will be saved'. It is certain, however, that this saving fire will be more terrible than all the sufferings that a man could endure in this life."

Who is telling the truth? Saint Augustine or we ourselves, who think more or less vaguely that purgatory is an outmoded notion of no interest at all?

Indeed, I would like to start from my animist African roots. Among my pagan ancestors, when a man died of an abrupt illness or in a tragic accident, the body was interrogated. They asked the deceased directly what caused his sudden death.

For example, I remember very clearly a pagan man, originally from a neighboring village, who had died in Ourous as the result of very serious burns. In order to enter his house, the funeral procession would have had to cross a river. But customs forbid crossing a river with a dead body. He was therefore buried not far from Ourous, in the bush. At the time of the funeral ceremonies, I saw those who were carrying his body go forward and then back, only to go suddenly to the right and to the left. I asked my mother the reasons for these strange movements. She explained to me that it was necessary to ask the dead man, who answered by the signs of the movements that he gave to the pallbearers. . . . I was very doubtful, but Mama repeated that the power of the dead man was the explanation for these gestures. I remember that the master of ceremonies posed a wide variety of questions to the deceased: the quality of his relationship with his wife, how well he observed customs, his honesty at work, or his respect for his ancestors. Indeed, animists believe that the soul goes wandering in misery and suffering, compelled to do humiliating servile tasks, until it is washed of all its earthly faults. Then, after this period of purification, it will be able to return to the village of the ancestors, which is the equivalent of paradise. Without this ritual, which is the moment of truth, the soul is liable to languish in boredom, isolated, without ties to his brethren. When the soul wanders, it can upset the peace of mind of the living and trouble their business; sacrifices and libations at the foot of sacred pillars are designed to help these souls to return to the village of the ancestors.

In many primitive religions, purgatory is a moment of wandering before "paradise", which man can experience if his soul is purified according to the traditional rules. Animists did not know revelation for many centuries, but they did have the natural insight into the necessity of a place of transition.

Saint Augustine grew up in a pagan culture, then made the decision to convert to Christianity. His vision of purgatory is therefore particularly interesting. In various passages in his works he explains this belief in more detail. He seems to have had great influence, especially on two points. On the one hand, Augustine fixes the time of the trial of purgatory in the next world: it takes place between the individual judgment, after the death of each man, and the collective judgment or Last Judgment at the end of time. On the other hand, he emphasizes that this trial that necessarily leads to paradise must not be imagined as an easy salvation, because it is very formidable.

For Christians, paradise is the place where men will live in perfect communion with God. It is not possible to reach that light as long as our soul bears the stains of its earthly sins. Purgatory is therefore a time of purification, a moment of preparation for the great journey to God. As during long boat trips, it is a sort of quarantine for sick souls.

We cannot approach God without having a soul that is completely purified; we must be completely refined by the fire of his love. In order to enter into the light of the Father, it is necessary to be irradiated.

Saint Thérèse of Lisieux wrote astonishing things about purgatory: "Listen, this is how great your confidence should be! It should make you believe that purgatory is not made for you, but only for the souls that failed to recognize God's merciful love or who doubted its power to purify. With those who strive to respond to this love, Jesus is 'blind' and 'does not count' [their sins], or rather, in order to purify them, he counts only on this fire of charity that 'covers all faults' and, especially, on the fruits of his perpetual Sacrifice. Yes, despite your little infidelities, you can hope to go straight to heaven, because the good Lord desires it even more than you do, and he will surely give you what you have hoped to receive of his mercy. Your confidence and your resignation are what he will reward; his justice, which knows your frailty, has been divinely arranged so as to achieve this. As you rely on this assurance, just make sure even more that he does not lose any love!"

Unquestionably, modern Western rationalism has great difficulty in understanding the reality of purgatory. In discussing such a topic, we can see the distance there can be between certain societies and the religious sphere. They can see only fairy tales in it.

Fundamentally, the man who does not want to understand purgatory is no longer able to know who God is. If God is love, then that love burns absolutely and immeasurably. When Moses meets God, he sees a burning fire from which comes a voice that says to him: "I am who am." The voice tells him not to come too near and to remove his dusty sandals.

We cannot approach God like romantics taking a stroll, seeking nice emotions in an English garden.... God demands that we be purified of all the disorderly states that weigh down our heart and darken our soul.

The saints are immediately in the joy of heaven. But for most human beings, purgatory is a difficult, arid antechamber on the way to our Creator, who wants to forgive our temporal faults. God does not render justice in a spirit of vengeance; his measure is not that of men. And so purgatory is a renewal of man. The old man goes away, and the new man comes into the purifying tenderness of God.

Purgatory, therefore, is born of divine love. It is a purifying fire that some identify with God himself.

Why do we sometimes have the feeling that God has fallen asleep?

To answer your question, I would like to quote first the words of Benedict XVI during his last Wednesday audience on February 27, 2013: "Eight years [after accepting the Petrine ministry] I can say that the Lord has truly led me, he has been close to me, I have been able to perceive his presence daily. It has been a portion of the Church's journey which has had its moments of joy and light, but also moments which were not easy; I have felt like Saint Peter with the Apostles in the boat on the Sea of Galilee: the Lord has given us so many days of sun and of light winds, days when the catch was abundant; there were also moments when the waters were rough and the winds against us, as throughout the Church's history, and the Lord seemed to be sleeping. But I have always known that the Lord is in that boat, and I have always known that the barque of the Church is not mine but his. Nor does the Lord let it sink; it is he who guides it, surely also through those whom he has chosen, because he so wished. This has been, and is, a certainty which nothing can shake. For this reason my heart today overflows with gratitude to God, for he has never let his Church, or me personally, lack his consolation, his light, his love."

We often ask this question about the absence of God when we look at the massive presence of evil in our world. When I traveled to the worst disaster sites on earth, to the Philippines after the typhoon or to Jordan in the camps for refugees from the war in Syria, it was not unthinkable to wonder where the Lord really was. If I consider the persecuted, hunted-down Christians who were driven from their homes, forced into exile with no belongings at all, abandoned and humiliated everywhere in the world, I know that despair is quite understandable. As in the Old Testament, we would like God to strike and destroy our enemies. Why does he not answer in such tragic moments?

And yet, day and night the anguished cries of our voices reach his ears: "For your sake we are slain all the day long, and accounted as sheep for the slaughter. Rouse yourself! Why do you sleep, O Lord? Awake! Do not cast us off for ever! Why do you hide your face? Why do you forget our affliction and oppression? ... Rise up, come to our help! Deliver us for the sake of your merciful love" (Ps 44:22–24, 26).

The words of Christ on the Cross echo our doubts precisely. At that time he asked his Father: "Lord, why have you abandoned me?" But Jesus' cry is an act of unfailing confidence, to tell God that he relies on him alone. This is not a cry of rebellion, but a filial lament. Today too, when we are lost, like the witnesses of the crucifixion, our doubt is still a hope. If we call out to God, it is because we have confidence. Christian doubt is not a moment of despair but another declaration of love.

God is not asleep; he is present despite our searching, which is sometimes too exclusively rational. We are like weeping children who do not understand that our Father remains at our sides forever.

The greatest saints, like Saint Thérèse of Lisieux or Mother Teresa of Calcutta, experienced trials of faith in which they felt abandoned. ...

Yes, Saint Thérèse had very painful experiences. When she was at the Carmel, it happened that she doubted the very existence of Jesus, the savior of mankind. She experienced terrible moments, dark nights in which God seemed strangely silent. Nevertheless, Thérèse always knew that she was not alone, that the light would finally appear at the end of the tunnel. She knew that God would not leave her indefinitely in darkness. All the saints experienced moments of great doubts. This feeling of abandonment resembles what went through the Heart of Jesus on the Cross: Golgotha alone is the summary of all our dark nights.

Doubt is a moment of purification and strengthening. Hence, just one question arises: Do we still believe when the night remains desperately dark? Do we keep hoping even beyond the easy times? Faith is trust or else it does not exist.

Mother Teresa regarded doubt as a way to discover God's true face. It is not possible to understand God in abundance and easy blessings. After her rebellion against the trials of poverty that she was experiencing every day, she understood that God never comes to console us for our little despairs or our selfish rebellions. God is absolute love; therefore he can reveal himself only in love.

As I traveled so often to battlefronts, to places of famines or earthquakes, I kept thinking, together with Thérèse of Lisieux, that the little voice of unfailing confidence in divine love was the only possible way.

Yes, we must believe, despite the horrible suffering and violence connected with human folly. Faced with so much pain, we have two options. Rebellion, which will always cause additional difficulties, and love, which will lead us closer to God.

Mother Teresa saw the worst atrocities. But she also understood that suffering could bring about new solidarity, unheard-of blessings, indomitable hope.

Incidentally, we often blame God for many evils without admitting our own responsibility.... Without God, the world would be a lasting hell. With God, there is grace; it is the tenderness and the caress of heaven.

How can we continue to believe, "despite the despites", as Saint Josemaría [Escrivá], the founder of Opus Dei, put it?

The Church must always remember the reality of our divine adoption. Thanks to it, we experience the joy and the peace that come from God, and even our weaknesses do not depress us.

We must never forget the moment of Jesus' death. Despair seemed to cover everything, and the darkness surpassed the light. The apostles were overwhelmed. Despite this enormous tragedy, the women did not renounce their faith. Mary and Mary Magdalen, the sinner from whom Jesus had expelled seven demons, wanted to take care of Jesus' body and make sure that he had a dignified burial. They could not believe that evil had conquered the Son of God. Mary remained present even after his death because her faith was a rock that no tide could sweep away; she went beyond what is humanly possible.

Today, too, we can get over the disappointments that we feel with regard to the Church or about any other human or Christian matter if we remain in union with God through prayer. We must continue to have absolute trust that we are not alone. Without God, we can do nothing.

Despite sufferings, despite failure, despite evil, our victory is our faith. Saint John writes: "This is the victory that overcomes the world, our faith. Who is it that overcomes the world but he who believes that Jesus is the Son of God?" (1 Jn 5:4–5).

Sometimes the relentless attacks against the words of the pope, against the teaching of the Church, or against morality can cause us to think that evil has won the battle. Some obscure philosophical forces wish to impose silence on the Church so as to govern the world more easily according to its selfish, mercenary, and cruel principles. We must not let down our guard against the noise that would like to annihilate man's whole interior life by brutalizing him with images and news that are veritable drugs.

It is necessary to believe in spite of everything, because that is our vocation as Christians. We must believe in the future of the Church, which has overcome many crises. We must believe that the victor is still Christ. We must believe with great and loving patience.

Once again, I turn to Saint Augustine, who speaks marvelously about our human condition: "He who wants to find in himself the cause of his joy will be sad, but he who wants to find in God the cause of his joy will always be joyful, because God is eternal. Do you want to have eternal joy? Cling to the One who is eternal."

IX

EVANGELII GAUDIUM, THE JOY OF THE GOSPEL ACCORDING TO POPE FRANCIS

Even God could do nothing for someone already full. You have to be completely empty to let Him in to do what He will.

—Mother Teresa of Calcutta

NICOLAS DIAT: *Following Paul VI, Francis likes to speak, in his first apostolic exhortation* Evangelii gaudium, *about the sweet, comforting joy of evangelizing.*

ROBERT CARDINAL SARAH: When a man communicates some good, it comes from his heart, like a source of water that spreads all around him. The good increases, the more he gives it. On the other hand, it is weakened if he refuses to share it.

The renewal of the faith and of Christian life exists only in mission. And this is a gift from God, who enlists us in his work of salvation. If the faith is communicated generously, it is strengthened because "one bears witness to the faith by handing it on", as John Paul II often said, following Saint Augustine. Once the Gospel is spread to the four corners of the world, the Word of God shines like the rays of the sun to enlighten us so that we might reject the deeds of darkness. Joy abounds as much in the hearts of the heralds of the Gospel as it does in the hearts of all who open the doors of their life to Christ.

Unfortunately, the number of those who do not know Christ and do not belong to the Church is growing continually. It has almost doubled since the end of the Council. With regard to this immense crowd of people whom the Father loves and for whom he sent his only Son Jesus Christ, the urgency of missionary activity is obvious. The blessing of seeing the Church grow should be a central concern for every baptized person. Whenever the joy of evangelization is not the heart of Christian life, we can only deplore a worrisome symptom of spiritual dryness. The only authentic Christian flourishing lies in the offering and gift of self for the cause of the Gospel. For there is more joy in giving than in receiving: giving Jesus and his Gospel, calling the attention of all mankind to the mystery of Christ expands the heart of every Christian. Christ's message does not belong to us; it exists in order to be offered to all mankind. To be fair, we must note also that the absolute number of baptized people in the world continually increases, and in certain countries the proportion of Catholics is even growing.

There are different levels in evangelization. We do not have to respond to the same thirst when strengthening the faith of baptized Catholics who have wandered from the Church as when the challenge consists of speaking about Christ for the first time to persons who do not know him at all.

Francis recalls that evangelization is part of the mandate that Christ has given to us. In his apostolic exhortation, he cites two important statements of Saint Paul: "The love of Christ urges us on" (2 Cor 5:14) and "Woe to me if I do not proclaim the Gospel!" (1 Cor 9:16). But the pope also explains that "in this regard, several sayings of Saint Paul will not surprise us" (EG 9). There are unquestionably countries where the words of the Apostle of the Gentiles are scarcely understood....

What exactly is meant by Christian joy?

It is important to recall that Christian joy has never resembled an effortless happiness, as on a path where we fly from one victory to the next. I do not want to forget the words of Saint Peter: "For we did not follow cleverly devised myths when we made known to you the power and coming of our Lord Jesus Christ, but we were eyewitnesses of his majesty" (2 Pet 1:16). As for the Apostle of the Gentiles, he considers evangelization a demanding duty. In fact, Paul often presents his ministry in terms of combat, sufferings, and trials. Adherence to Christ always involves great joy, but also a communion in the mystery of his Passion, death, and Resurrection: "Now I rejoice in my sufferings for your sake, and in my flesh I complete what is lacking in Christ's afflictions for the sake of his body, that is, the Church, of which I became a minister according to the divine office which was given to me for you, to make the word of God fully known" (Col 1:24–25). The Word of God very often causes him to be "in toil and hardship, through many a sleepless night, in hunger and thirst, often without food, in cold and exposure. And, apart from other things, there is the daily pressure upon me of my anxiety for all the churches" (2 Cor 11:27–28).

And so Francis, taking Paul VI as his inspiration, writes: "An evangelizer must never look like someone who has just come back from a funeral! Let us recover and deepen our enthusiasm, that 'delightful and comforting joy of evangelizing, even when it is in tears that we must sow.... And may the world of our time, which is searching, sometimes with anguish, sometimes with hope, be enabled to receive the good news not from evangelizers who are dejected, discouraged, impatient, or anxious, but from ministers of the Gospel whose lives glow with fervor, who have first received the joy of Christ'" (EG 10, citing *Evangelii nuntiandi* 75).

Moreover, it is important to recall that the Second Vatican Council marked a turning point in the concept of mission. During a colloquium organized by the Catholic Institute of Higher Studies of the Diocese of Luçon, in March 2013, on the topic of "The Fiftieth Anniversary of Vatican Council II, a Hermeneutic of Continuity", I tried to emphasize that Vatican II was the first reflection on mission within the framework of an ecumenical council. The work had begun at Vatican I, but it was not brought to completion. In the decree *Ad gentes* on the missionary activity of the Church, there is a change of perspective through the statement that the foundation of this mission is found not solely in the mandate from Jesus, but in the Trinity: "The pilgrim Church is missionary by her very nature, since it is from the mission of the Son and the mission of Holy Spirit that she draws her origin, in accordance with the decree of God the Father" (AG 2).

If we do not clearly establish the basis for the missionary mandate in the Trinity, there is a risk of reducing the missions to multiple activities of a social nature, to projects for economic development or progress, to political involvement to promote the liberation of oppressed peoples, or to a mere struggle against exclusion. Good things, all of them, and sometimes necessary, but they are distinct from the mission that Jesus entrusted to his disciples. To be a missionary, indeed, does not mean giving things but communicating the foundation of the trinitarian life: the love of the Father, of the Son, and of the Holy Spirit. To be a missionary is to lead people toward a personal experience of the immeasurable love that unites the Father, the Son, and the Holy Spirit so as to allow oneself to be seized at the same time by the ardent furnace of love that manifested itself so sublimely on the Cross. To be a missionary is to help others to become true disciples of Jesus, to experience a profound friendship with Jesus, and to become one and the same being with Jesus (Rom 6:5).

And so, what happens between Jesus and his disciples is by analogy exactly what happens between the fire and the iron: there really is between Christ and his disciples an ineffable communion of life, of love, of reciprocal knowledge, a union so close that Jesus acts in them and consumes them as though in a blaze. Through the image of iron and fire, which we find in her last manuscript, Saint Thérèse of the Child Jesus perceived this symbolic dimension of the depths of the bonds of love between Jesus and those whom he loves. Fire alone has the power to penetrate iron, to imbue it with its own burning substance, to transform it into itself, to make it incandescent so that the iron seems to be identified with the fire and to become one with it. The disciple who is united to Jesus and plunges into the blaze of his pierced Heart can be compared to the burning log that dries out and eliminates all its impurities before being transformed into fire. Missionary work consists not only of communicating a message but also of helping people to encounter Christ and to have an intimate experience of his love.

At the origin of Saint Paul's conversion there is a discovery: despite his wanderings, Jesus loved him and gave himself up for him, he says to the Galatians. Paul knew that he was a great sinner, but he became aware that God loved him despite his sins. Hence, he understood that nothing was more important than to reveal to the pagans the love of God. For the rest of his life he would meditate on the decisive event on the road to Damascus, in which he experienced God's merciful love for him personally.

The source of mission is summed up by Saint John: "That ... which we have heard, which we have seen with our eyes, which we have looked upon and touched with our hands, concerning the Word of life ..., we proclaim also to you, so that you may have fellowship with us; and our fellowship is with the Father and with his Son Jesus Christ. And we are writing this that our joy may be complete" (1 Jn 1:1, 3–4).

Francis insists, moreover, on the necessary "missionary transformation of the Church". This challenge was the focus of your work at the Congregation for the Evangelization of Peoples, was it not?

The pope thinks that the Church must make an effort to set out for the missions beyond her traditional frontiers, so as to concentrate one part of her work on places and persons that she might tend to neglect. In the Old Testament, Abraham, Moses, and Jeremiah set out on journeys at God's command. The apostles themselves never ceased to be astonished at the roads that Christ followed. Thus the Holy Father can write: "Evangelization takes place in obedience to the missionary mandate of Jesus: 'Go therefore and make disciples of all nations, baptizing them in the name of the Father and of the Son and of the Holy Spirit, teaching them to observe all that I have commanded you' (Mt 28:19–20). In these verses we see how the risen Christ sent his followers to preach the Gospel in every time and place, so that faith in him might spread to every corner of the earth" (EG 19).

The incentive to go out of oneself in order to evangelize is a short summary of what it means to be Christian. We cannot help radiating our joy in speaking about God to people who do not know him. The Church is in the first place a community of missionary disciples. The peripheries about which the pope speaks call us to make a commitment with regard to Christ and his sacrifice on the Cross. I adopt as my own these forceful words: "God's word is unpredictable in its power. The Gospel speaks of a seed which, once sown, grows by itself, even as the farmer sleeps (Mk 4:26–29). The Church has to accept this unruly freedom of the word, which accomplishes what it wills in ways that surpass our calculations and ways of thinking. The Church's closeness to Jesus is part of a common journey; 'communion and mission are profoundly interconnected'", Francis reminds us (EG 22–23).

The missionary transformation of the Church is not a human way but, rather, a call by the Holy Spirit who lights our paths like a burning torch that shines in the darkness of this world.

It was a privilege for me to work for nine years in the service of evangelization, and I was able to observe with joy the fine, rapid growth of the young Churches of the mission countries in Africa and Asia as well as in Oceania.

In this same apostolic exhortation, the pope often mentions the idolatry of money that runs through the history of mankind but that has seemed to reach distressing levels in recent years. How do you react to his reflection?

Francis considers it important to recall that "the culture of prosperity deadens us; we are thrilled if the market offers us something new to purchase. In the meantime all those lives stunted for lack of opportunity seem a mere spectacle; they fail to move us. One cause of this situation is found in our relationship with money, since we calmly accept its dominion over ourselves and our societies" (EG 54–55).

Christ himself possessed nothing and unceasingly denounced worship of the golden calf as well as the vendors in the Temple. The missionary must be the enemy of easy money, for which he has little use in carrying out his work. Of course some financial means are necessary for day-to-day life. But the privileged instrument of mission work is still grace.

From her origins, the Church has always fought so that money might be at the service of man. I am extremely shocked to see how often industrial and financial groups exploit in Africa, with no moral principles whatsoever, the natural resources of countries where people live in dire poverty. They do not care at all about the misery of the populations. The Church's social doctrine, however, has always maintained that justice applies to all phases of economic activity, because it always concerns man and his needs. The discovery of resources, financing, production, consumption, and the other phases of the economic cycle inevitably have moral implications. And so every economic decision has consequences of a moral character and involves the demands of justice.

The pope wished to denounce once again the cynicism of materialistic societies that reduce the human being to one function—consumption—and try to limit man's spiritual development by all the means of domination in their possession. The powers that rely on money inaugurate the reign of a horizontal world in which transcendence is denied, disparaged, or ridiculed.

A society that takes material development as its only guide inevitably drifts toward slavery and oppression. Man is not born to manage his bank account; he is born to find God and to love his neighbor.

Francis criticizes the sterility of egotism. What in particular does he mean by his denunciation of selfish acedia?

Acedia is a sickness of the soul that is expressed in boredom, distaste for prayer, slackening or abandoning one's penitential practices, neglecting the heart, and indifference toward the sacraments. These symptoms are often a passing trial, but acedia can also lead to genuine spiritual torpor.

In moral theology, acedia is one of the seven capital sins.

Francis has all the more reason to be alarmed by a problem that is so serious that it is reaching worrisome levels in the West. On this point, his speech to the European Parliament in Strasbourg, in November 2014, was particularly clear.

What other explanation is there for the collapse of the Church's missionary efforts, if not the self-centeredness and complacency of our hearts? Christians have the vocation to become the salt and light of the world. Nowhere in the Gospel is it written that we were supposed to keep the Word of God for our own petty personal convenience. Selfish flight and a lack of generosity often conceal a lack of maturity and a very impoverished vision of human nature.

It is unthinkable that a Christian would not agree to become involved in a work of transmitting the faith. Francis often vehemently lectures the priests and religious who have become functionaries of the faith, in a rigid form of withdrawing from their identity as priests. No doubt, the priest who builds for himself a comfortable, secure world runs the risk of no longer responding even to the call of his priesthood. The pope asks everyone to set out into the deep so as to embark on the missionary adventure, which means taking risks for the sake of others and being bold for God. The missionary wake-up call will blow open the offices in which the lukewarm or bureaucratic priest may shut himself. A priest who is stingy with the time he spends on his flock is going through a real spiritual storm.

In the same way, personally, I bitterly denounce those priests who, ultimately, are responding only to a desire for human success, for power and personal ambition, for recognition in politics and the media. The cleric is here on this earth to speak about God, to serve God, and nothing else. Fear, feverish activity, and vanity remain the fierce enemies of men who have given their lives to God.

Similarly, the pope is not afraid to say that the greatest threat is " 'the gray pragmatism of the daily life of the Church, in which all appears to proceed normally, while in reality faith is wearing down and degenerating into small-mindedness.' A tomb psychology thus develops and slowly transforms Christians into mummies in a museum. Disillusioned with reality, with the Church, and with themselves, they experience a constant temptation to cling to a faint melancholy, lacking in hope, which seizes the heart like 'the most precious of the devil's potions'. Called to radiate light and communicate life, in the end they are caught up in things that generate only darkness and inner weariness, and slowly consume all zeal for the apostolate. For all this, I repeat: Let us not allow ourselves to be robbed of the joy of evangelization!" (EG 83).

With the same energy, Francis criticizes and rejects what he calls "sterile pessimism". . . .

Francis insistently mentions this because he is unwilling to let believers be hemmed in by the difficulties of everyday situations. The pope does not want Christ's disciples to be prisoners of conflicts, disagreements, and mutual hatreds. These days the Church is no doubt going through many storms, but she has survived even worse spiritual or temporal tragedies. It is important for baptized Catholics to keep the beautiful, holy joy of little children. Pessimism brings forth sterility and destruction, whereas hope proceeds from the Holy Spirit. Everyday problems, as weighty as they may be, must not become excuses for restraining our missionary involvement. Christ himself went through very severe trials. The difficulty of the moment can be transformed into strength, and it points to the horizon that will allow us to grow.

It is necessary to keep the faith perspective. Doubt is not Christian. The apostles faced multiple uncertainties, and they understood that they had to go forward without turning back. Christians are called to abandon themselves into the hands of God, who is the true teacher of evangelization.

We will always be fragile, inept instruments; but we must stay the course of hope in God. He urged his people to leave Egypt so as to set out for the Promised Land. In the desert, some wanted to go back, out of nostalgia for "the fish, the cucumbers and the onions", and especially out of fear of crossing through large spaces that were so inhospitable, but

Moses encouraged his brethren not to doubt God and to keep the faith. In difficulties, the example of courageous, intrepid missionaries is still indispensable. How can a priest forget that the ultimate priestly ambition is the salvation of all men?

Francis uses a particularly appropriate image when he calls on Christians to be "living sources of water from which others can drink" (EG 86): "'Behold, the days are coming,' says the Lord GOD, 'when I will send a famine on the land; not a famine of bread, nor a thirst for water, but of hearing the words of the LORD'" (Amos 8:11). "There is nothing corporeal about this hunger; nothing earthly about this thirst", Saint Leo the Great comments. The pope is right to recall that being a vessel can turn into a heavy cross; but let us not forget that it was precisely on the Cross that the Lord gave himself to us as a source of living water. Indeed, from the Heart of Jesus flowed torrents of love to irrigate a world parched by hatred, violence, suspicions, and wars....

The Holy Father rejects the pitfall of pessimism and invites all to envisage the future in a positive way, does he not?

In his apostolic exhortation, Francis decided to quote the address of John XXIII at the opening of the Council. Good Pope John, by his character and experience, always looked at the human scene with optimism. He spoke as follows in his characteristic tone of voice: "At times we have to listen ... to the voices of people who, though burning with zeal, lack a sense of discretion and measure. In this modern age they can see nothing but prevarication and ruin.... We feel that we must disagree with those prophets of doom who are always forecasting disaster, as though the end of the world were at hand. In our times, divine Providence is leading us to a new order of human relations which, by human effort and even beyond all expectations, are directed to the fulfillment of God's superior and inscrutable designs, in which everything, even human setbacks, leads to the greater good of the Church" (quoted in EG 84).

Nevertheless, being optimistic does not prevent us from being clear-sighted. Benedict XVI was a master of lucidity. I am thinking in particular of the words of that great pope at the end of his pontificate, in October 2012, concerning the fiftieth anniversary of the opening of the Council: "We are also happy today, we hold joy in our hearts but

I would say it is perhaps a more measured joy, a humble joy. In these fifty years we have learned and experienced that original sin exists and that it can be evermore expressed as personal sins which can become structures of sin. We have seen that in the field of the Lord there are always tares. We have seen that even in Peter's net there were bad fish. We have seen that human frailty is present in the Church, that the barque of the Church is even sailing against the wind in storms that threaten the ship, and at times we have thought: 'the Lord is asleep and has forgotten us'. These are some of the experiences of the past fifty years, but we have also had a new experience of the Lord's presence, of his goodness and of his strength. The fire of the Holy Spirit, the fire of Christ, is not a voracious, destructive fire; it is a silent fire, a small flame of goodness and of truth that transforms, that gives light and warmth. We have seen that the Lord does not forget us. Even today in his humble way the Lord is present and warms our hearts, he shows life, creates charisms of goodness and charity that illuminate the world and are a guarantee for us of God's goodness. Yes, Christ is alive, he is with us even today, and we can be happy today too because his goodness will not be extinguished; it is still strong today!" This explains why Benedict XVI spoke so much about Christian joy and why his face was illuminated by a tender, profound smile marked with kindness.

In a similar way, Francis keeps questioning attitudes of "spiritual worldliness". This last theme seems to be at the heart of your own reflection.

The pope shows true courage when he speaks in these words. For in the Church, more particularly in her government, there can be persons who indulge in worldly behavior and habits.

Spiritual worldliness hides behind religious, spiritual appearances, but nevertheless it is a veritable denial of Christ. The Son of God came to bring salvation to mankind, not a few brief pleasures in lounges decorated with beautiful crimson velvet. A priest who seeks material well-being, worldly comfort, or his own glory instead of Christ's is working for the devil. A priest who uses the appearances of his priesthood to enjoy more fully the pleasures of this world is a renegade. A priest who forgets that true power comes from God alone breaks the promises that he made at his ordination.

In many respects, the various forms of spiritual worldliness almost fall into a form of Pelagianism. The worldly cleric, indeed, relies on his own strength and his freedom, while setting aside the authentic power of grace.

In fact, worldliness is the most perverse enemy of the missionary spirit; it can go so far as to be a formidable subversion of it.

The priest is servant, he is not a god; the priest does not command troops, he leads his flock to God by his example. The priesthood is not a quest for glory or any sort of human prestige, because it derives its strength from God alone: "Non nobis Domine, non nobis: sed nomini tuo da gloriam" (Not to us, O LORD, not to us, but to your name give glory) (Ps 115:1).

Benedict XVI had understood perfectly the extent of this problem. During an address in Freiburg im Breisgau on September 25, 2011, he declared: "In order to accomplish her true task adequately, the Church must constantly renew the effort to detach herself from her tendency towards worldliness and once again to become open towards God. In this she follows the words of Jesus: 'They are not of the world, even as I am not of the world' (Jn 17:16), and in precisely this way he gives himself to the world. One could almost say that history comes to the aid of the Church here through the various periods of secularization, which have contributed significantly to her purification and inner reform. Secularizing trends—whether by expropriation of Church goods, or elimination of privileges or the like—have always meant a profound liberation of the Church from forms of worldliness, for in the process she as it were sets aside her worldly wealth and once again completely embraces her worldly poverty. In this she shares the destiny of the tribe of Levi, which according to the Old Testament account was the only tribe in Israel with no ancestral land of its own, taking as its portion only God himself, his word and his signs. At those moments in history, the Church shared with that tribe the demands of a poverty that was open to the world, in order to be released from her material ties: and in this way her missionary activity regained credibility. History has shown that, when the Church becomes less worldly, her missionary witness shines more brightly. Once liberated from material and political burdens and privileges, the Church can reach out more effectively and in a truly Christian way to the whole world, she can be truly open to the world. She can live more freely her vocation to the ministry of divine worship and service of neighbor. The missionary task, which is linked to Christian worship and should determine its structure, becomes more clearly visible. The Church opens herself to the world, not in order to win men for an institution with its own claims to power, but in order to lead them to themselves by leading them to him of whom each person can say with Saint Augustine: he is closer to me than I am to myself (cf. *Confessions*, III, 6, 11). He who is infinitely above me is yet so deeply within me that he is my true interiority. This form of openness to the world on the Church's part also serves to indicate how the individual Christian can be open to the world in effective and appropriate ways."

I will conclude by asking three questions: How could a priest who lacks nothing resemble Christ? How can a priest who possesses a superabundance of material comfort claim to be an associate of Christ? How can anyone forget Christ's words: "A scribe came up and said to him, 'Teacher, I will follow you wherever you go.' And Jesus said to him, 'Foxes have holes, and birds of the air have nests; but the Son of man has nowhere to lay his head'" (Mt 8:19–20)?

Of course, in a cynical or merely superficial world, the media love to make people think that Jesus was not born in a poor stable when Mary and Joseph were turned away everywhere. The powers that dislike Jesus cannot tolerate such an omen; for them the wretched stable must be a sentimental myth. They also forget that at his death Jesus did not even have a place in which to be buried. He was laid hastily in the tomb intended for Joseph of Arimathea....

Due to his experience in Latin America, Francis assigns a very special place to "the evangelizing power of popular piety". Based on your pastoral experience in Africa, what is your view of these expressions of faith?

The enthusiasm of African Catholics is manifested during beautiful eucharistic celebrations, long pilgrimages, ancestral processions, or on the feast days of major saints. Francis rightly recalls the importance of this piety, inasmuch as some people who are puffed up by rationality would like to tone down their importance.

The witness of the people is beautiful because it is expresses outwardly an intense interior life. Popular piety publicly manifests what Christ accomplishes in the secret depths of their hearts. Hence it is easy to understand that the powers-that-be want to minimize their impact....

Often popular piety is a way of inculturating the faith. In this way Christ enters into communion with the roots of a people who did not know him a little while ago. Popular piety is central to an authentic process of evangelization. I remember that Benedict XVI, during a private audience, confided to me that his most beautiful memory of his journey to Brazil was the touching piety of the people.

In Guinea, I wanted to start a penitential pilgrimage to Our Lady of Guinea, in Boffa. Some of the faithful may walk more than 125 miles to reach the shrine. The Catholics from the most distant regions travel more than 250 miles on foot, in particular those who come from my village of Ourous. The first few years, the local people who saw us walking asked whether we were fugitives, victims of an epidemic or a war.... Today, the welcome extended by all, Christians and Muslims, is tremendous. Although they are far from my land, I do not overlook the shrine of Kibeho in Rwanda, or the pilgrimages connected with the martyrs of Uganda.

For me, a son of an African country that is so poor, my first trip to Lourdes was unforgettable. Even today I cannot go to Paray-le-Monial, Ars, Lisieux, or the chapel on the rue du Bac without considerable emotion. I am impressed by the filial affection expressed by pilgrims of all ages who, in Fatima or Czestochowa, advance toward the Blessed Virgin or go around her icon on their knees, with a rosary in hand.

I am not surprised that Francis could write: "To understand this reality we need to approach it with the gaze of the Good Shepherd, who seeks not to judge but to love. Only from the affective connaturality born of love can we appreciate the theological life present in the piety of Christian peoples, especially among their poor. I think of the steadfast faith of those mothers tending their sick children who, though perhaps barely familiar with the articles of the creed, cling to a rosary; or of all the hope poured into a candle lighted in a humble home with a prayer for help from Mary, or in the gaze of tender love directed to Christ crucified. No one who loves God's holy people will view these actions as the expression of a purely human search for the divine. They are the manifestation of a theological life nourished by the working of the Holy Spirit who has been poured into our hearts (cf. Rom 5:5)" (EG 125).

I myself was deeply moved in July 2014, at Châteauneuf-de-Galaure, as people left church after Mass, when little Sibylle, with a big smile, offered me a drawing she had made. It was Christ on the Cross. I could make out Jesus very clearly, his hands and feet nailed to the Cross. At the top of the Cross, instead of the usual inscription "INRI", Sibylle had written "Jerusalem". And at the foot of it she had drawn the Virgin Mary, hands outstretched, with this caption: "Mary is weeping *(sic)* because Jesus died on the cros *(sic)*." Children are marvelous! They sense the Heart of God and the mysteries of his love that meet us even in our serious sins and petty weaknesses.

Yes, the poor importune us, and the simple folk oblige us. Their joys are always interior. These people already experience a bit of the joy of heaven, and they will discreetly go there ahead of us.

How are we to understand what Francis calls "reverence for truth"?

God is truth; through his Son, he intends to draw us toward this truth. Attachment to and love of the truth are the most authentic, the most righteous, and the noblest attitude that a man could ever want on this earth. Conversely, the absence of truth is man's real poverty, for the rejection of the truth paralyzes and falsifies his activity. Thus, the man who is not in the truth of God finds himself a prisoner of his own ego. Without truth, we are strangers to ourselves, cut off from the depths of our being, cut off from God, prisoners in our own darkness.

In his encyclical *Evangelii nuntiandi*, Paul VI declared that evangelization is supposed to quench a thirst that could be summed up as a threefold search, for the truth about God, the truth about man, and the truth about the world (see EN 78). We are neither the authors nor the masters of the truth, but rather its stewards and servants. Reverence for the truth is the true spiritual worship that we must render to God.

In the Gospel of John, we find these extraordinary words: "Jesus then said to the Jews who had believed in him, 'If you continue in my word, you are truly my disciples, and you will know the truth, and the truth will make you free'" (Jn 8:31–32).

By building his life on the truth, man becomes a rock, because God is love and truth. He never disappoints. Conversely, if mankind chooses to build on sand, it runs the risk of suffering major interior and external losses.

Furthermore, concerning the problem of fidelity to the truth, Francis writes: "Certainly, to understand properly the meaning of the central message of a text we need to relate it to the teaching of the entire Bible as handed on by the Church. This is an important principle of biblical interpretation which recognizes that the Holy Spirit has inspired not just a part of the Bible, but the Bible as a whole, and that in some areas people have grown in their understanding of God's will on the basis of their personal experience. It also prevents erroneous or partial interpretations which would contradict other teachings of the same Scriptures. But it does not mean that we can weaken the distinct and specific emphasis of a text which we are called to preach. One of the defects of a tedious and ineffectual preaching is precisely its inability to transmit the intrinsic power of the text which has been proclaimed" (EG 148).

Francis decided to entitle one chapter of his apostolic exhortation "Realities are more important than ideas." How do you interpret this analysis?

The pope wishes to make it clear to us that the Church feels urgently obliged to perceive reality. This leads us to the truth, whereas an idea often proves to be proud and self-sufficient.

Thus, some people are very set in their ideas about the Church, the bishop, or the liturgy. I think that it is important to say that the reality of the faith seems more important to me than ideas about the faith....

The pope writes: "There ... exists a constant tension between ideas and realities. Realities simply are, whereas ideas are worked out. There has to be continuous dialogue between the two, lest ideas become detached from realities. It is dangerous to dwell in the realm of words alone, of images and rhetoric. So a third principle comes into play: realities are greater than ideas. This calls for rejecting the various means of masking reality: angelic forms of purity, dictatorships of relativism, empty rhetoric, objectives more ideal than real, brands of ahistorical fundamentalism, ethical systems bereft of kindness, intellectual discourse bereft of wisdom" (EG 231).

I think that Francis ardently wishes to give the Church a taste for reality, inasmuch as some Christians and even some clerics can sometimes be tempted to hide behind ideas in order to forget the real situations of persons.

Conversely, some worry that this concept of the pope endangers the integrity of the Magisterium. The recent debate on the problem of the divorced and remarried has often been prompted by this sort of tension.

For my part, I do not believe that the pope means to endanger the integrity of the Magisterium. Indeed, no one, not even the pope, can destroy or change Christ's teaching. No one, not even the pope, can set pastoral ministry in opposition to doctrine. That would be to rebel against Jesus Christ and his teaching.

The marriage covenant by which a man and a woman establish between themselves a lifelong partnership was raised by Christ the Lord to the dignity of a sacrament (*Code of Canon Law*, can. 1055). Moreover, in his preaching, Jesus taught unequivocally the original meaning of the union of man and woman, as the Creator willed it in the beginning.

In this way he abolished the concessions allowing the dismissal of one's spouse that had crept into the Law of Moses. And so the marital union of the man and the woman is indissoluble; God himself decreed it: "What God has joined together let no man put asunder" (Mt 19:6).

This unequivocal insistence on the indissolubility of the matrimonial bond may have perplexed Jesus' disciples, to whom it seemed like an unrealistic demand (Mt 19:10). Even so, Christ did not impose on married couples a burden that is impossible to carry. Since he came to reestablish the initial order of creation, which had been disrupted by sin, the Son of God gives the strength and the grace to live a married life in the new dimension of the kingdom of God.

By following Christ, by renouncing themselves and taking up their cross each day, married couples will be able to understand the original meaning of marriage and live it out with his help. The grace of Christian marriage is a fruit of the Cross of Christ.

The apostle Paul tries to help us understand this reality by writing: "Husbands, love your wives, as Christ loved the Church and gave himself up for her, that he might sanctify her" (Eph 5:25–26). Then he adds: "For this reason a man shall leave his father and mother and be joined to his wife, and the two shall become one flesh. This is a great mystery, and I mean in reference to Christ and the Church" (Eph 5:31–32).

Certainly, but divorce is very widespread today....

On the question of divorce, the Church's teaching has been constant. Divorce and remarriage are an occasion of great scandal. Vatican Council II, in *Gaudium et spes*, calls divorce "a plague" (*GS* 47). Likewise, the *Catechism of the Catholic Church* teaches that divorce is immoral because of the disorder it introduces into the family and society. This rupture always results in serious harm: to the spouse who is abandoned, to the children who are traumatized by the separation of their parents and often torn between them; and "because of its contagious effect which makes it truly a plague on society" (CCC 2385). "Divorce is a grave offense against the natural law ... [and] does injury to the covenant of salvation, of which sacramental marriage is the sign. Contracting a new union, even if it is recognized by civil law, adds to the gravity of the rupture: the remarried spouse is then in a situation of public and permanent adultery" (CCC 2384). Christ's words are forceful: "I say to you: whoever divorces his wife, except for unchastity, and marries another, commits adultery" (Mt 19:9).

Saint Basil, in his *Moralia* 73, writes: "If a husband, separated from his wife, approaches another woman, he is an adulterer because he makes that woman commit adultery; and the woman who lives with him is an adulteress, because she has drawn another's husband to herself."

Of course, today there are many Catholics who resort to divorce according to the civil law and contract a new civil union. The Church, out of fidelity to the Word of Jesus Christ, upholds his position: "Whoever divorces his wife and marries another commits adultery against her; and if she divorces her husband and marries another, she commits adultery" (Mk 10:11–12). It is not possible to recognize a new union as valid if the first marriage was. Divorced persons who have remarried civilly are in a situation that is objectively contrary to God's law. Consequently, they cannot receive Eucharistic Communion as long as this situation persists. For the same reason, these men and women cannot exercise certain responsibilities in the Church. Reconciliation in the Sacrament of Penance can be granted only to those who have repented of having violated the sign of Christ's covenant and fidelity and are committed to living in complete continence (CCC 1650).

Some might argue that divorce is so common today that it no longer gives scandal.... According to that reasoning, we could therefore admit divorced and remarried persons to Holy Communion. In the opinion of these zealots of a strange sort of progress, no one would be shocked! This sort of argument is based on a misunderstanding of the very notion of scandal. It is not a psychological shock but, rather, an action that deliberately draws others into sin. In no case should a sinner tempt or pressure someone else to sin. Now the abundance of divorces and remarriages are sins that result in social situations and institutions that are contrary to God's goodness.

The "sinful situations" that are thus created are the expression and the effect of personal sins. They induce others to commit evil in turn. Christ's disciples find themselves in an increasingly difficult setting that weakens their faith, their attachment, and their fidelity to God's teaching. The Church constantly exhorts them to resist and firmly to oppose the structures of sin. She reminds them that a married couple can be founded only on the relationship shared by one man and one woman. The overall plan for mankind cannot be carried out apart from the man-woman duality. Is this not the point where we must look constantly to Christ, the one who ultimately reveals man?

The Son of God alone reveals to man and to woman their true common nature, their true and equal dignity, by restoring to perfection the ties of reciprocal love, mutual aid, and complementarity that were inscribed in the depths of their being, from the beginning, by the Creator.

In Africa, too—even though some peoples practiced polygamy before the Christians arrived—in the pure ancestral tradition, monogamous and indissoluble marriage is the center of existence. It is not only the covenant of the husband and the wife but, at the same time, the covenant of their families and clans, sealed with the word that is given and the "blood" of the kola nut that is shared together. The kola nut, the seed of the kola tree, is the symbol of the definitive and indissoluble union of the matrimonial bond. It is made up of two parts that are firmly joined to each other. The future spouses divide it, and each one munches on his part. The master of ceremonies then asks the spouses to restore the kola nut to its initial state. The impossibility of doing so symbolizes the definitive bond of marriage. The couple, indissolubly constituted and associated to the families by the bonds of marriage, also becomes generational, so as to be registered in the immortal line of the preceding generations. Through their children and their children's children, the parents continue to exist, thanks to a bond of solidarity that Christians call the communion of the living and the dead.

Do you think that this vision of marriage and of the indissolubility of the conjugal bond is shared by all African ethnic groups?

Yes, there is not even any doubt about this question. For example, in the Fon culture, in Benin, the term *Sesi* refers to the first wife who is exchanged for a dowry and is married as a virgin, and facing her there must always be the *Sesu*, the first husband married in the first wedding. At the time of the woman's funeral, it becomes quite clear that monogamy and indissolubility are traditional, firmly anchored in the African practice of marriage.

We encounter the term *Sesi* precisely within the framework of the funeral ceremonies that are designed to send the deceased woman off on her journey from this world toward that of the Supreme Being. The funeral ceremonies of a deceased wife require certain gestures and rituals of her husband, in particular the rite of clothing. A woman is often buried with a number of loincloths. The tradition welcomes loincloths from family members, friends, acquaintances, and successive husbands that she may have had. Nevertheless, the rite of clothing is carried out only in the presence of the very first husband, the *Sesu*. Until he is there, the ceremony cannot proceed. Moreover, whatever wealth the other successive husbands may own, the first husband, even if he is poor and miserable, has the right to perform the role of spouse for the woman and to clothe her with a view to her passage to the next world. She is in fact *Sesi*. And he is the one who determines the hour of the burial. Thus, in this cultural context, it is clear that a woman is destined to marry only one man by a true wedding, just as her family accepts a dowry for her only once. The other husbands are considered as lovers and friends. The moment of truth at death helps us to grasp the profound sense of purposefulness underlying the Black African cultural universe.

We can declare with certainty that, in the African cultural context, a woman, after having served as a wife to other men besides her first husband, with the knowledge and ready agreement of the group, finds herself at the end of her life restored to her original status.

I would like to conclude this mention of the African tradition by paying my respects to John Paul II, who in *Familiaris consortio* definitively sealed the teaching and discipline of the Church that are founded on Sacred Scripture. Today, I think that we should stop discussing this question like disrespectful intellectuals, giving the impression of disputing the teaching of Jesus and the Church. Some Western governments, with great disdain for God and nature, are passing insane laws about marriage, family, and human life. For her part, the Church cannot behave frivolously in God's sight.

We seem to forget sometimes that a synod of bishops gave rise to the apostolic
exhortation Familiaris consortio.

You are absolutely right! Many questions relating to the very beautiful reality of the family that God created were discussed in it. Among
other topics, it spoke about divorced Catholics. In *Familiaris consortio*
John Paul II wrote: "Together with the Synod, I earnestly call upon
pastors and the whole community of the faithful to help the divorced,
and with solicitous care to make sure that they do not consider themselves as separated from the Church, for as baptized persons they can,
and indeed must, share in her life. They should be encouraged to listen
to the word of God, to attend the Sacrifice of the Mass, to persevere in
prayer, to contribute to works of charity and to community efforts
in favor of justice, to bring up their children in the Christian faith, to
cultivate the spirit and practice of penance and thus implore, day by
day, God's grace. Let the Church pray for them, encourage them, and
show herself a merciful mother, and thus sustain them in faith and hope.
However, the Church reaffirms her practice, which is based upon Sacred
Scripture, of not admitting to Eucharistic Communion divorced persons
who have remarried. They are unable to be admitted thereto from the
fact that their state and condition of life objectively contradict that union
of love between Christ and the Church which is signified and effected
by the Eucharist. Besides this, there is another special pastoral reason:
if these people were admitted to the Eucharist, the faithful would be
led into error and confusion regarding the Church's teaching about the
indissolubility of marriage.... Similarly, the respect due to the sacrament
of Matrimony, to the couples themselves and their families, and also
to the community of the faithful, forbids any pastor, for whatever reason or pretext even of a pastoral nature, to perform ceremonies of any
kind for divorced people who remarry. Such ceremonies would give
the impression of the celebration of a new sacramentally valid marriage,
and would thus lead people into error concerning the indissolubility of
a validly contracted marriage. By acting in this way, the Church pro-
fesses her own fidelity to Christ and to His truth. At the same time she
shows motherly concern for these children of hers, especially those who,
through no fault of their own, have been abandoned by their legitimate
partner. With firm confidence she believes that those who have rejected
the Lord's command and are still living in this state will be able to obtain

from God the grace of conversion and salvation, provided that they have persevered in prayer, penance, and charity" (FC 84).

Finally, Francis often speaks about "the missionary power of intercessory prayer". What is your view on this subject?

The pope wrote an admirable passage when he reminded us: "The great men and women of God were great intercessors. Intercession is like a 'leaven' in the heart of the Trinity. It is a way of penetrating the Father's heart and discovering new dimensions which can shed light on concrete situations and change them. We can say that God's heart is touched by our intercession, yet in reality he is always there first. What our intercession achieves is that his power, his love, and his faithfulness are shown ever more clearly in the midst of the people" (EG 283).

If man does not lift up his sights toward God, by praying and interceding, he dries out and dies to himself. The same thing also applies, in a similar way, to the success of missionary work.

Saint Paul addresses this topic very often. In his Letter to the Ephesians, he strongly exhorts them: "Pray at all times in the Spirit, with all prayer and supplication. To that end keep alert with all perseverance, making supplication for all the saints, and also for me, that utterance may be given me in opening my mouth boldly to proclaim the mystery of the gospel, for which I am an ambassador in chains; that I may declare it boldly, as I ought to speak" (Eph 6:18–20). The urgent necessity of intercessory prayer appears repeatedly in Paul's teaching. He asks the first Christians to pray for him and to intercede with the saints so that his work of evangelization might be abundant and effective: "Continue steadfastly in prayer, being watchful in it with thanksgiving; and pray for us also, that God may open to us a door for the word, to declare the mystery of Christ, on account of which I am in prison, that I may make it clear, as I ought to speak" (Col 4:2–4).

The prayer of monks and nuns is one of the most productive foundations of the Church. Monasteries are absolutely prodigious centers of evangelization and mission. The ardent, continual prayer of Carmelite, Benedictine, Cistercian, or Visitation nuns, to mention only a few congregations, assists and mightily supports the work of priests. The modern world and even some clerics, inebriated by their feeling of power, often think that cloistered monks and nuns serve no purpose. Ultimately, that is the noblest compliment we can offer the contemplatives who have withdrawn behind the high walls of their cloisters; they serve nothing in particular here below, but simply God alone. This is the simple, beautiful secret of their prayers, which support the whole world.

How can we forget Christ's saying: "The harvest is plentiful, but the laborers are few; pray therefore the Lord of the harvest to send out laborers into his harvest. Go your way; behold, I send you out as lambs in the midst of wolves. Carry no purse, no bag, no sandals; and salute no one on the road" (Lk 10:2–4). The first thing to do when laborers are lacking is not to apply our intelligence to restructuring a diocese, to reorganize the parishes by consolidating them—which is not to deny the possible usefulness and appropriateness of such a project. Instead, it is necessary to pray that God will raise up many holy vocations to the priestly ministry and the consecrated life.

Do we really pray ardently for vocations? Do we pray every day that God will send priests?

We must ask God ceaselessly to raise up great mission workers among his people. Missionary work is not a human endeavor; it can only come from God. Intercessory prayer is gentle and confident. The Holy Ghost Fathers of my childhood had successful missions because they were constantly immersed in prayer, asking God to grant them his protection and to make their work as sowers of the word productive. Humanly speaking, how could anyone imagine for an instant that such poor men could have succeeded in communicating Christ's words in the most remote parts of Africa? Only the missionary power of intercessory prayer of which Francis speaks can explain their magnificent achievements....

During the three years of his public life on this earth, Jesus often took the apostles aside to pray. The mission of Christ and of the early Christians was already God's work. The suffering that can sometimes accompany missionary work is transformed into victory by intercessory prayer.

Francis ultimately wants the Gospel to penetrate into the life of every person. The Word of God is not an idea or an ideal; it exists to circulate through the whole human being, in all his dimensions, and in so doing the Gospel can set out for the farthest corners of the world. The Holy Father's desire is realistic, because he is in complete agreement with the will of Christ. Certainly Francis is seeking to apply the words of Saint James, who clearly stated: "Show me your faith apart from your works, and I by my works will show you my faith. You believe that God is one; you do well. Even the demons believe—and shudder" (Jas 2:18–19).

Evangelization would remain just an idea that would not fit into the concrete situations of life if we did remain closely united to God through prayer.

In *Lumen fidei*, his first encyclical, Francis writes: "There is an urgent need, then, to see once again that faith is a light, for once the flame of faith dies out, all other lights begin to dim. The light of faith is unique, since it is capable of illuminating *every aspect* of human existence. A light this powerful cannot come from ourselves but from a more primordial source: in a word, it must come from God" (LF 4).

The source is God, through constant prayer. God is always our admirable strength, our serene joy, and our luminous hope.

X

GOD DOES NOT SPEAK, BUT HIS VOICE IS CLEAR

The world is the greatest of all visible things, just as God is the greatest of all that is invisible. But we see that the world is, and we believe that God is. That God made the world we can believe from no one with greater certainty than from God himself, who said in the Sacred Scriptures through the words of the prophet: "In the beginning, God created the heavens and the earth."

—Saint Augustine, *City of God* 11, 4

NICOLAS DIAT: *In the midst of so many responsibilities, requests, and worries in the papal administration, how does Africa continue to be for you a spiritual rock?*

ROBERT CARDINAL SARAH: I must admit that when I was called to the Roman Curia by John Paul II, in October 2001, I was not very enthusiastic. I had to leave a little country where there were only three of us bishops, and our Church remained very poor. I kept thinking about that difficult saying in the Gospel: "To every one who has will more be given, and he will have abundance; but from him who has not, even what he has will be taken away" (Mt 25:29).

Worse yet, several weeks later, my first Christmas far from my country and from the Christians of Guinea was horrible. I was nostalgic, sad to be far away from my cathedral, from joyous songs and the warmth of African Christmases. At the Pontifical Urban University, on the Janiculum Hill where I was living then, I celebrated Midnight Mass for a handful of seminarians. Then, on December 25, all the young men left for their parishes or to stay with the families of friends. I was overwhelmed by the solitude. I could no longer find the salt of African fervor.

During those first months in Rome, I felt rather like an uprooted tree. Then, with time, I appreciated God's call for me to carry out a new mission in the service of the pope. Even though I still felt homesick, the face of Bernardin Cardinal Gantin, that great servant of Africa, was constantly before my eyes. In the depths of my heart, I heard the sonorous echo of his very moving words: "All my Christian love is summed up in these simple words: God, Jesus Christ, the pope, the Blessed Virgin: supreme realities that Rome caused me to discover, love, and serve. For this too, how can I ever thank the Lord enough?" I did not forget Africa, but I was happy with the scope of my task. I know that I benefited from many graces because of the very special mission of the Congregation for the Evangelization of Peoples. Every day, I could meet with the bishops of dioceses from all over the world who came to Rome to speak to us about their missionary achievements and progress. God snatched me away from my beloved country, but I had the honor of working in the service of his entire flock.

When the health of my former prefect, Cardinal Dias, declined, I went alone to the various discussions with Benedict XVI so as to submit to him the possible episcopal appointments he had to make according to the studies and the proposals of the congregation, which were examined meticulously by the Assembly of the *Ordinaria*. How can I forget the richness, the simplicity, and the depth of my conversations with this great pope? It is quite clear to me that I never would have experienced such moments if I had stayed in Conakry.

From then on my attachment to my native land was doubled by an obligation to defend it against the threats looming over it because of globalization and the new global ethic promoted by the secularized West. As part of its identity, Africa is open to transcendence, to adoration, and to the glory of God. The African peoples respect human life, but they look beyond it by seeking eternity. The soul of Africa always opens toward God. Unlike a large part of the West, this continent has a fundamentally theocentric vision. Material concerns are always secondary. In this life, the African knows that he is only a sojourner.

Despite the more or less underground programs that seek to destroy its spiritual resources, the springtime of God remains for a good part of Africa. I know that Benedict XVI understood the features of the African soul profoundly when he wrote: "Africa is the depository of an immense treasure ... [it] constitutes an immense spiritual 'lung' for a humanity that appears to be in a crisis of faith and hope."[1] If my land continues to suffer, it is because its springtime is continuing according to the divine plan.

Before leaving Rome to return to his native country, Benin, Cardinal Gantin said that he was like a banana tree. When this tree has yielded its fruits, people cut it down. But there is always a shoot that sprouts up; indeed, he thought that I was that new shoot.... The cardinal was a marvelous example. He conveyed to me the greatness and nobility of his sentiments toward our continent, and I cannot forget how well he understood the depth of African sincerity with respect to the invisible. Bernard Gantin used to say: "God does not ask me for success, but for love. Now true love does not come primarily through words but through the heart. Everything else is secondary and perishable. God alone is essential and eternal. And love allows us to resemble him a little."

And so the men and women of Africa try to resemble God a little. They see in this quest the most wonderful adventure that man can experience here below. Their eyes are not fixed on earthly realities, and I know that this spiritual search is fruitful. Because despite the wars, the poverty, the harshness of nature, God gives much to his children who seek him, and even more than what they dare to ask from him. Africa loves to lift up its eyes toward heaven, and God often sends beautiful messages to those who truly love him.

What is the finest achievement of the Church?

God alone knows! In any case, the charitable activity of the Church on behalf of the poor and the needy is extraordinary. The Church has always fought to reduce the material and spiritual poverty of the peoples. The network of the 165 branches of Caritas throughout the world, Catholic charitable structures and organizations (such as the Order of Malta) that strive to put the Gospel into practice, the Church's commitment to education and healthcare and to the defense of the dignity of the human person, her goodwill efforts placed at the service of the poorest of the poor, are a peerless army that work to relieve sufferings. God has granted us success in our exceptional charitable work for the weakest.

---

[1] Homily for the opening Mass of the Synod of Bishops, Second Special Assembly for Africa, October 4, 2009, reprinted in French in *Africae Munus*, no. 13.

If I had not benefited from the Church's aid, I would not be with you right now. From her origins, the Spouse of Christ always chose to go to the farthest limits of the world to help people who owned nothing. The Holy Ghost Fathers in my little village were part of that remarkable tradition of priests magnetized by the breath of God to such an extent that they were capable of things that were humanly impossible.

Over the course of the centuries, God's greatest gift is to have sent, after Christ, saints who gave their lives for the poorest of the poor. Saint Vincent de Paul, Saint John Bosco, Saint Daniel Comboni, and Mother Teresa of Calcutta thought of those who were no longer of interest to anyone. The Church's victory is engraved on the hearts of all the poor people she has saved for generations.

Thousands of priests and religious showed a matchless tenacity, despite serious obstacles, in carrying out their missions of charity. And the greatest charity of all is to reveal God manifested in his Son on the Cross. Thanks to the example of these men and women of God, the work of evangelizing and humanizing our societies met with great success.

It is important to understand the impact of charitable activity. For Christians, the essential thing is never the material and social assistance in itself, but the fight against spiritual poverty. From this perspective, as a corollary to the immense gift that God has given her, the Church has the serious obligation never to give up.

The most beautiful action on this earth, therefore, is still to restore to men their equal dignity as children of heaven and their ability to be open to the eternal light.

Thanks to the poor, the Church's victory is always humble and hidden, far from deceptive trappings.

What have been the Church's defeats?

If you are referring to the Church as a society and not to her essential reality as the Mystical Body of Christ, one fatal error would be to emphasize social, economic, or, worse, political work to the detriment of evangelization. Francis' first words, in the Sistine Chapel, a few hours after his election to the See of Peter, are especially eloquent: "We can walk as much as we want, we can build many things, but if we do not profess Jesus Christ, things go wrong. We may become a charitable NGO, but not the Church, the Bride of the Lord. When we are not walking, we stop moving. When we are not building on the stones, what happens?

The same thing that happens to children on the beach when they build sandcastles: everything is swept away, there is no solidity." When Christ is no longer proclaimed, it is therefore no longer about the Church. Because the Church is holy, apostolic, and missionary.

In his book Threshold of Hope, *John Paul II wrote that "God is always on the side of the suffering."²* *How do you interpret this sentence?*

When God appeared to Moses, he told him: "I have seen the affliction of my people who are in Egypt, and have heard their cry because of their taskmasters; I know their sufferings, and I have come down to deliver them" (Ex 3:7–8).

God always sides with those who weep. In how many psalms do we read that God never abandons the poor? From a human perspective, we often have a feeling of rebellion when divine aid appears to be absent in the face of adversity. But throughout my journeys in the poorest countries of the world, I have observed that God remained much more present that we could ever have imagined. Indeed, through these trials and physical miseries, I have seen with my own eyes how God transforms the souls of the poor through obscure, humble sufferings that cleanse their wounds. In observing the poor, I too have learned to say, in poverty: My God, I am glad about all the trials I have experienced, and I thank you in advance for all the ones yet to come. I hope they will help to bandage the wounds of the world.

I am not forgetting the great saints whom God sent to die with the poor, such as Father Damien. After arriving on May 10, 1873, in Molokai, in the Hawaiian Islands, Saint Damien Josef de Veuster volunteered to be God's presence in the midst of the lepers whom no one wanted to visit. Damien knew perfectly well that he had no chance of returning alive from such an adventure. After ten years of mission work in the midst of those unfortunate creatures, who had been corralled, like livestock waiting for the slaughterhouse, he contracted leprosy, which began to gnaw away at him, and it inevitably destroyed him. Yet he had chosen to give his all to the dying of Molokai for the love of God. He celebrated his last Mass, completely exhausted by leprosy, on March 28, 1889, a few days before being carried off to the Father of all mercies.

²John Paul II, *Crossing the Threshold of Hope,* trans. Jenny McPhee and Martha McPhee (New York: Alfred A. Knopf, 1994), 66.

When I had the opportunity to converse with Mother Teresa, I saw a woman who was completely immersed in God. Her face had no special human beauty, but a simple, magnificent interior light, the reflection of a fire that can shine through only by ongoing contact with God. Within her dwelt a presence, a simplicity, and a serenity that came from Christ, whom she contemplated in the tabernacle for hours. Indeed, Mother Teresa attracted people, because a little bit of heaven had already come down into her soul. Her humility was that of the comrades and friends of God. The frailty of her voice and the power of her words were the tangible sign of a woman who was literally immersed in God.

Mother Teresa was acutely aware of God's true tenderness for men and his loving care for the poor.

Often, to reassure ourselves, we say that God writes straight with crooked lines. . . .

Considering my own journey, I can say that nothing was simple. My life was a genuine pilgrimage from one continent to another, from one country to another, from one seminary to another, from a simple parish to the Archdiocesan See of Conakry, in complex national political circumstances, then from my dear Guinea to the Eternal City. God willed this difficult path, the better to teach me that here below men are never definitively at home.

As Christ's disciples, we are constantly on an exodus. Christians always remain nomads, in search of God, on a difficult but rewarding pilgrimage. It is important for them to remain attentive to God's will.

Often, like Abraham, we do not know where God is leading us. Whereas we would like a stable, perfect universe, the human path is torturous, winding, and muddy, like the one that leads to my poor village of Ourous. However, we must never forget that man is never alone. Despite the most difficult appearances, God ultimately leads us toward perfection, sanctity, and the complete fulfillment of our own vocation. A life can seem to be a tragedy, but God knows the exact meaning of everything. Our Father is carrying out a plan for each of us. He simply asks man to be docile and attentive to the messages that he ceaselessly sends us. He may subject us to insults or overwhelming slander in order to teach us gentleness and humility.

Along this path, we must not forget God's magnificent words to Abraham: "Walk before me, my child, and be blameless" (cf. Gen 17:1). There is a hope of God in man, and a hope of man in God.

I personally am the work of God's hope and of the hope of his collaborators, those men who assisted me in my priestly formation and my human maturation. Through them, I often heard God say to me repeatedly: "Walk before me, my child, and be blameless."

Do you suppose that the little child from the bush that I was could have imagined for one moment that he would leave one day for Rome to become a cardinal? At the major seminary in Nancy, when I met Cardinal Tisserant for the first time, I thought I would never ever again hear one of the pope's colleagues speak. How could my grandmother Rose have imagined what sort of life I would have? God's mysterious ways are not without humor. The apostles who surrounded Christ were the first ones to be surprised by the vagaries of God. The Gospels are full of the unexpected....

Which is your favorite evangelist?

Without any possible doubt, I like Saint John more than all the others. I think he entered so profoundly into the Heart of Jesus that he became a loving interpreter of his words. John discovered the radical character of the supporting pillar of Christ's teaching, love even unto the gift of self. His Gospel continues magnificently in his Letters.

For me, John is the heart of the Christian message in which God reveals himself as a loving Father. John was at the foot of the Cross on that day when the Son died for love of us. He saw the pierced Heart of Jesus and the torrents of love pouring out on mankind. He contemplated the blood of the Lamb washing us of all stains. He listened to the very last Words of Jesus, and these words then were slowly engraved on his loving heart.

With the Virgin Mary and Mary Magdalen, John experienced extreme suffering after the death of the Son of God. They prayed with "prayers and supplications, with loud cries and tears" (Heb 5:7), and turned to the Father as much as men can.

What do the prayers of monks mean to you, and even more: their choice of the contemplative life?

The monastic life is physically difficult, but it aspires to be completely immersed in the peace of God. Monks have chosen an active, silent life entirely consecrated to God. Little by little their days should become an uninterrupted prayer; in it the monk remains united with God during all his occupations. The true purpose of monastic life is to attain a more or less habitual state of prayer and penance, of liturgy and study, of manual labor and worship. As Thomas Merton wrote in *The Sign of Jonas*, silence and solitude, listening and meditation on the word, continually place the monk's soul under the direct influence of the divine action.[3]

On this earth, monks must become the most humble, most patient laborers in their knowledge of the spiritual life.

Father Jérôme, who was a Trappist monk for almost sixty years at Sept-Fons Abbey, wrote realistic, admirable lines about the life of monks. In his *Écrits monastiques*, he remarked: "You do not become a monk in one day! It takes ten, thirty, sixty years. The young monk, the novice, is a bud in early spring, when the branches are still black and cold from the winter, when the fruit is still only a promise."[4]

Apart from God and faith, monks are incomprehensible. We must not be afraid to say that they are useless. However, the monk knows that his vocation is mysteriously useful, because it is mysteriously efficacious for men; he recognizes that his poor existence is an imperfect participation in the life, Passion, and sorrowful death of Jesus Christ. Yet his soul must not lose sight of our Lord's wounds.

Concealing his prayer in the great prayer of Jesus, the monk intercedes for all mankind, living and deceased, believers and unbelievers, unknown or very dear to him; not so that the wicked may become good, but so that they might have access to happiness and truth.

On October 9, 2011, in his homily during Evening Prayer at the historical Charterhouse of Serra San Bruno, where the mortal remains of the founder of the Carthusian Order are preserved, Benedict XVI spoke very fitting words about the essence of the Carthusian life and, in broader terms, about the greatness of contemplative life. For my part, I consider it one of the finest passages by the former pope: " '*Fugitiva relinquere et aeterna captare*': to abandon transient realities and seek to grasp that which is eternal. These words from the letter your Founder addressed to Rudolph, Provost of Rheims, contain the core of your spirituality (cf. *Letter to Rudolph*, no. 13): the strong desire to enter in union of life with

---

[3] Thomas Merton, *The Sign of Jonas* (New York: Harcourt, Brace, 1956).
[4] Père Jérôme, *Écrits monastiques* (Montrouge: Sarment, 2002).

God, abandoning everything else, everything that stands in the way of this communion, and letting oneself be grasped by the immense love of God to live this love alone. Dear brothers you have found the hidden treasure, the pearl of great value (cf. Mt 13:44–46); you have responded radically to Jesus' invitation: 'If you would be perfect, go, sell what you possess and give to the poor, and you will have treasure in heaven; and come, follow me' (Mt 19:21). Every monastery—male or female—is an oasis in which the deep well, from which to draw 'living water' to quench our deepest thirst, is constantly being dug with prayer and meditation. However, the charterhouse is a special oasis in which silence and solitude are preserved with special care, in accordance with the form of life founded by Saint Bruno and which has remained unchanged down the centuries. 'I live in a rather faraway hermitage ... with some religious brothers', is the concise sentence that your Founder wrote (*Letter to Rudolph 'the Green'*, no. 4). The Successor of Peter's Visit to this historic Charterhouse is not only intended to strengthen those of you who live here but the entire Order in its mission, which is more than ever timely and meaningful in today's world. Technical progress, especially in the area of transport and communications, has made human life more comfortable but also more keyed up, at times even frenetic. Cities are almost always noisy; silence is rarely to be found in them because there is always background noise, in some areas even at night. In recent decades, moreover, the development of the media has spread and extended a phenomenon that had already been outlined in the 1960s: virtuality risks predominating over reality. Unbeknownst to them, people are increasingly becoming immersed in a virtual dimension because of the audiovisual messages that accompany their life from morning to night. The youngest, born into this condition, seem to want to fill every empty moment with music and images, out of fear of feeling this very emptiness. This is a trend that has always existed, especially among the young and in the more developed urban contexts, but today it has reached a level such as to give rise to talk about anthropological mutation. Some people are no longer able to remain for long periods in silence and solitude. I chose to mention this socio-cultural condition because it highlights the specific charism of the Charterhouse as a precious gift for the Church and for the world, a gift that contains a deep message for our life and for the whole of humanity. I shall sum it up like this: by withdrawing into silence and solitude, human beings, so to speak, 'expose'

themselves to reality in their nakedness, to that apparent 'void', which
I mentioned at the outset, in order to experience instead Fullness, the
presence of God, of the most real Reality that exists and that lies beyond
the tangible dimension. He is a perceptible presence in every creature:
in the air that we breathe, in the light that we see and that warms us, in
the grass, in stones.... God, *Creator omnium*, passes through all things but
is beyond them and for this very reason is the foundation of them all.
The monk, in leaving everything, 'takes a risk', as it were: he exposes
himself to solitude and silence in order to live on nothing but the essential, and precisely in living on the essential he also finds a deep communion with his brethren, with every human being. Some might think that
it would suffice to come here to take this 'leap'. But it is not like this.
This vocation, like every vocation, finds an answer in an ongoing process, in a life-long search. Indeed it is not enough to withdraw to a place
such as this in order to learn to be in God's presence. Just as in marriage
it is not enough to celebrate the Sacrament to become effectively one,
but it is necessary to let God's grace act and to walk together through the
daily routine of conjugal life, so becoming monks requires time, practice and patience, 'in a divine and persevering vigilance', as Saint Bruno
said, they 'await the return of their Lord so that they might be able to
open the door to him as soon as he knocks' (*Letter to Rudolph 'the Green'*,
no. 4); and the beauty of every vocation in the Church consists precisely in this: giving God time to act with his Spirit and to one's own
humanity to form itself, to grow in that particular state of life according
to the measure of the maturity of Christ. In Christ there is everything,
fullness; we need time to make one of the dimensions of his mystery our
own. We could say that this is a journey of transformation in which the
mystery of Christ's resurrection is brought about and made manifest in
us, a mystery of which the word of God in the biblical Reading from
the Letter to the Romans has reminded us this evening: the Holy Spirit
who raised Jesus from the dead and will give life to our mortal bodies
also (cf. Rom 8:11) is the One who also brings about our configuration
to Christ in accordance with each one's vocation, a journey that unwinds
from the baptismal font to death, a passing on to the Father's house. In
the world's eyes it sometimes seems impossible to spend one's whole life
in a monastery but in fact a whole life barely suffices to enter into this
union with God, into this essential and profound Reality which is Jesus
Christ. This is why I have come here, dear Brothers who make up the

Carthusian Community of Serra San Bruno, to tell you that the Church needs you and that you need the Church! Your place is not on the fringes: no vocation in the People of God is on the fringes. We are one body, in which every member is important and has the same dignity and is inseparable from the whole. You too, who live in voluntary isolation, are in the heart of the Church and make the pure blood of contemplation and of the love of God course through your veins. *Stat Crux dum volvitur orbis* [the Cross is steady while the world is turning], your motto says. The Cross of Christ is the firm point in the midst of the world's changes and upheavals. Life in a Charterhouse shares in the stability of the Cross which is that of God, of God's faithful love. By remaining firmly united to Christ, like the branches to the Vine, may you too, dear Carthusian Brothers, be associated with his mystery of salvation, like the Virgin Mary who *stabat* [stood] beneath the Cross, united with her Son in the same sacrifice of love. Thus, like Mary and with her, you too are deeply inserted in the mystery of the Church, a sacrament of union of men with God and with each other. In this you are singularly close to my ministry. May the Most Holy Mother of the Church therefore watch over us and the holy Father Bruno always bless your community from Heaven."

Certainly, the life of a hermit may seem too rigorous, almost unsuitable in our age. But we must never forget that Bruno wanted to see God in an intimate face-to-face conversation. The founder of the Carthusians could not wait for death and eternity to respond to the urgency of his thirst. Indeed, Carthusians are impatient men.

In a letter to Jacques and Raïssa Maritain, Léon Bloy wrote: "Whatever the circumstances may be, always put the Invisible before the visible, the Supernatural before the natural; if this rule is applied to all your actions, we know that you will be equipped with strength and bathed with deep joy." Without meaning to, the writer summed up the essence of the monk's ambition.

Monks are shining stars that silently guide mankind toward the paths of the interior life. Their whole life, down to its minutest practical details, is centered on God. We must not be surprised that this absolute gift can produce effects that surpass mere rationality. We do not give our life to God without consequences.

Saint Benedict was obsessed with truly pleasing God. In reading biographies devoted to him, I have always been struck by his joy of living in

God's sight. He thought of solitude as a proof of love. He devised rules that allow monks to wield the weapons suited to waging the difficult combat of the interior life. His ambition was to give his monks the means to dwell in the sight of God. With the ardor of the meek, this great saint was consumed by the desire to be in God. The Order that he founded has held a very important place in Church history, even in recent times; I would not be divulging a secret if I told you that the example of the Benedictines was decisive for Joseph Ratzinger. His thirst for God alone resembles that of monks in all respects.

When I was archbishop of Conakry, for ten years I looked for sons of Saint Benedict who would agree to settle in my country. Every day I begged the Lord to grant me that grace. In 1994, I finally managed to bring some Benedictine nuns from Maumont Abbey, in the Diocese of Angoulême. Previously I had tried to enlist the good offices of the monks of Solesmes for my project. Finally, the Senegalese monastery of Keur Moussa yielded to my insistent appeals by founding a priory in Guinea. God has worked marvels, and he has exceeded my expectations.

Indeed, I considered that there is no substitute for the prayers of the monks to arouse an unceasing search for God and to foster the spiritual life of my people. Now, whenever I return to Guinea, I never fail to devote at least two days to the Benedictine monks and nuns. I love monasteries because they are God's citadels, strongholds where we can find him more easily, walls where the Heart of Jesus tenderly keeps watch.

There, those who seek God can say with the psalmist: "Domine, dilexi habitaculum domus tuae et locum habitationis gloriae tuae.... Unum petii a Domino, hoc requiram: ut inhabitem in domo Domini omnibus diebus vitae meae, ut videam voluptatem Domini et visitem templum eius" (Ps 26:8; Ps 27:4) (O LORD, I love the habitation of your house, and the place where your glory dwells.... One thing have I asked of the LORD, that will I seek after; that I may dwell in the house of the LORD all the days of my life, to behold the beauty of the LORD, and to inquire in his temple). In monasteries we rediscover purity of heart, *munditia cordis.*

I am firmly convinced that the Church continues on her path thanks to the intercession, day and night, of contemplative monks and nuns. The Bride of Christ is radiant with the invisible prayer of the soldiers who have hitched their lives to the vaults of heaven.

Today, despite the collapse of many traditions in the modern world, some men continue to base their whole lives on the love of God. In his treatise *De amore Dei* (*On the Love of God*), Saint Bernard wrote poetically: "The measure with which to love God is to love without measure."

On May 24, 2009, during his visit to Monte Cassino, Benedict XVI spoke these incomparable words about Benedict: "To live no longer for ourselves but for Christ: this is what gives full meaning to the life of those who let themselves be conquered by him. This is clearly demonstrated by the human and spiritual life of Saint Benedict. who, having abandoned all things, set out to follow Jesus Christ faithfully. Embodying the Gospel in his life, he became the pioneer of a vast movement of spiritual and cultural rebirth in the West. I would like here to mention an extraordinary event in his life related by Saint Gregory the Great, his biographer, and which is certainly well known to you. One might almost say that the holy Patriarch was also 'carried up into Heaven' in an indescribable mystic experience. On the night of 29 October 540, we read in the biography, while leaning out of the window, 'his eyes fixed on the stars and rapt in divine contemplation, the Saint felt that his heart was burning ... for him the starry firmament was like the embroidered curtain that veiled the Holy of Holies. At a certain point, his soul felt transported to the other side of the veil, to contemplate unveiled the Face of the One who dwells in inaccessible brightness' (cf. A. I. Schuster, *Storia di san Benedetto e dei suoi tempi* [Milan: Ed. Abbazia di Viboldone, 1965], 11ff.). Of course, similarly to what happened for Paul after he had been taken up into Heaven, for Saint Benedict too subsequent to this extraordinary spiritual experience, a new life had to begin. Indeed, although the vision was but fleeting, the effects endured; his features themselves, the biographers say, were altered by it, his expression always remained serene and his behavior angelic, and although he lived on earth, it was obvious that his heart was already in Paradise."

How do you understand the words of Christ: "I am with you always"?

In the first place, the presence of Jesus exists through the Church. I get the sense that we very quickly forget these words from the Gospel of Matthew: "Again I say to you, if two of you agree on earth about anything they ask, it will be done for them by my Father in heaven. For where two or three are gathered in my name, there am I in the midst of them" (Mt 18:19–20). Through the Church, Christ's promise has been kept continually since his death.

We can perceive his presence in the sacraments, also. We are baptized in the name of Christ. Similarly, the Eucharist is the Body of Jesus, and confession fulfills the will of the Son of God to remit the sins of mankind. Finally, in the Gospels, he is the one who speaks through his apostles.

The Vatican II Constitution on the Sacred Liturgy, *Sacrosanctum concilium*, explains as follows: "To accomplish so great a work Christ is always present in His Church, especially in her liturgical celebrations. He is present in the sacrifice of the Mass not only in the person of His minister, 'the same now offering, through the ministry of priests, who formerly offered himself on the cross', but especially in the Eucharistic species. By His power He is present in the sacraments so that when a man baptizes it is really Christ Himself who baptizes. He is present in His word since it is He Himself who speaks when the holy scriptures are read in the Church. He is present, lastly, when the Church prays and sings, for He promised 'Where two or three are gathered together in my name, there am I in the midst of them' (Mt 18:20). Christ indeed always associates the Church with Himself in this great work where God is perfectly glorified and men are sanctified. The Church is His beloved Bride who calls to her Lord and through Him offers worship to the Eternal Father. Rightly, then, the liturgy is considered as an exercise of the priestly office of Jesus Christ. In the liturgy the sanctification of the man is signified by signs perceptible to the senses and is effected in a way which corresponds with each of these signs; in the liturgy the whole public worship is performed by the Mystical Body of Jesus Christ, that is, by the Head and His members. From this it follows that every liturgical celebration, because it is an action of Christ the priest and of His Body which is the Church, is a sacred action surpassing all others; no other action of the Church can equal its efficacy by the same title and to the same degree" (SC 7).

Christ is also present alongside the poor and the suffering. It is impossible to forget Christ's radical words when he spoke to his disciples about his Second Coming: "When the Son of man comes in his glory, and all the angels with him, then he will sit on his glorious throne. Before him will be gathered all the nations, and he will separate them one from another as a shepherd separates the sheep from the goats, and he will place the sheep at his right hand, but the goats at the left. Then the King will say to those at his right hand, 'Come, O blessed of my Father, inherit the kingdom prepared for you from the foundation of the world; for I was hungry and you gave me food, I was thirsty and you gave me drink, I was a stranger and you welcomed me, I was naked and you clothed me, I was sick and you visited me, I was in prison and you came to me.' Then the righteous will answer him, 'Lord, when did we see you hungry and feed you, or thirsty and give you drink? And when did we see you a stranger and welcome you, or naked and clothe you? And when did we see you sick or in prison and visit you?' And the King will answer them, 'Truly, I say to you, as you did it to one of the least of these my brethren, you did it to me.' Then he will say to those at his left hand, 'Depart from me, you cursed, into the eternal fire prepared for the devil and his angels; for I was hungry and you gave me no food, I was thirsty and you gave me no drink, I was a stranger and you did not welcome me, naked and you did not clothe me, sick and in prison and you did not visit me.' Then they also will answer, 'Lord, when did we see you hungry or thirsty or a stranger or naked or sick or in prison, and did not minister to you?' Then he will answer them, 'Truly, I say to you, as you did it not to one of the least of these, you did it not to me.' And they will go away into eternal punishment, but the righteous into eternal life" (Mt 25:31–46).

Saint John Chrysostom always vigorously takes up the defense of the poor and the unfortunate. He likes to recall that Christ never came to terms with the scandal of the wealth and luxury that were displayed before the eyes of the poor. In his *Homilies on Matthew* he wrote: "Do you want to honor Christ's body? Then do not scorn him in his nakedness, nor honor him here in the church with silken garments while neglecting him outside where he is cold and naked. For he who said, 'This is my body', and made it so by his words, also said: 'You saw me hungry and did not feed me', and, 'inasmuch as you did not do it for one of these, the least of my brothers, you did not do it for me.' What we do here in the church requires a pure heart, not special garments; what we do outside requires great dedication.... Of what use is it to weigh down Christ's table with golden cups, when he himself is dying of hunger? First, fill him when he is hungry; then use the means you have left to adorn his table. Will you have a golden cup made but not give a cup of water? What is the use of providing the table with cloths woven of gold thread, and not providing Christ himself with the clothes he needs? What profit is there in that? Tell me: If you were to see him lacking the necessary food but were to leave him in that state and merely surround his table with gold, would he be grateful to you or rather would he not be angry? What if you were to see him clad in worn-out rags and stiff from the cold, and were to forget about clothing him and instead were to set up golden columns for him, saying that you were doing it for his honor? Would he not think he was being mocked and greatly insulted?"

Saint John Chrysostom shows Christ in the poor man and has him say: "I could feed myself, but I prefer to wander about as a beggar, to hold out my hand before your door, in order to be fed by you. It is for love of you I act this way." The archbishop of Constantinople vehemently protests against slavery and the alienation that goes with it: "What I am going to say is sad and horrible, nevertheless I must say it. Put God in the same rank as your slaves.... Set Christ free from hunger, need, prison and nakedness. Ah! You shudder at my words!"[5] When Saint John Chrysostom speaks about Christ present among us, there is reason to be afraid! His words are blunt, harsh, and unyielding. The whole man is there in his words. He does not speak in order to hear his own voice or to beguile. He writes to instruct, to exhort, to reform, anxious to combat pagan customs and to instill the morality of the Gospel. Saint John Chrysostom is a true pastor who educates and feeds his people, explains the Sacred Scriptures and applies them to everyday life.

Finally, what is holiness?

In his First Letter to the Thessalonians, Saint Paul declares: "Brethren, we beg and exhort you in the Lord Jesus, that as you learned from us how you ought to walk and to please God, just as you are doing, you do so more and more. For you know what instructions we gave you through the Lord Jesus. For this is the will of God, your sanctification: that you abstain from immorality; that each one of you know how to control his own body in holiness and honor, not in the passion of lust like heathens who do not know God; that no man transgress, and wrong his brother in this matter, because the Lord is an avenger in all these things, as we solemnly forewarned you. For God has not called us for uncleanness, but

---

[5] Trans. in *The Liturgy of the Hours* (New York: Catholic Book Pub. Co., 1975), 4:182–83.

in holiness. Therefore whoever disregards this, disregards not man but God, who gives his Holy Spirit to you" (1 Thess 4:1–8).

What are the ways to achieve holiness? The first is the humble acceptance of a gift from heaven. Indeed, holiness is in the first place a grace that comes from God. We must strive to accept it and to cooperate with it. In the *Imitation of Christ* we find this magnificent passage: "There can be no holiness, then, Lord, if you withdraw your supporting hand. No wisdom can be of any help, once you cease to guide it; no courage can support us, if you cease to keep it in being. . . . No, when you leave us, we sink and perish; when you visit us, we are raised up and restored to life. We have no sure footing, but through you we are made firm; we grow cold at heart, but you stir us once more into flame."[6]

Nevertheless, I think that there is a privileged way, the way of love and charity. This always leads man to perfection; it is the surest road to holiness. This connection between charity, perfection, and holiness is very important. People therefore must advance in faith by living in charity.

Demanding as they are, the words that Jesus speaks to us are full of love. This is why he tells us: "You must be perfect, as your heavenly Father is perfect" (Mt 5:48). Indeed, in agreeing to be Christians, we must constantly act without thinking about petty objectives of prestige or ambition or about ends that may appear nobler, such as philanthropy or humanitarian kindness. The Christian is a person who unceasingly reflects on the ultimate and radical end of love, which Jesus Christ manifested to us by dying for us on the Cross. Hence holiness consists of living exactly as God wants us to live, by being conformed more and more to his Son, Jesus Christ. Saint Paul already warned us without mincing words when he wrote: "Put on then, as God's chosen ones, holy and beloved, compassion, kindness, lowliness, meekness, and patience, forbearing one another and, if one has a complaint against another, forgiving each other; as the Lord has forgiven you, so you also must forgive. And over all these put on love, which binds everything together in perfect harmony. And let the peace of Christ rule in your hearts, to which indeed you were called in the one body" (Col 3:12–15).

God deeply desires that we might resemble him by being saints. Charity is love, and holiness is a sublime manifestation of the ability to

---

[6] Thomas à Kempis, *The Imitation of Christ*, trans. Ronald Knox and Michael Oakley (New York: Sheed and Ward, 1959), 120.

love. It is an identification with Christ and therefore the fulfillment of
our vocation to be a son or daughter of God.

What precisely are angels?

From the Bible we know that the angels are pure spirits, messengers
of God, endowed with extraordinary intelligence and bathed in God's
light. The angels truly live with God, forming around him a celestial
court that never stops praising the Creator.

They are the protectors and natural guides of men. I find it particularly important to be aware of the existence of our guardian angel, who
watches over us at every moment. Christ often mentions the angels,
revealing to us that "there is joy before the angels of God over one sinner who repents" (Lk 15:10). The Son of God asks us to make sure to
love children, "for I tell you that in heaven their angels always behold
the face of my Father who is in heaven" (Mt 18:10).

The example of the angels reminds men of the necessity of living a
holy life, one that is honest and pure. In heaven we will be brought to
live in their company, lost in the glory of God. Indeed, Christ tells the
Sadducees: "The sons of this age marry and are given in marriage; but
those who are accounted worthy to attain to that age and to the resurrection from the dead neither marry nor are given in marriage, for they
cannot die any more, because they are equal to angels and are sons of
God, being sons of the resurrection" (Lk 20:34–36).

Mankind truly needs to be assisted by these mysterious beings. I am
not unaware of the fact that it may be difficult to speak about angels in a
world that is set in its rationalistic, narcissistic ways.

Nonetheless, the Bible explains that in God's eyes man is superior
to the angels. God did not become incarnate in an angel. Although he
selected the Archangel Gabriel to be the messenger of his Incarnation, he
chose to come down to earth in human flesh. The Letter to the Hebrews
declares: " 'What is man that you are mindful of him, or the son of man,
that you care for him? You made him for a little while lower than the
angels, you have crowned him with glory and honor, putting everything
in subjection under his feet.' Now in putting everything in subjection
to him, he left nothing outside his control. As it is, we do not yet see
everything in subjection to him. But we see Jesus, who for a little while
was made lower than the angels, crowned with glory and honor because

of the suffering of death, so that by the grace of God he might taste death for every one" (Heb 2:6–9).

Man's greatness is found in the Incarnation, and the angels who freely accepted this great mystery praise God eternally.

With his sublime sense of pedagogy, Benedict XVI explained in a homily to religious and seminarians of Bavaria (September 11, 2006): "To be with Jesus and, being sent, to go out to meet people—these two things belong together and together they are the heart of a vocation, of the priesthood. To be with him and to be sent out—the two are inseparable. Only one who is 'with him' comes to know him and can truly proclaim him.... Pope Gregory the Great, in one of his homilies, once said that God's angels, however far afield they go on their missions, always move in God. They remain always with him."

It is significant that in the Vatican gardens Pope Francis, together with Benedict XVI, decided to bless a statue of Saint Michael and to place the Vatican under the protection of that archangel.

Finally, I cannot forget the fine, strong words that Francis spoke in September 2014 during his morning meditation: "Satan is subtle: the first page of Genesis says so.... He presents things as if they were good, but his intention is destruction.... The angels defend us: they defend man and they defend God-man, the superior man, Jesus Christ, who is the perfection of humanity, the most perfect one. [This is why] the Church honors the angels, because it is they who will be in the glory of God ... because they defend the great hidden mystery of God, that is, that the Word came in the flesh."

Our interview will soon come to an end. Can you tell us about your appointment by Pope Francis to head one of the most important dicasteries in the Roman Curia, the Congregation for Divine Worship and the Discipline of the Sacraments?

Every time the successor of Peter has been so kind as to entrust to me a responsibility for the service of the Church, I have always had the sense of my shortcomings and my inadequacy.

Although I feel the all-too-heavy weight of the mission that is entrusted to me, because of my objective weaknesses, nevertheless I hear flowing from my heart an immense thanksgiving to the Lord, who as a rule chooses what is nothing in the world's sight in order to accomplish his work.

I therefore thank the Lord who grants me the privilege of working with him and for him for the purpose of helping the people of God to enter fully into the mystery that he celebrates in the holy liturgy.

Humbly I thank the pope. I also feel genuine gratitude toward my coworkers in the Congregation for Divine Worship and the Discipline of the Sacraments. Together, with God's help and through his active presence—for the eucharistic liturgy, *Sacramentum caritatis* recalls, "is essentially an *actio Dei* which draws us into Christ through the Holy Spirit"—we work so that the celebrations of worship and the sacraments might always be experienced in the presence of God and in wonder at his salvific action, encompassing not only the individual but the whole Church, all of society, the whole universe, in the great movement that causes mankind and the world to pass from death to life in the mystery of the Lord's Passover. Together, we seek to make people understand that the liturgy is determined by God himself and not by men. Indeed, man cannot simply fabricate worship *ex nihilo*. For "we do not know with what we must serve the LORD until we arrive there" (Ex 10:26). If God does not reveal himself, man only embraces emptiness.

Joseph Ratzinger has indicated that the liturgy must show Christ, allow him to shine through in his transforming presence through the signs, the gestures, and the words that the Church has handed down to us in her rites. How do you understand this analysis?

Joseph Ratzinger tried to explain further what *Sacrosanctum concilium* asserts with great clarity: "The liturgy is the outstanding means whereby the faithful may express in their lives, and manifest to others, the mystery of Christ and the real nature of the true Church" (SC 2). He stated that "God acts in the liturgy through Christ, and we, as the Church, can act only through him, with him, and in him."[7] In the Church, if the liturgy really is the epiphany or manifestation of Christ, the prolongation, as Saint Leo the Great puts it, of what the Lord experienced in Palestine— his birth, his preaching, his miracles, his teaching the disciples, his Passion, death, and Resurrection—then it is fundamentally a mystical and contemplative reality. But it is also a reality made up of signs, gestures and

---

[7] *Une Histoire de la messe: Introduite par deux conférences du Cardinal Joseph Ratzinger à Font-gombault* (Le Nef, 2009), 26.

words, so as to put us in permanent contact with the redeeming work of Christ, and so that thus his transfiguring presence appears through "our lives ... now hidden in God with Christ" (see Col 3:3).

Through the liturgy, Jesus enters into our hearts. Priests therefore must see to it that he has the first place so as to allow him to shine through; only in this way will people who look at us see Jesus. Christ must be seen through us.

In a world that constantly takes us out of ourselves, imprisoning man in sensory and material goods, sometimes totally depriving him of what is essential, the liturgy truly is the door to our union with God through our union with Jesus. It prepares us for the heavenly liturgy that will allow us to contemplate God unveiled, face to face, so as to love him without end. In the liturgy, we experience the manifestation and the operative presence of Jesus Christ, if the priest enters fully into the Paschal Mystery, which is celebrated with faith, devotion, and beauty in the Holy Eucharist.

On July 7, 2007, Benedict XVI promulgated Summorum Pontificum, *the Motu proprio on the Roman liturgy previous to the reform in 1970. What is your point of view on this document?*

I personally welcomed *Summorum Pontificum* with confidence, joy, and thanksgiving. It is, so to speak, a sign and a proof that the Church, *Mater et Magister* (our Mother and Teacher), is still attentive to all her children, taking into account their different sensibilities. Benedict XVI intended to promote the wealth of various spiritual expressions, provided they lead to a real, genuine ecclesial communion and a more luminous radiance of the Church's sanctity.

I think that this beautiful *Motu proprio* is right in line with the will of the Council Fathers. And so we must not pretend to forget that *Sacrosanctum concilium* declared: "For the liturgy is made up of immutable elements divinely instituted, and of elements subject to change. These not only may but ought to be changed with the passage of time if they have suffered from the intrusion of anything out of harmony with the inner nature of the liturgy or have become unsuited to it" (SC 21).

In the letter that accompanied *Summorum Pontificum*, Benedict XVI wrote: "For that matter, the two Forms of the usage of the Roman Rite can be mutually enriching: new Saints and some of the new Prefaces can and should be inserted in the old Missal.... The celebration of the Mass according to the Missal of Paul VI will be able to demonstrate, more powerfully than has been the case hitherto, the sacrality which attracts many people to the former usage. The most sure guarantee that the Missal of Paul VI can unite parish communities and be loved by them consists in its being celebrated with great reverence in harmony with the liturgical directives. This will bring out the spiritual richness and the theological depth of this Missal."

Probably in the celebration of Mass according to the old missal, we understood better that the Mass is an act of Christ and not of men. Similarly, its mysterious and mystagogical character is more immediately evident. Even if we participate actively in the Mass, it is not our action but Christ's. In *The Spirit of the Liturgy*, Cardinal Ratzinger wrote: "What does this active participation come down to? What does it mean that we have to do? Unfortunately, the word was very quickly misunderstood to mean something external, entailing a need for general activity, as if as many people as possible, as often as possible, should be visibly engaged in action. However, the word 'part-icipation' refers to a principal action in which everyone has a 'part'. And so if we want to discover the kind of doing that active participation involves, we need, first of all, to determine what this central *actio* is in which all the members of the community are supposed to participate.... By the *actio* of the liturgy the sources mean the Eucharistic Prayer. The real liturgical action, the true liturgical act, is the *oratio*.... This *oratio*—the Eucharistic Prayer, the 'Canon'—is really more than speech; it is *actio* in the highest sense of the word. For what happens in it is that the human *actio* (as performed hitherto by the priests in the various religions of the world) steps back and makes way for the *actio divina*, the action of God" (171–72).

The *Motu proprio Summorum Pontificum* attempts to reconcile the two forms of the Roman rite and above all seeks to help us rediscover the sacrality of Holy Mass as an *actio Dei* and not a human act. We are touching here on an extremely important point: the problem of the widespread lack of discipline, the lack of respect and of fidelity to the rite, which can also affect even the validity of the sacraments.

Some people are alarmed about a crisis of the liturgy in the Church. Are they right?

Alas, I think that they are right to be worried and to fear the worst.... We observe more and more that man seeks to take the place of God.

The liturgy then becomes a mere human game. If eucharistic celebrations turn into human celebrations of ourselves and places where we apply our pastoral ideologies and partisan political preferences, which have nothing to do with spiritual worship that is to be celebrated as God wills, the danger is immense. For then God disappears.

Last December [2014] Reinhard Cardinal Marx, president of the German Bishops' Conference, said: "Throughout the world, the search for a theologically responsible and pastorally appropriate way of assisting Catholics who are divorced or divorced and civilly remarried is one of the urgent challenges for pastoral ministry to families and married couples in the context of evangelization." What is your viewpoint on this subject, which figured among the questions at the last synod in October 2014?

I have a lot of respect for Reinhard Cardinal Marx. But this very general statement seems to me to be the expression of mere ideology that they want to impose hastily on the whole Church. In my experience, specifically after twenty-three years as archbishop of Conakry and nine years as secretary of the Congregation for the Evangelization of Peoples, the question of "Catholics who are divorced or divorced and civilly remarried" is not an urgent challenge for the Church of Africa or Asia. On the contrary, this is an obsession of some Western Churches that want to impose so-called "theologically responsible and pastorally appropriate" solutions that radically contradict the teaching of Jesus and of the Church's Magisterium.

The primary urgent task in mission countries is to design a pastoral ministry whose sole objective is to answer the question: What does it mean to be truly Christian in the present historical and cultural situation of our globalized societies? How can we form fearless, generous Christians, zealous disciples of Jesus? For a Christian adult, faith in Christ cannot be an intuition, an emotion, or a feeling. For a Christian, the faith must become the shape, the mold of his whole life, private and public, personal and social.

Whatever the current difficulties may be, Christ's disciples must assert the demands of faith in Christ without reticence and without compromise, in theory and in practice, because they are the demands and precepts of God.

The second urgent task is to form solid Christian families, for the Church, which is God's family, is built on the foundation of Christian families that are sacramentally united and witnesses to this momentous mystery that Christ has given to us eternally.

The truth of the Gospel must always be lived out in the difficult crucible of involvement in social, economic, and cultural life as a whole. Faced with today's moral crisis, in particular the crisis of marriage and the family, the Church can contribute to the search for just and constructive solutions, but she has no other option but to take part in that search by vigorously citing the unique and distinctive things that faith in Jesus Christ brings to the human enterprise. In this sense, it is not possible to imagine any conflict or tension whatsoever between magisterial teaching and pastoral practice. The idea of putting magisterial teaching in a beautiful display case while separating it from pastoral practice, which then could evolve along with circumstances, fashions, and passions, is a sort of heresy, a dangerous schizophrenic pathology.

I therefore solemnly state that the Church in Africa is staunchly opposed to any rebellion against the teaching of Jesus and of the Magisterium.

If I may make a historical reference: in the fourth century, the Church of Africa and the Council of Carthage decreed priestly celibacy. Then, in the sixteenth century, that same African Council served as the foundation on which Pope Pius IV based his arguments against pressures from the German princes, who asked him to authorize the marriage of priests. Today, too, the Church of Africa is committed in the name of the Lord Jesus to keeping unchanged the teaching of God and of the Church about the indissolubility of marriage: what God has joined, let no man put asunder.

How could a synod go back on the constant teaching that was unified and explained in greater depth by Blessed Paul VI, Saint John Paul II, and Benedict XVI?

I place my trust in the fidelity of Francis.

In January 2015, I had the honor of accompanying him during his journey to Sri Lanka and the Philippines. In Manila, his talk on the family was particularly forceful: "Let us be on guard against colonization by new ideologies. There are forms of ideological colonization which are out to destroy the family. They are not born of dreams, of prayers, of closeness to God or the mission which God gave us; they come from without, and for that reason I am saying that they are forms of colonization. Let's not lose the freedom of the mission which God has given us, the mission of the family. Just as our peoples, at a certain moment of their history, were mature enough to say 'no' to all forms of political colonization, so too in our families we need to be very wise, very shrewd, very strong, in order to say 'no' to all attempts at an ideological colonization of our families. We need to ask Saint Joseph, the friend of the angel, to send us the inspiration to know when we can say 'yes' and when we have to say 'no'.... I think of Blessed Paul VI. At a time when the problem of population growth was being raised, he had the courage to defend openness to life in families. He knew the difficulties that are there in every family, and so in his Encyclical he was very merciful towards particular cases, and he asked confessors to be very merciful and understanding in dealing with particular cases. But he also had a broader vision: he looked at the peoples of the earth and he saw this threat of families being destroyed for lack of children. Paul VI was courageous; he was a good pastor and he warned his flock of the wolves who were coming. From his place in heaven, may he bless this evening!"

In November 2014, on returning from a journey to Lebanon, you posed a particularly difficult question: "Why is it possible for God to allow the children who are most faithful to him to be massacred, even to make a painful offering of their lives?" How are we to understand this question?

The martyrs are the sign that God is alive and always present among us. His merciful love is manifested visibly and tangibly in Jesus Christ, who promised never to leave his Church and those who have chosen to follow him faithfully: "Behold, I am with you always, to the close of the age" (Mt 28:20). Now his presence is tangible in his persecuted disciples: " 'Saul, Saul, why do you persecute me?' And he said, 'Who are you, Lord?' And he said, 'I am Jesus, whom you are persecuting' " (Acts 9:4–5). The martyrs are not only the physical presence of Jesus in a hostile world that is impervious to the Gospel; they are also man's most radical response to God's love. Indeed, there is no greater proof of love than to give one's life for those whom one loves. God really gave himself for us, even unto death. It is through death that we respond truly and totally to God's love.

In *Deus caritas est*, Benedict XVI wrote forcefully: "In the Old Testament, the novelty of the Bible did not consist merely in abstract notions but in God's unpredictable and in some sense unprecedented activity.

This divine activity now takes on dramatic form when, in Jesus Christ, it is God himself who goes in search of the 'stray sheep', a suffering and lost humanity. When Jesus speaks in his parables of the shepherd who goes after the lost sheep, of the woman who looks for the lost coin, of the father who goes to meet and embrace his prodigal son, these are no mere words: they constitute an explanation of his very being and activity. His death on the Cross is the culmination of that turning of God against himself in which he gives himself in order to raise man up and save him. This is love in its most radical form" (DCE 12).

Today again, in the cruel deaths of so many Christians who are shot, crucified, decapitated, tortured, and burned alive, this "turning of God against himself" is accomplished again for the uplifting and salvation of the world.

According to statistics published by the Pew Research Center Study in January 2014, in one-third of the 198 countries where surveys were conducted, serious persecutions against Christians were reported. Many of those who profess allegiance to Christ are being persecuted throughout the world. Many historians even say that half of all the Christian martyrs in the history of the Church were killed in the twentieth century.

But the blood of Christian martyrs speaks a different language from that of Abel (Heb 12:24). It demands neither vengeance nor punishment, but tells of forgiveness and reconciliation. The martyr is a witness to love and an example of faith for those who are open to the God of mercy and truth. This explains the unexpected success in France of the film *Des hommes et des Dieux* (*Of Gods and Men*), which tells the story of seven Cistercian monks from the monastery in Tibhirine who were massacred in March 1996.

Besides, how can we not admire the words of the last testament of Shahbaz Bhatti, a Pakistani Catholic politician who was killed because of his faith in March 2011? He wrote: "High-ranking positions in government have been offered to me, and I have been asked to put an end to my battle, but I have always refused, even at the risk of my own life. My response has always been the same. I do not want popularity, I do not want positions of power. I only want a place at the feet of Jesus. I want my life, my character, my actions to speak of me and say that I am following Jesus Christ. This desire is so strong in me that I consider myself privileged whenever—in my combative effort to help the needy, the poor, the persecuted Christians of Pakistan—Jesus should wish to accept the sacrifice of my life. I want to live for Christ, and it is for Him that I want to die."

We get the impression that we are hearing again about the martyrdom of Saint Ignatius of Antioch, who came to Rome to suffer the worst outrages, ground up by the teeth of ferocious beasts.

Similarly, I cannot forget the faces of Shahbaz Masih, aged thirty, and of his wife Shama Bibi, who was twenty-four, who were burned alive, thrown into a kiln where bricks were being baked, on November 4, 2014, in the province of Punjab, in Pakistan, leaving three children, and while Shama was pregnant. Shahbaz Masih and Shama Bibi died in silence, as holocausts offered up to the God of Love. But the victims' silence does not justify guilty indifference with regard to the fate of thousands of Christians who die every day. How can we ignore the sorrowful cry of the prophet Isaiah: "The righteous man perishes, and no one lays it to heart; devout men are taken away, while no one understands" (Is 57:1)?

While Christians are dying for their faith and their fidelity to Jesus, in the West, men of the Church are trying to reduce the requirements of the Gospel to a minimum.

We go so far as to exploit the mercy of God, stifling justice and truth, so as to "welcome" homosexual persons—as the *Relatio post disceptationem* from the last Synod on the Family in October 2014 puts it—who "have gifts and qualities to offer to the Christian community". Moreover, this document goes on to say that "the question of homosexuality requires serious reflection on how to devise realistic approaches to affective growth, human development, and maturation in the Gospel, while integrating the sexual aspect." In fact, the real scandal is not the existence of sinners, for mercy and forgiveness always exist precisely for them, but rather the confusion between good and evil caused by Catholic shepherds. If men who are consecrated to God are no longer capable of understanding the radical nature of the Gospel message and seek to anaesthetize it, we will be going the wrong way. For that is the real failure of mercy.

While hundreds of thousands of Christians are living each day filled with fear, some are trying to keep the divorced and remarried from suffering: they would feel discriminated against if they were excluded from sacramental communion. Despite their ongoing state of adultery, despite their state of life that testifies to a refusal to abide by the Word that raises up those who are sacramentally married to be the revelatory sign of Christ's Paschal Mystery, some theologians want to grant admission to Eucharistic Communion to the divorced and remarried. The divorced and remarried took it upon themselves to transgress Christ's command: "What God has joined together, let no man put asunder" (Mt 19:6), and consequently they are forbidden to receive sacramental communion; to abolish this prohibition would clearly mean the denial of the indissolubility of sacramental marriage.

Aline Lizotte, a renowned theologian and director of the Karol Wojtyła Institute, correctly argues in *L'Obéissance du Christ et le mystère de piété*: "The truth of the conjugal union is practiced only within a marriage involving a stable union of one man and one woman, whose expressed public consent implies a radical communion of the gifts of both with a view to handing on the mystery of the person in offspring. Within Christ's Church, other forms of sexual union, even if they include elements that enable them to resemble sacramental marriage, are, objectively speaking, obstacles to the fullness of conjugal life as it is willed by the Creator and affirmed by Christ. For a baptized person, to say that a *de facto* union, concubinage, or merely civil marriage can objectively be positive elements leading toward sacramental fullness is to try to rewrite the history of salvation backward!"[8]

Today there is a confrontation and a rebellion against God, a battle organized against Christ and his Church. How is it comprehensible that Catholic pastors should put doctrine to a vote: the law of God and the Church's teaching on homosexuality, on divorce and remarriage, as though from now on the Word of God and the Magisterium had to be sanctioned and approved by majority vote?

Men who devise and elaborate strategies to kill God, to destroy the centuries-old doctrine and teaching of the Church, will themselves be swallowed up, carried off by their own earthly victory into the eternal fires of Gehenna.

At the next Synod on the Family, what path would we be trying to take if we separated worship, law, and ethics? In *The Spirit of the Liturgy*, Joseph Ratzinger already wrote: "In the ordering of the covenant on Sinai, ... there is an essential connection between the three orders of worship, law, and ethics. Law without a foundation in morality becomes

---

[8] Aline Lizotte, *L'Obéissance du Christ et le mystère de piété* (Avignon: Éd. AFCP, 2007).

injustice. When morality and law do not originate in a God-ward perspective, they degrade man, because they rob him of his highest measure and his highest capacity, deprive him of any vision of the infinite and eternal. This seeming liberation subjects him to the dictatorship of the ruling majority, to shifting human standards, which inevitably end up doing him violence.... [W]orship and law cannot be completely separated from each other. God has a right to a response from man, to man himself, and where that right of God totally disappears, the order of law among men is dissolved, because there is no cornerstone to keep the whole structure together."[9]

The West urgently needs to set its sights on God and the Crucified Lord, to look "on Him whom they have pierced", to rediscover their trust in and their fidelity to the Gospel, to overcome its weariness, and to stop refusing to hear "what the Spirit says to the Churches", even if they are African....

Eternity, in three words?

Life, love, and communion.

Eternity is a great wheeling motion, exaltation forever, plunging into the life of God, into the love of God, and into God's trinitarian communion.

Eternity is the present moment. Eternity is in the palm of your hand. Eternity is a sowing with fire, which suddenly takes root and breaks down the barriers that prevent our hearts from being a deep abyss.

Eternity is you, Lord. And we find you in love and communion: you in me and I in you and you in them and them with me for eternity.

What made it possible for Saint Augustine to write in The City of God *this magnificent statement: "God does not speak, but his voice is clear; he illuminates little, but his light is pure"?*

God is a silent lover and a lighthouse so bright that it remains invisible. Genuine love does not speak. Are not wordless smiles the most beautiful? God's silence is a voice, the most profound of all.

[9] Joseph Ratzinger, *The Spirit of the Liturgy*, trans. John Saward (San Francisco: Ignatius Press, 2000), 18–19.

All creation speaks of God, thanks to its marvelous silence. In the Paschal night, all our lives are born.

Our life of faith most often walks in the night. The more faith has to confront trials, the stronger it becomes. Nights of faith always end with finding the little light of God.

In the life of Saint Augustine, God was always present. In the times when he was straying, heaven might appear to have been less obvious. Nevertheless, God never ceased to watch over him, and Augustine ended up responding to a voice that was not speaking. Then he never stopped seeking him until he took his final breath. In the *Confessions*, the bishop of Hippo writes these extraordinary words:

> *Late have I loved you, O Beauty ever ancient, ever new,*
> *late have I loved you!*
> *You were within me, but I was outside,*
> *and it was there that I searched for you.*
> *In my unloveliness I plunged*
> *into the lovely things which you created.*
> *You were with me, but I was not with you.*
> *Created things kept me from you;*
> *yet if they had not been in you they would not have been at all.*
> *You called, you shouted, and you broke through my deafness.*
> *You flashed, you shone, and you dispelled my blindness.*
> *You breathed your fragrance on me; I drew in breath and now I*
> *   pant for you.*
> *I have tasted you, now I hunger and thirst for more.*
> *You touched me, and I burned for your peace.*
> *When once I shall be united to you with my whole being,*
> *I shall at last be free of sorrow and toil.*
> *Then my life will be alive, filled entirely with you.*
> *When you fill someone, you relieve him of his burden,*
> *but because I am not yet filled with you, I am a burden to myself.*[10]

Our world is often astray, as was young Augustine.

It ardently searches without knowing where truth is found.

---

[10] Trans. in *Liturgy of the Hours* 3:273–74.

It searches along a thousand paths, trying to believe in
   eternal life.
Through many artificial paradises it searches for joy,
   simplicity, and beauty.
In fog and sunlight, our world is searching for its Father and
   its God.
For, in the human heart, one that knows him or one that
   is still searching for him, there is already the luminous
   presence of God.